EUCALYPTUS

Reaktion's Botanical series is the first of its kind, integrating horticultural and botanical writing with a broader account of the cultural and social impact of trees, plants and flowers.

Published
Apple Marcia Reiss
Ash Edward Parker
Bamboo Susanne Lucas
Berries Victoria Dickenson
Birch Anna Lewington
Cactus Dan Torre
Cannabis Chris Duvall
Carnation Twigs Way
Carnivorous Plants Dan Torre
Cherry Constance L. Kirker and Mary Newman
Chrysanthemum Twigs Way
Eucalyptus Stephen D. Hopper
Geranium Kasia Boddy
Grasses Stephen A. Harris
House Plants Mike Maunder
Lily Marcia Reiss
Moss and Lichen Elizabeth Lawson
Mulberry Peter Coles
Oak Peter Young
Orchid Dan Torre
Palm Fred Gray
Peony Gail Harland
Pine Laura Mason
Poppy Andrew Lack
Primrose Elizabeth Lawson
Rhododendron Richard Milne
Rose Catherine Horwood
Rowan Oliver Southall
Snowdrop Gail Harland
Sunflowers Stephen A. Harris
Tulip Celia Fisher
Weeds Nina Edwards
Willow Alison Syme
Yew Fred Hageneder

EUCALYPTUS

Stephen D. Hopper

REAKTION BOOKS

For the late M.I.H. (Ian) Brooker AM (1934–2016),
eucalypt taxonomist, mentor and friend

Published by
REAKTION BOOKS LTD
2–4 Sebastian Street
London EC1V 0HE, UK
www.reaktionbooks.co.uk

First published 2025
Copyright © Stephen D. Hopper 2025

EU GPSR Authorised Representative
Logos Europe, 9 rue Nicolas Poussin, 17000, La Rochelle, France
email: contact@logoseurope.eu

Printed and bound in India by Replika Press Pvt. Ltd

A catalogue record for this book is available from the British Library

ISBN 978 1 83639 111 1

Contents

Foreword *by Ron (Doc) Reynolds* 7

Foreword

✻

Having lived in Esperance on the south coast of Western Australia for the most of my life and being actively engaged in community affairs and cultural heritage protection regimes over forty years, I have met many wonderful people over this time. Professor Stephen Hopper is one of them, and his humble, warm-hearted nature and willingness to share his vast knowledge and experience make it a pleasure to be in his company.

Steve came on one of my eco-cultural discovery tours, then returned, wanting to learn more about what my old people had told and shown me, in particular around Gabtoobitch (Cape Arid). He showed me that he was genuine in engaging with my people to share and learn in a reciprocal way. It is a pleasure to walk with him on country as he plucks plants up and points out the various plant species. On a Gabbie Kylie (Esperance) field school, looking over a large granite outcrop, we located a small eucalypt that had never been properly documented before. Steve was over the moon. To me it was just another bush. Steve explained to us all that there are still many plant species not recorded, and he said that it was particularly exciting to come across a new eucalypt, which is being named as *Eucalyptus sweedmaniana* subsp. *noongaring* to honour our Elders past and present.

On another occasion, I was showing him some bush foods. I harvested this rare water plant from a *gnamma* (rock pool) on top of a granite outcrop and started eating the plants, which Steve pointed out were quite rare. My response: 'Nice tucker bro.' On another occasion, at a very significant site, Steve was excited that we had found another rare plant, a small kangaroo paw, which only grows to about 15 centimetres (6 in.) high.

As Steve sits down after a field trip and sorts through the many plant species he has harvested, I can only look on with awe. He meticulously and artistically cuts and places the small specimens of plants on clear tape to stick into a new journal to add to the many other journals he has collected across the world.

My people have known eucalypts for countless millennia and regard them as our friends and teachers. They care for us. As a child, I was once badly burned on the arm when I rolled on to a campfire while asleep. My parents quickly found a eucalypt and applied the fresh leaves as a poultice. It healed my arm, to the point where no scar is seen today. These trees nurture people in so many ways. They deserve attention and respect, and will always be part of the living spirit of our *boodja* (country).

I now class Professor Stephen Hopper as a close friend and an expert accomplice on my many trips into the bush. The information and stories he shares in this book on *Eucalyptus* are a testament to the man who recognizes that the cultural significance of eucalypts is of utmost importance for future generations, alongside many other aspects that are now understood for these spiritual trees and shrubs.

I look forward to the many journeys as we open up new engagement between Aboriginal people and non-Aboriginal people along the country we know as *Tjaltjraak boodja. Tjaltjraak* is, of course, a eucalypt of great significance to my people as a geographical marker of our country (*boodja*). We have named our Native Title organization after this tree.

I am pleased to recommend this book to all who have an interest in the great Australian eucalypts, useful in so many ways, but also strongly connected to country and spirit, forever.

Ron (Doc) Reynolds
Senior Cultural Advisor for Wudjari people
Esperance, Western Australia

Introduction

✻

*E*ucalyptus. The name is thoroughly European, a product of the Enlightenment and the age of global exploration. The plant is Antipodean in origin, predominantly Australian, but today it is also found planted in many other countries across Eurasia, North and South America, and Africa, and on many islands.

This book aims to explore aspects of Aboriginal and Western scientific knowledge systems pertaining to the eucalypts. The object is to synthesize the burgeoning information available on these trees, mallees and shrubs (illus. 1, 2) in a way that pays due respect to Aboriginal priority and insights. The book explores the natural history and naming of eucalypts, and their ethnobiology, and reviews biological, cultivation and conservation studies. Overall, I hope the book will advance understanding about how we might care for and manage eucalypts in the future.

The genus *Eucalyptus* includes the world's tallest flowering plants. A few species today soar 90–100 metres (300–330 ft) above the forest floor, but they were perhaps even higher in the past, before logging, burning and clearing for agriculture eradicated the record.[1]

By 2010 more than 850 species of eucalypt were recognized, now in four genera (758 in *Eucalyptus*, 57 in *Corymbia*, 36 in *Blakella* and 10 in *Angophora*).[2] Another fifty species have been described since or recognized but not named, making a current total of more than nine hundred eucalypts. The scientific inventory of eucalypts is an ongoing task.

1, 2 Eucalypts range in size from the world's tallest flowering plants
in the form of trees reaching more than 80 metres (263 ft) (*yowork*,
Eucalyptus regnans, in Victoria and Tasmania, *left*) to multi-stemmed mallees
(such as *jinjulu* or *kunyalyka*, *E. glomerosa*, Great Victoria Desert, *above*).

All but twelve of the eucalypts are endemic to Australia and found
nowhere else. Eucalypt geographical distribution ranges from the
continent-wide river red gum (*E. camaldulensis*) to such extremely rare
and localized species as Southwest Australia's rose mallee (*E. rhodantha*).
Among even the most famous, such as *yorgum* (red-flowering gum,

Corymbia ficifolia; illus. 3), there are species with globally significant narrow ranges.

Worldwide, eucalypts are both revered and reviled. Celebrated in its main country of origin, *Eucalyptus* has been dubbed the 'universal Australian'.[3] In Australia, eucalypts have become the object and backdrop of countless pieces of art and science, novels and verse, films and photographs.[4] Their hard timber has made fortunes from wild harvest and transformed landscapes beyond recognition in exotic plantations.

3 The flowers of eucalypts attract a range of pollinators. Seen here are copulating flower wasps (the male with wings) on *yorgum* (red-flowering gum, *Corymbia ficifolia*), which is confined to a tiny area of the south coast of Western Australia.

4 Exceptional diversity of dried eucalypt nuts, buds and flowers from temperate, desert and tropical regions of Western Australia.

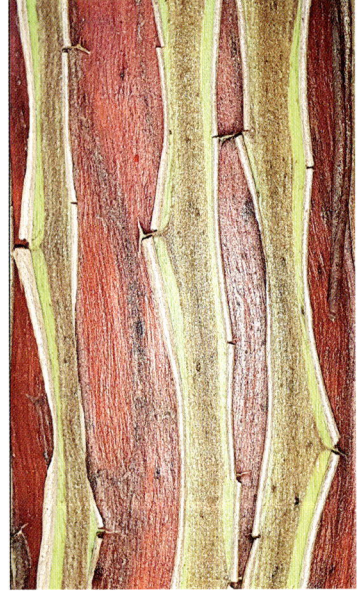

5–8 Colourful bark is a feature of many eucalypts. *Clockwise from top left:*
Eucalyptus subcrenulata (Tasmania); *E. virginea* (Southwest Australia); *E. orbifolia*
(Western Australia); and *E. viminalis* (Tasmania).

Their use has inspired new industry, mobilized public protests and toppled governments. Their aromatic oil-filled leaves have restored human health and fed the fury of wildfires.

Eucalypts provide habitat, food and shelter for myriad animals, plants and fungi, their roots binding the soil, their leaves converting carbon dioxide into oxygen, their canopies moderating climate and helping to replenish the earth with rainfall. The volatile oils emitted from their pendent leaves during hot summer days create a haze that led to the naming of the Blue Mountains that flank the inland side of the Sydney Basin.[5]

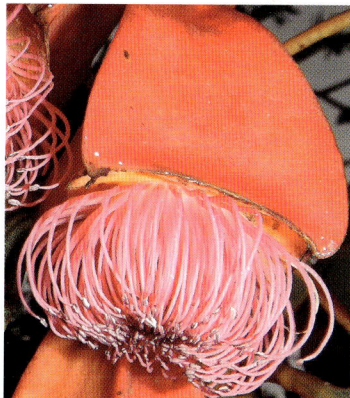

9–12 Floral diversity in *Eucalyptus. Clockwise from top left*:
Eucalyptus rameliana (Western Australia); *E. incrassata* (South Australia);
E. tetraptera; and *E. lehmannii* (both Southwest Australia).

No other continent is so bedecked and dominated by what was a single genus of trees across all but its most arid and inhospitable habitats.[6] The seeming uniformity of grey-green eucalypt canopies are a hallmark of Australia, belying and hiding a riot of diversity that requires a mature and perceptive eye to comprehend fully. What appears at first relatively invariant, boring to some, becomes on closer inspection a cornucopia of diversity, resilience, colour and wonder (illus. 4–12).

The name *Eucalyptus* derives from the ancient Greek for 'well covered', alluding to the cap (operculum or calyptra) that covers the floral parts as they develop in the bud (illus. 13). Strictly, in Greek, *Eucalyptus* should be pronounced 'eff-cal-ip-toos', but the initial 'eu' has been anglicized to sound as 'yoo' in English.

In some ways the protective bud cap symbolizes the allure and mystery of eucalypts. It protects, hides and nurtures the transient

13 *Eucalyptus* means 'well covered', alluding to the bud cap, which comprises united petals and sepals that protect the developing stamens and style of the young flower (seen here in *E. caesia* subsp. *caesia*).

potential for new life that each bud offers, eventually falling away to reveal the mature glories of the multi-stamened blossoms, inviting pollinators to sup nectar while helping to start the next generation of trees.

This book is organized around three themes. First, Aboriginal perspectives and European discovery are explored. There is a substantial body of cultural knowledge of eucalypts now documented for Aboriginal people. Reviewed here for the first time, this knowledge stands often in stark relief to our understanding of how *Eucalyptus* became known to Western scientists. The book then turns to natural history and science, examining new research on where eucalypts are known to occur, what their major life history attributes are and how they evolved on the Australian continent during significant continental movement, climate change, faunal evolution and landscape development over the past 60 million years. Growing, using and conserving eucalypts make up a third theme that touches on the widespread cultivation of eucalypts for horticulture, street trees, land care and plantation forestry. Eucalypts are now grown in many countries, with varying results and acceptance. Many uses can be made of this remarkable group of trees, in medicine, the arts, industry and culture. The somewhat tumultuous history of conservation of eucalypts is outlined, and modern conservation strategies described. While some species are widespread, many are more localized, including about 10 per cent of known species that occupy very narrow geographical areas. Nearly a quarter of known species are threatened with extinction. How might we best conserve this extraordinary arborescent heritage?

Overall, drawing on a plethora of published works, the book offers some novel perspectives on *Eucalyptus* when compared with previous publications. In it, I explore themes that have emerged as revelatory in my own intellectual development and studies of the genus. I hope the book will stimulate others to wonder about, and care for, one of the most important genera of plants on Earth.

14 Aboriginal Australian language groups mapped according to Tindale (1974) and Horton (1996).

one
Eucalypt Dreaming on Mainland Australia

❋

E ucalypts loom large in Aboriginal Dreaming stories across Australia. They are seen as the primary structural elements of ancestral spirit-scapes, sacred trees, known and protected as individuals. Australian Aboriginal people have been divided into about 250 language groups (illus. 14) and there are more than nine hundred species of eucalypt across Australia, so, considering the patchiness of the ethnographic and linguistic record and oral history, we can only glimpse a profoundly diverse and rich multicultural Aboriginal heritage.[1]

To appreciate the profoundly spiritual, yet eminently practical, world view of Aboriginal cultures across mainland Australia, I will discuss examples of eucalypt Dreaming and uses. The chapter begins with a brief introduction to the concept of the Dreaming. We then go to Sydney, where the D'Harawal people have shared one of the clearest stories on eucalypts in a cultural context. From there, the rich ethnographic literature of Australia's tropical north is reviewed before we turn to Victorian accounts of eucalypts in Aboriginal culture. We then explore eucalypt stories from Australia's largest inland river system, the Murray-Darling. The central desert and western desert regions are then highlighted, before the chapter concludes with one of the biggest stories reaching across the continent: Seven Sisters Dreaming. Given the special eucalypts and cultures embraced by Tasmania and Southwest Australia, Aboriginal cultures in these areas are considered in subsequent chapters.

Why is this sequence important? Aboriginal people have occupied Australia for 55,000–70,000 years, during which time they have developed a deep and diverse knowledge of eucalypts.[2] Equally, traditional storytelling by Elders of ancestral law and proper behaviour, incorporating self-restraint and self-sacrifice during life, may include spirit beings that are trees imbued with human characteristics or providing settings for appropriate behaviour.[3] We shall see that sophisticated relationships with eucalypts have been achieved through their incorporation not only in daily life as sources of useful products, but as signs of the ever-present old ways of deeply respected ancestors – the Dreaming.

Note that this chapter draws on the published record only of Aboriginal Dreaming stories and eucalypts. While this approach often separates individual families from their stories, causing personal loss of agency, it was considered important to summarize such knowledge rather than ignore its content. This situation is rectified in the next chapter, which deals with the oral tradition of just one family in Southwest Australia, to highlight the richness and empowerment that tying stories to named people and place yields. I also start below with a Sydney D'Harawal people story by Dr Frances Bodkin, which beautifully illustrates the power of place-based storytelling by individual Elders.

The Dreaming

Eucalypts feature prominently in the creation stories and law of Aboriginal people, a never-ending connection between ancestral spirits who created the land, plants, animals and people, present-day country and life, and the future.[4] Although the idea is difficult to translate into English, 'the Dreaming' is an approximation of this complex world view and is now widely used. It is best explained by Aboriginal people themselves. For example, Yami Lester, a northwest South Australian Yakuntjara Elder, explains what *wapar* (the Dreaming) is all about:

Aboriginal culture cannot be separated from the land. On the land are stories, Aboriginal stories that explain why people, rock holes, the hills and the trees came to be there. The land is full of stories. Every square mile is just like a book, a book with a lot of pages, and it's all a story for the children to learn. The old people always tell stories about it, and at an early age the children start learning from that land.

The land holds the people together. The people lived there together and they enjoy the land and know the stories of the land. They know where the rock holes and water holes are, and they go hunting on the land. The relationship with the land is part of their life. It's their spiritual meaning. They feel sad and sick if something happens to their place.

In the *wapar* the land was made. Our culture, the language, the land we live in, our relationship with people and the religious system that controls our everyday life, comes from the *wapar*. Learning our culture is learning about the *wapar*. The land is full of the stories.[5]

The Seven Peacekeepers of the D'Harawal people

Because of Sydney's rich eucalypt flora, it is perhaps no surprise that one of the best Dreaming stories recorded about eucalypts comes from the D'Harawal people. D'Harawal land extends from Botany Bay southwards down the coast of New South Wales to Jervis Bay and adjacent coastal mountains. D'Harawal Elder Dr Frances Bodkin introduces her edited compendium of *Gurugal* (= a long time before, Dreaming Law) stories by noting that their purpose and meaning are multilayered.[6] Sacred and secret layers are reserved for those people who are at a level of cultural initiation equal to that of the storyteller. These stories are remembered and not told to a broad audience. A second layer relates to cultural law, extrapolating from the telling of the legend in a separate discussion of what it means and tells us about the expected behaviour of D'Harawal people. Lastly, the third layer is the publicly relayed legend itself, spoken and written in plain language so that children and a wide public can follow the story and work out for themselves what it might mean in terms of solving life's problems and challenges.

Bodkin's book, beautifully illustrated by Lorraine Robertson, exemplifies a growing literature by Aboriginal authors published in a similar style, sometimes bilingual, with sufficient words in their native language to introduce non-speakers to key terms. Such literature gives first voice and due recognition to Elders of the people from whom the Dreaming stories originate, and generously shares Dreaming Law with people other than their own people and kin.

An important point, emphasized by many Elders and anthropologists, among them Ronald Berndt, is that each family may have its own variant of a Dreaming story, or part of a story, a fact that necessitates the hearing of several independent renditions.[7] All versions are equally legitimate, however. Such dynamic diversity is to be expected in a strong oral tradition, allowing individual flair and innovation in the telling while ensuring that the thrust and theme remain as shared by the ancestral spirits and passed down through generations.

Bodkin's story about eucalypts is called 'Maridyulu'boola Yandel'mawa', the Seven Peacekeepers. It tells of people in the past arguing and fighting over territory, and the D'Harawal selecting a wise warrior – Boo'nah, who was fluent in many local languages – to become the Peacemaker, Yandel'bana. They also selected seven brave, strong lawmen to help Yandel'bana, and called them the Yandel'mawa, the Warriors of Peace. Together they consulted widely and gathered evidence, enabling Yandel'bana to assemble the Elders of warring tribes and set the terms of peace. Much of the trouble was caused by spirit sorcerers called the Wiree. Their powers weakened as peace settled across the lands. They travelled to Yandel'ora, a special place where no weapons were allowed, and aimed to attack the unarmed peacemakers there. Yandel'ora had a significant spirit keeper, the Gorronj, who sensed that the Wiree were up to no good and turned the Yandel'mawa into tall trees, leaving Yandel'bana as a man. The story relates how Yandel'bana and the Yandel'mawa were able to see through the tricks of the Wiree, and surround and trap them in a *gnwi-yang* or *gwee-un* (fire), even though the Wiree tried to escape as a *williwilli* (whirlwind). The Wiree disappeared as harmless sparks rising from the campfire.

The seven tall trees are important local eucalypts of D'Harawal country. Each has its own warrior name, and each has special uses. Each also contributed special parts to the campfire that burned up the Wiree, and each had a special wound after the battle with these spirit sorcerers.

Boo'angi, the spotted gum (*Blakella maculata*; illus. 15) makes excellent *wumara* and *woomeras* (spear-throwers and shields). It contributed gum to the fire and blood was on Boo'angi's arm after the battle. *Mai'andowi*, the smooth-barked grey gum (*Eucalyptus punctata*), has special medicines to ward off evil spirits, contributed a branch to the Wiree fire and was missing a little finger afterwards. The tree is found from the Blue Mountains down to the coast in D'Harawal country. *Bai'yali*, the white stringybark (*E. globoidea*), holds the secrets of fire-making in its bark and had skin missing from his leg. *Bourrounj*, the Sydney peppermint (*E. piperita*), found good food to keep the warriors strong, gave nectar from its flowers to the campfire and had swollen, wet eyes after the battle. *Terri'yergo*, the scaly-barked gum (*E. squamosa*), is best for boomerangs, provided a woody root for the fire and had a toe missing afterwards. It is the warrior with the narrowest geographical range, being confined to sandstone plateaus, such as those in Royal National Park south of Botany Bay and Ku-rin-gai Chase National Park north of Sydney.[8] *Kai'yeroo*, the ribbon gum (*E. viminalis*), makes excellent spears, provided gum nuts to burn on the Wiree fire and was missing a tooth afterwards. In D'Harawal country the tree occurs inland in the Blue Mountains and westwards.[9] Lastly, *Mugga'go*, Beyer's ironbark (*E. beyeri*), provided shelter that kept evil spirits at bay, shed leaves for the campfire and lost some of its hair in the battle. This is a third Blue Mountains species among the seven Warriors of Peace, found inland to the west

16–19 Life-cycle components of *marri* or *kardan* (*Corymbia calophylla*), a Southwest Australian endemic, known as bloodwood or red gum. *Clockwise from top left:* adult leaves, buds and fruits; juvenile leaf; seedling; seeds.

and northwest in D'Harawal country, but approaching the coast around Jervis Bay.

These characterizations of the Warriors of Peace in tree form have practical as well as moral implications. *Kai'yeroo*, for example, the ribbon gum tree, produces tall, straight saplings that are ideal for spears, and the missing tooth alludes to tooth evulsion as a rite for the transition to manhood during *yulang yirabadjang* (initiation), or to womanhood on marriage. *Mai'andowi* missing a little finger alludes to the special fishing

15 *Opposite: Boo'angi* (spotted gum, *Blakella maculata*) from the story of Yandel'mawa, the seven Warriors of Peace, of the D'Harawal people.

powers of some *guragalungalyung* (girls), who were selected for this rite of early amputation using spider silk to cut circulation, and who became women called *malgun*.[10]

Megababang (women) are also mainly responsible for the medicinal use of plants, and grey gum (*E. punctata*) is useful in that regard. Bloodwoods (*Corymbia*), such as *marri* (*C. calophylla*) from Western Australia and *boo'angi* from Sydney, ooze red gum of medicinal value from wounds on their trunks (illus. 16–20). *Bourrounj*, the Sydney peppermint, offers a sweet, mildly intoxicating drink when its flowers are soaked in water, and its aromatic, oil-rich leaves offer relief from eye infections. The sinuous *terri'yergo* (scaly-barked gum) is suitably

20 Red gum oozing from wounds on the stump of *marri* (*Corymbia calophylla*).

21 Birrpai man Charlie Murray removing bark in an early stage of *nuwi* (canoe) manufacture near Port Macquarie on the central coast of New South Wales, *c.* 1905.

curvaceous for boomerang manufacture where the roots join the stump – hence the toe chopped away in the Dreaming story. The tough *muggaʾgo* (ironbark) offers waterproof bark strips for constructing huts and *nuwi* (canoe) hulls (illus. 21–3). *Baiʾyali*, the white stringybark, also provides long *lamandra* (strips of bark, hence the skin missing from his leg) that is used for waterproofing *gonye* (huts), building *nuwi*, making dilly bags and *yung* (shields) and the fine tinder needed to light fires.

27

22 Birrpai men Charlie Murray (left) and Neil Morcom (right) shaping a *nuwi* (canoe) after smoking the bark following its removal from the tree, near Port Macquarie on the central coast of New South Wales, *c.* 1905.

23 Birrpai man Peter Budge in a finished *nuwi* (canoe), with Charlie Murray and Neil Morcom on the branch, near Port Macquarie on the central coast of New South Wales, *c.* 1905.

This Dreamtime story in the public form relayed by Bodkin makes it clear that eucalypts are strong allies, shared by many Aboriginal people across their lands, and are not to be feared or shown disrespect. Medicines, kindling for fire, bark for shelter and canoes, sweet drinks and useful material for wooden tools and weapons are all provided by these trees, which are richly diverse in the Sydney region, requiring a discerning eye to recognize the different species and their uses. Morally, the story highlights that good spirits who cooperate and pool their resources will win over evil, and that wide consultation with evidence from disputees considered carefully by intelligent and wise Elders helps with decisions that can bring lasting peace if obeyed by the people. It also argues that the D'Harawal are especially suited to such strong peacemaking.

The Aboriginal recognition and names of different eucalypt species and even hybrids in the Sydney region were documented by George Caley in 1805–9.[11] He hired an agile bilingual Darkinyung teenager, Moowat-tin, as a tree-climber and collector of eucalypt specimens. Some thirty of Moowat-tin's names for eucalypts have been passed down to the present day through notes on Caley's herbarium sheets in Vienna, London and elsewhere.[12] These include *banga'ly* for the common coastal *E. robusta* and *burrar'gro* for a natural hybrid of *burragro-derrobarry* (ironbark, *E. siderophloia*) and *baril'gora* (grey box, *E. moluccana*). The Darkinyung taxonomy conveyed by Moowat-tin indicates a level of sophistication in understanding eucalypt diversity that took settler botanists more than a century to comprehend fully.[13]

Eucalypts featured prominently in male initiation rituals – the *Bunan* ceremonies – carried out by coastal peoples from Sydney southwards. Earth walls connecting circular areas enclosed representations of animal and other spirits, including Dharramoolun or Dharamoolan, a one-legged thunder-voiced male spirit of prime importance to initiation rites. Eucalypts growing adjacent to the earth walls were marked with significant geometric patterns, and their burls (warty excrescences on trunks, known as *dhunnunggalung*) were considered to be resting places for Dharramoolun. More prosaically, small burls were also

24 Birrpai man Charlie Murray observing Neil Morcom engaged in the removal of a burl from the trunk as part of a bowl construction process on the central coast of New South Wales, c. 1910. The small burls being harvested from a eucalypt will be made into wooden containers and drinking vessels called *cudji* or *cogie* by the Blue Mountains Gundungurra people.

harvested (illus. 24) and hollowed out to form small wooden containers and drinking vessels called *cudji* or *cogie* by the Gundungurra people of the Blue Mountains.[14]

Eucalypt Dreaming from Tropical Australia

Thawurr denmesri (rough-leaved bloodwood, *Corymbia dunlopiana*), a small tree with bright red flowers found at the northwestern end of the Northern Territory, is named after lightning that occurred during the creation of country (*yek* or *rak* respectively) by the Marri Ngarr and Magati Ke coastal people near the Moyle River.[15] Lightning stories also apply to particular trees of *lunja* or *wimbad* (snappy gum, *E. brevifolia*; illus. 25) from the Jaru people's border country of the Western Australian Kimberley and adjacent western Northern Territory. This tree sometimes has lightning flickering out of its branches, said to be a harbinger of bad things.[16]

25 Special trees of snappy gum (*Eucalyptus brevifolia*), known as *lunja* or *wimbad* to the Jaru people of the tropical Western Australian/ Northern Territory border country, forecast bad things. Barramundie Eggs Hill, Argyle, in the Kimberley region of Western Australia.

The Marri Ngarr and Magati Ke people use the slender, straight, termite-hollowed trunks of *thawurr denmesri* for making didgeridoos, and sugarbag (honey from social native bee nests) is found in the cavities of the trees (illus. 26, 27). Other bloodwoods, such as *nandji arrwu* (*C. confertiflora* or *C. papuana*), yield a fine ash when the bark is burned, and this is used as an additive in chewing tobacco. Digging sticks come from *nandji rtadimer* (*C. foelscheana*) and *nandji warlan* (*C. porrecta*). Edible seeds are enjoyed from *nandji akan* (woollybutt, *E. miniata*; illus. 28, 29).

An important food from the red bloodwoods (section *Septentrionales* within *Corymbia*) across northern and central Australia is known to the Marri Ngarr and Magati Ke people as *a-ngurrmu* (bush coconut).[17] These are roundish galls up to 9 centimetres (3½ in.) in diameter formed by eriococcid bugs, three species in the genus *Cystococcus*.[18] The hard outer wall of the gall is broken open and the fleshy interior eaten, as well as the very sweet-tasting insects themselves. Female *Cystococcus* inside the galls give birth to males first, then females. Young sisters cling to their winged brothers when they leave the gall in search of mates, so

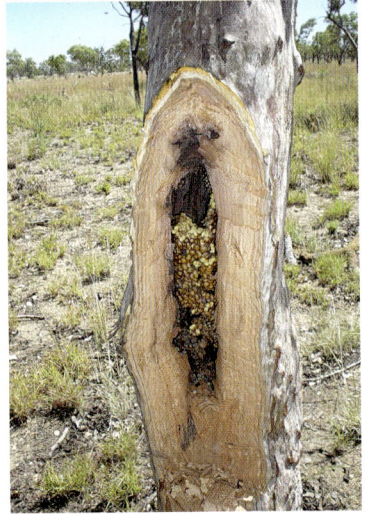

26 *Left*: Food from tropical Western Australian eucalypts: *laju, bardi* or *wichetty* grub (*Eucalyptus victrix*), Walmajarri people, near Paraku, Kimberley.
27 *Right*: Sugarbag honey of native trigonid bees (on *E. brevifolia*), Gija people, near Greenvale, East Kimberley.

28 *Nandji akan* (woollybutt, *Eucalyptus miniata*) of the Marri Ngarr and Magati Ke coastal people near the Moyle River, in woodland near Berry Springs, Northern Territory.

both sexes disperse across red bloodwood populations. *Nandji venhnhi* (*Corymbia polycarpa*) is the prime source of *a-ngurrmu*.

An unusually playful use of *nandji nadimelh* (swamp bloodwood, *C. ptychocarpa*), a species with large pink flowers that attract honey-eaters and lorikeets, is to blow up the soft new leaves to form a small balloon. Marri Ngarr and Magati Ke people bite the edges of these leaves and blow into the hole, the tissue being elastic enough to expand, balloon-like. Such young leaves of several eucalypts are also used by many people across Australia to make a kazoo-like vibrating valve for gum leaf music, as well as to mimic bird calls. As with Tasmanian and southern mainland people, sheets of *nandji wesri* (stringybark, *E. tetrodonta*) are stripped during the monsoonal summer wet season when sap is flowing, lightly burned (see illus. 22) and dried hard, so

29 *Eucalyptus miniata*, illustrating various details including its edible seeds.

that they become waterproof. The bark sheets are then laid over a wooden frame to make *wuwup* (shelters). *Nandji mimir* (baskets) could also be made from *nandji wesri* for carrying material and babies, to keep them dry in wet weather.

A white gum with *nandji arrwu* (smooth bark, *E. umbrawarrensis*) is found on sandstone ridges and ranges only in the tropics of the Northern Territory.[19] When dry, its bark is burned, and the resulting white ash improves the flavour and strength of chewing tobacco.

A connection to the Dreaming is implied by a use of the red sap of *ngendil* or *dan*, the smooth-stemmed bloodwood (*Corymbia bleeseri*), by Northern Territory Malakmalak and Matngala people, who live around the lower reaches of the Daly River southwest of Darwin.[20] The sap is painted on didgeridoos made from the wood of *menyikerrik* or *menykerrwek* (*C. ferruginea*), *didinbuk* or *yuwer* (Darwin woollybutt)

(*E. miniata*; see illus. 28, 29) and especially the hill woollybutt (*E. phoen-icea*). Elders have said that the red sap of *ngendil* makes didgeridoos 'look good and gives them special powers'.[21] Since this is all that has been published, those special powers are presumably sacred and secret knowledge only for initiated people.

C. *bleeseri* also features prominently in the Dreaming of the Wunambal Gaambera people of the northwestern Kimberley coast, around the Mitchell River in far northern Western Australia. Known as *burungurr*, the bloodwood was the launch point for Cheinmora ancestors, who 'leapt from this tree into the Milky Way'.[22]

Southern Victoria

Diagonally southeast across the nation, on the outskirts of Melbourne in temperate Victoria, eucalypt Dreaming has a special place in the cosmology of the Wurunjerri or Woiworung people, whose country is transected by the Birrarung/Yarra River. In the late nineteenth century the anthropologist Alfred William Howitt was told of a spiritual land in the sky known as Tharangalk-bek, the gum-tree country.[23] The great creator ancestor and spirit wedge-tailed eagle Bunjil arrived there with his family atop a *williwilli*. Bunjil is the star Altair in the Eagle Constellation, and the spirits of dead people ascend to Tharangalk-bek. This story is shared by other Kulin people, such as the Wathaurong, throughout western central Victoria. *Tharangalk* is *Eucalyptus viminalis*, the manna gum (illus. 30), which provides edible sugary insect secretions of manna and lerp on its leaves.

Although Howitt and his colleagues were keen to align Aboriginal beliefs with the Christian concept of a supreme being in heaven – or perhaps their informants sensed this and emphasized it in the stories of Bunjil – many Aboriginal cultures have Dreaming stories that end with ancestral heroes becoming part of the night sky.[24] This is consist-ent with meticulous attention to the spatial relationships of features on land and in the night sky for helpful navigation. The Dreaming provides a cosmology suitable for an oral tradition that fully integrates

30 *Tharangalk* (manna gum, *Eucalyptus viminalis*). In Victoria,
near Melbourne, Wurunjerri people believe that the spirits of dead
people ascend to Tharangalk-bek, gum-tree country in the sky.

travelling on country, respecting and following the journeys of ancestral beings, and translating the practical and moral implications of
these journeys into a rich tapestry of social relations and expected
behaviour.

The practical uses of eucalypts in this area were similar to those
for the Sydney region and tropical Australia, such as bark for canoes
and shelters, gum (*kino*) for medicine and wood for fire.

Inland People of the Murray-Darling Basin
and the Mighty River Red Gum

Several cultures saw the Milky Way as a great river lined with river
red gums (*E. camaldulensis* subsp. *camaldulensis*), the ultimate resting
place for spirits of the dead.[25] For Gamilaraay/Kamilaroi-speaking
Ualarai people near Angledool in northern inland New South Wales,

Warrambool was the Milky Way, and a river red gum features in their night-sky Dreaming as Yarraan-doo/the Southern Cross. It was the

> first *Minggah*, or spirit tree[,]a huge *Yaraan*, which was the medium for the translation of the first man who died on earth to the sky. The white cockatoos which used to roost in this tree when they saw it moving skywards followed it, and are following it still as *Mouyi*, the pointers. The other *Yaraan* trees wailed for the sadness that death brought into the world, weeping tears of blood. The red gum which crystallises down their trunks is the tears.[26]

The river red gum is the most widespread of all eucalypts on mainland Australia. Famous in art, photography and river lore, it has a long history in Aboriginal Dreaming. The vast network of rivers, creeks and floodplains of the Murray-Darling basin are dominated by the red gum, and the tree features in the creation stories of many languages. For example, the Wemba Wemba people, who live upstream and either side of the Murray from Swan Hill, 50 kilometres (31 mi.) southeast of the junction with the Murrumbidgee River, describe the creation of the Mile/Murray River as a great battle near Merteruk-pert/Swan Hill between a mighty hunter, Totyerguil, of the mallee country of northwestern Victoria, and Otchout, a huge Murray River cod. Totyerguil's two *wuthu payingguk* (young sons), in search of wattle gum, came across the big fish in a waterhole and ran back to tell their *marn* (father). Totyerguil quickly built a *yungwity* (canoe) and speared the resting fish in the back, but it rushed to the banks and formed a channel to another waterhole, where it hid and rested overnight. Totyerguil located the cod the next morning and speared it in the back again, but another channel was formed as the giant fish escaped to another waterhole. This was repeated over many days, all the way to Murray Bridge in South Australia, where Otchout hid in a very deep pool before escaping into the sky as the *turt* (star) Delphinus. Totyerguil, who had by this time run out of spears, went to the banks and stood his *yungwity* and *wak* (paddle) upright on their ends. The canoe became a huge *piyal* (river red gum) and the paddle a *kalpen* (Murray pine, *Callitris columellaris*). The ridge of spines along the back of the cod are there to remind people of this heroic chase in the Dreaming, and all know that canoes are best made from the *mityuk* (bark of *piyal*), and paddles from *kalpen*.[27]

As Australia's largest permanent river system, the Murray-Darling has proved a major refuge for Aboriginal people during the climatic dynamism of the late Pleistocene and Holocene, supporting large permanent populations for approximately 40,000 years.[28] Today's canoe and fishing cultures along the rivers and tributaries have an ancient ancestry. The forests of river red gum are deeply steeped in Dreaming stories and revered almost universally, with individual trees 'recognised, recorded and protected'.[29]

The Yorta Yorta people, upstream neighbours of the Wemba Wemba and Baraba Baraba, care for some of the largest stands of *bala* (river red gums) in the Paam/Barmah forest along the Dungala/Murray River near Goulburn. Their creation story, *Ina Yillian*, alludes to the great ancestral hero Baiami, who suggests that a hungry old woman, Gumuk Winga, should dig some yams across a vast misty flat landscape.[30] Gumuk Winga is unsuccessful and tired, dragging her digging stick behind her, so Baiami summons the spirit snake Gane to help and follow her. Gane cuts a deep, sinuous furrow through the landscape, creating hills and valleys, giving colour to all things, following the trail of the digging stick. Then it rains incessantly, the landscape floods and the great river Dungala flows.

Well north of the Murray, the anthropologist Robert Hamilton Mathews recorded that river red gums and other eucalypts feature in the Dreaming of the Wiraidyuri people of the western plains and rivers of New South Wales. For Sydney Basin people, Dhurramulan, a half-brother of the supreme ancestor Baiaimi, is an important character, especially to do with male initiation rites. He was also known as Ngullagelung/Ngulla (tree), alluding to his common abode. With a voice like thunder, he was responsible for separating young adolescent initiates from their mothers and teaching lore and law during *burbung* ceremonies. Tooth evulsion was part of his domain, the upper incisors of boys in the Dreaming becoming the *gunabillang* (crystals) used as sacred stones during initiation rites. *Muddhiga* (bullroarers), flat, narrow pieces of wood that were swung around the head on lengths of string to make a deep humming sound, were other sacred items for the eyes of male Elders only, emulating the thunderous voice of Dhurramulan. Moreover, he often sat upon gnarly outgrowths or burls of eucalypts, 'worn smooth by Dhurramulan's repeated occupation', from which position he behaved as a transforming trickster, destroyer and regen-erator.[31] Certain eucalypts themselves became sacred as such platforms and homes for Dhurramulan/Ngullagelung.

The Ngemba/Ngiyampaa people near Brewarrina, the furthest navigable point on the Darling River east of Bourke in western New South Wales, had an unusual marriage system that divided people into 'blood' and 'shade' groups. Mathews learned that camping and resting places under the shade of large river red gums were regulated by group according to the particular shade cast by the trees:

> The shadow thrown by the butt and lower portion of the tree is called '*nhurrai*', that cast by the middle portion of the tree is '*wau-gue*'; whilst the shade of the top of the tree, or outer margin of the shadow is '*winggu*' . . . Again, the men[,]women and children, whose prescribed sitting places are in the butt and middle shades of the trees are called '*guai mundhan*', or sluggish blood, while those who sit in the top or outside shade are des-ignated '*guai gulir*', or active blood . . . [the latter] are supposed to keep a strict watch for any game which may appear in sight, the approach of friends or enemies, or anything which may require vigilance in a native camp.[32]

This system of bloods and shades was widely adopted across western New South Wales, indicating the central importance of river red gums in the daily lives and marriages of these people.

Trees in Trees of the Barwon River
Palaeochannels near Walgett, New South Wales

The flat, featureless terrain of the Barwon River palaeochannel is dominated by woodlands including *buubaya* (bimble box, *E. populnea*), *gulabah* (coolibah, *E. coolabah*) and *guburruu* (black box, *E. largiflorens*). These trees become hollowed out by termite attack, and the local river-dwelling Kamilaroi, Euahlayi (Yuwaalayay) and Wailwan people enlivened their homelands by culturally modifying the eucalypts. They created bowls enriched with termite droppings within the base of the eucalypts, in which plants of different genera were planted and watered to commemorate individuals who had passed away. This created a tree (guest)-in-tree (host) combination, reflecting totems of the deceased and bedecked with markings corresponding to the cicatrices (scar tissue) possessed by the individuals concerned.

The most common guest species and their families found in a recent survey included peach bush (*Ehretia saligna* in the family Boraginaceae), wilga (*Geijera parviflora*, Rutaceae), currant (*Apophyllum anomalum*, syn. *Capparis anomala*, Capparaceae), boonaree (*Alectryon oleifolius*, Sapindaceae) and native orange (*Capparis mitchellii*, Capparaceae).[33] The guest trees would extend their roots downwards into the soil, and many persisted for centuries, eventually splitting the host eucalypt apart. These 'trees in trees' enlivened the often featureless, flat terrain, affording landmarks and meaning to campsites and country that reinforces a deep sense of place among the riverside people.

Most of the eucalypts in this region have other common practical uses, including (local Euahlayi (Yuwaalayay) names first) – *buubaya* (see above for bimble box *E. populnea*), *gulabah*, *guburruu*, *gaywuwildhaa* (long-fruited bloodwood, *Corymbia dolichocarpa*), *thiinyaay* (ironbark, *Eucalyptus melliodora*), *gundhi* (red stringybark, *E. macrorhyncha*), *dhani* (manna gum, *E. viminalis*), *yarraan* (river red gum, *E. camaldulensis*), *bibil* (grey box, *E. moluccana*, white box, *E. albens* and yellow box, *E. melliodora*), *bulamin* (apple tree, *Angophora floribunda*) and *gaabiin* (carbeen, *Blakella tessellaris*). These uses ranged from food, water, shelter, firewood, habitat for wildlife (especially edible possums, koalas, goannas), medicine (for example, poultices, disinfectant to treat wounds or bruising), oil, timber (for spears, coolamon, woomera, boomerangs) and bark (canoes, shields, burial slabs, tabletops).[34] Special uses included hollow branches for the musical instrument the didgeridoo (*gaywuwildhaa*, C. *dolichocarpa*; *bibíl*, *E. albens*). Small branches (*bungun*) of *bibíl* were used as decorations for ceremony (*corroborees*), while the young roots of *bibíl* can be eaten when pounded. Plant gum (*dhani*) of this species can tan hides. *Girran gírra*, the small leaves of *gulabah* (*E. coolabah*), are used to stun fish, and can treat headaches, sore throat, fever and sore eyes. The inner bark of *gulabah* when pounded can form a poultice for snake bite. Roots of *gulabah* hold water that can quench thirst. Perhaps the most versatile species is river red gum (*yarraan*, *E. camaldulensis*). Apart from other uses above, its *nganda* (bark) forms a chewing tobacco, for example. Deep understanding of local eucalypts and their utility is evident here.

Central Australians

In the central Northern Territory, Tommy Kngwarraye Thompson outlined the fundamental importance of river red gums in the Dreaming of his Kaytetye people from Barrow Creek, 250 kilometres (155 mi.) north of Alice Springs:

> in the Dreamtime . . . river red gum leaves were laid out on the ground and then they were turned over. They were not ordinary leaves. They were laid out one by one, and each was counted as it was laid out. First one girl – the eldest sister – then her younger sister, then their youngest sister, and then the youngest ones. They were groups of sisters related as aunts and nieces to each other. The leaves were decorated with their own ceremonial designs . . . Then they spoke their language. It was *Kaytetye*. The leaves were girls from the Dreamtime called *Kwerrimpe*. They told each other Dreamtime stories,

special stories that had the power to create. From these stories the *Kaytetye* language and people were born.[35]

Individual river red gums are named, revered and protected in many central Australian cultures. They play a signal role in the Caterpillar Dreaming of the Arrernte people around Mparntwe/Alice Springs. The caterpillars, of three species, originated at Anthwerrke/Emily Gap in the MacDonnell Ranges southeast of Mparntwe.[36] Caterpillar Dreaming is about women's business and the east side of town and the Todd River. The west side is Dingo Dreaming, men's business, and Ntaripe/Heavitree Gap, where the Todd courses through the MacDonnell Ranges, is a special place that women traditionally avoided. The caterpillars moved northwards from Anthwerrke across the country, creating various topographical features on the eastern side of Mparntwe.

The Arrernte people regard *apere* (river red gums) as being imbued with ancestral spiritual power. Some trees are a *kwekatye* (uninitiated boy or adolescent), involved in a songline that extends across the continent from Port Augusta in South Australia to the north coast. On the female side, many *apere* in the Todd River represent ancestral caterpillars from Urlatherrke/Mt Zeil 100 kilometres (62 mi.) to the west, who became lost on their way east to Anthwerrke. When the Urlatherrke caterpillars of the *Yeperenye* species camped overnight in the Todd on the north side of town, they ate *Ayepe* vine at a rock outcrop known as Atnelkentyarliweke Athirnte. There they painted up and devised ceremonies that future Arrernte people could observe to ensure the continuance of Caterpillar Dreaming and of the species. The river red gums thus make children strong through spiritual power, each child being connected intimately to the ancestral Dreaming, a sacred unity.

Apart from their strong role in Dreaming stories, the uses of *apere* by Central Australian people are extensive.[37] The scale-like sugary coating of sap-feeding *aperaltye* (lerps), *Psylla eucalypti*, is plucked from the leaves and eaten, and a sweet drink is made by soaking bark on which the exudate of another lerp has accumulated. The edible cater-pillars (*laju, bardi* or *wichetty* grubs) of a cossid moth are extracted from the trunks of *apere* and *ankerre* (western coolibah, *E. victrix*; see illus. 26), and the tasty *ahernenge* (caterpillars) of a hepialid moth (*Trictena argentata*) and the larvae of a cicada beetle (*Tropha* sp.) come from the roots of the *apere. Coolamons* (carrying bowls) are painstakingly crafted from curved roots or burls on the trunk. The dead wood is used for fire and the dry bark provides ash for mixing with the drug from *pituri* (*Duboisia hopwoodii*). Boys make a crude type of boomerang from the fresh bark and a wheel for spear practice. The leaves are used by girls and women for various games and in love magic rituals. Gum nuts of *apere* (river red gum) are also placed in the hair as adornments and to keep flies at bay, while the bud caps are assembled into necklaces by children. Armbands and legbands loaded with leaves make a rustling sound during dance. The branches make shady shelters and clean floors for food processing, and a medicinal drink or wash is obtained from the bark steeped in water.

Other central Australian eucalypts provide edible seeds. In Arrernte language, these include *ankerre* (western coolibah, *E. victrix*) and *uleperre* (blue mallee, *E. gamophylla*). The Warlpiri people also eat the seed of mallees, such as *yirruwu* (Normanton box, *E. normantonensis*) and *jitilypuru* (red mallee, *E. pachyphylla*).

Desert bloodwoods (*Corymbia opaca* and *C. chippendalei*; illus. 31) have similar uses to those outlined for people from Sydney and the tropical north of Australia.[38] Known as *arrkernke* by the Arrernte people, bloodwoods provide *arrkipangkwerle* (bush coconuts) with their large edible grubs and the inner flesh of the gall itself. The sugary lerp are consumed, and the flowers soaked in water afford a sweet drink. Honey ('sugarbag') from hives of stingless trigonid bees is a much-favoured delicacy. Water is found in the roots and trunk cavities. The gum mixed with water (or an ointment made from the crushed bark) heals burns, sore eyes and lips, wounds and sore throats; mixed with kangaroo dung, the gum forms a cement for repairing wooden tools and bowls. The red sap tans kangaroo-skin waterbags, while the wood is favoured for fires and the burls are made into water bowls. The nuts and buds become decorative hairpieces or are threaded into necklaces, while the leaves are attached to arms and legs in ceremonies. Peter Latz found that the Warlpiri people use smoke from the leaves of bloodwoods (*wirrkali* in their language) mixed with the hair of a murder victim to detect a killer from the direction in which the smoke blows.[39]

Returning to Dreamtime stories, desert bloodwoods feature prominently, as Latz relays:

the crumbly bark of a certain sacred tree plays an important part in a particular *Pitjantjatjara* grass-seed increase ceremony, and some unusual trees with large boles on the trunk sometimes represented mythological ancestors. There is a sacred tree growing near a certain *Pitjantjatjara* settlement. It is believed anyone falling asleep under this tree will soon die.[40]

31 The vast central and western deserts of the Eremaean North have relatively few eucalypts. Most are found in rocky ranges or along rivers and creeks, but also atop extensive sand-dune systems, as seen here with sand-dune bloodwoods (*Corymbia chippendalei*), alive and burned dead, in the Little Sandy Desert of Western Australia.

32 *Wirnda ngarda*, the windswept trees (*Eucalyptus camaldulensis × E. rudis* genetically stabilized intergrades) of the Greenough Flats on Australia's west coast north of Perth, are a notable tourist attraction, as well as being significant to Aboriginal Dreaming.

The naming of unusual red gums (*E. camaldulensis*) extends across the wide geographical range of the species. The spectacular bent trees of the Greenough Flats on the west coast north of Perth (illus. 32) are called *wirnda ngarda* (tree; crouched, hanging down, bent, uncomfortably bent, crooked, lying in an awkward position) by the Wadjarri and coastal Noongar people. This prosaic name undoubtedly belies more profound ceremonial meanings that are not shared publicly. These bent trees are included in *E. camaldulensis* subsp. *arida*, but form part of a genetically stabilized hybrid intergrade between *E. camaldulensis* and its southwest rough-barked relative *E. rudis*.

The plant collector and ethnologist Augustus Oldfield spent several months further north in the late 1850s with the Watchandie Nanda people around what is now Kalbarri National Park, near the mouth of the Murchison River. He recorded the centrality of song in cementing social ties, even with a foreign botanist:

> The Watchandies, seeing me much interested in the genus *Eucalyptus*, soon composed a song on this subject:

Toota babeen, Yandre babeen,
Collaille babeen, Warrigeera.[41]

This can be translated – less elegantly than the sonorous native language – as 'spearwood [*E. arachnaea*] friend, family of shrubby mallee eucalypts friends, river gum [*E. camaldulensis*] friend, [as is] woody pear [*Xylomelum angustifolium*, family Proteaceae]'. Powerful in its simplicity, the song would have been wonderfully evocative, sung around the campfire by several men, the women also 'singing and keeping time by beating with sticks on their skin cloaks done up into tight bundles', a tribute to the professional zeal of their British companion.[42]

Eucalypts are also enspirited trees, full of cultural meaning, so the Watchandie people may have noted that this white man was unusual in wanting to learn the names of such important trees. He was told the names, but not deeper stories, which were reserved for initiated men. Oldfield was oblivious to this, misreading the pervasive influence of religion and special knowledge throughout Aboriginal life, mistaking the simple information given to him as indicative of simple minds. In fact, every tree had a story; some were powerful, some to be avoided, some markers of songlines traversed by ancestral spirits.

For example, further north on the Beasley River of the arid Pilbara region, the Yinhawangka people recognize a *marralha* (river red gum, *E. camaldulensis* subsp. *refulgens*) tree as a *jibalarda* (increase site). One old tree in particular is known as a *Baby Thalu* site, a spiritual woman's place. The community researcher and campaigner Lorraine Injie eloquently described the significance of the site as a special place in her country:

The women that wanted to have babies came here to visit the *Baby Thalu* . . . A long time ago, the old people used to come here to wake up the babies, they say they could hear the babies crying, it was alive with their spirit. They hit the tree with small, leafy branches [and] talk in language, saying they have come to visit to make their request. Even when my Mum was alive she brought a couple of women that couldn't have babies to this tree and they ended up having kids ... There are many species of the gum tree: the *Wilhu* (white gum) [*E. victrix*], the *Mayigam* (snappy gum) [*E. brevifolia*] and the river *Marralha* (red gum), we boil the leaves and drink it as tea.[43]

Here we see eucalypts as active players in the Dreaming of people, sharing their power if addressed respectfully and appropriately, providing the gift of spirit children and life-giving tea. Such connections in some Aboriginal cultures were reinforced following childbirth. The Joondaburri people of Bribie Island near Brisbane and the Dalla people near the Blackall Range rubbed mothers and week-old babies all over with ash of the grey ironbark (*E. siderophloia*).[44] This continued for a week, until mother and child rejoined the family in the camp. A physical and protective connection with eucalypts was thus established even before the babies were seen by their fathers. Tree-climbing, too, was commenced at an early age, as recorded by the settler Charles Archer in 1844 on the first pastoral lease in Dalla country: 'We have several little black boys staying with us and you would be astonished to see a child not more than four years old climbing up a high tree which I am sure I couldn't ascend[,] looking for honey.'[45]

Wati Nyiinyii Tjukurpa (Zebra Finch Men Dreaming) and the Water Mallees of the Spinifex People

The Spinifex people of the Great Victoria Desert to the north of the Nullarbor Plain are among the last of the Aboriginal cultures to have made contact with European Australians. Some families remained isolated right up to the 1980s. Consequently, their culture has proved to be one of the best-documented in terms of the details of traditional life.[46] Eucalypts feature in the *Tjukurpa* (Dreaming) of the Wati Nyiinyii (Zebra Finch men), along an *iwarra* (songline) from interior desert dunes across the Nullarbor to the Southern Ocean. The broad path of the *iwarra* is taken separately by the two main kinship groupings of the Spinifex people: *Purungu* or fathers, the sun people, who take the exposed northern side; and *Narrupa* or sons, the shadow people, who take lower ground sheltered mainly by eucalypts.

Wati Nyiinyii Tjukurpa hinges on the bad behaviour of a selfish old man, who hoards water and uproots trees. This occurs especially at one location, where the life-giving water-bearing roots of water/red mallee (*E. socialis*) are broken and the land floods to the south through underground aquifers. The Wati Nyiinyii travel south to stop the flood and return their water to the north. As they travel through dune country and past waterholes, they are reminded of their red colours by the red bark and new growth of other mallees (*E. alatissima*, *E. pachyphylla*). On the way they leave many stone arrangements, which are brushed reverently with mallee branches by living Spinifex people following the *iwarra*. At the base of the Nullarbor cliffs the Wati Nyiinyii erect thousands of spears to hold back the floodwaters, so that perhaps the Dreaming here represents an ancient oral history of sea-level rises in the early Holocene.[47]

Seven Sisters Dreaming

This Dreaming transcends local cultures and traverses the nation east to west, from southeastern Queensland to the Pilbara of northwestern Western Australia and southwest to Albany. It consists of several songlines, handed down through family oral histories. The Seven Sisters are spirit women who are chased across the continent by two lustful spirit men, Wati Nyiru, creating country as the long journey unfolds. The Seven Sisters end up in the sky as the Pleiades constellation, although in Albany they were turned to stone at prominent granite outcrops.[48]

One part of their journey runs southwest from Angas Downs Station 120 kilometres (75 mi.) east-northeast of Uluru/Ayers Rock across the Northern Territory's southern border into South Australia to the beautifully painted Walinynga/Cave Hill 80 kilometres (50 mi.) south-southeast of Uluru.[49] The remarkable flat-topped mesa known as Atila/Mt Connor lies midway along this 150-kilometre (93 mi.)

route. There the Sisters see Nyiru, the two lustful spirit men, spying on them. The Sisters flee south to Witapula waterhole, where, frightened, they go underground and follow subterranean aquifers, surfacing to the southwest. Nyiru are there waiting, so the Sisters run to Walinynga and build a spinifex grass shelter that becomes Cave Hill. Pressed by the Nyiru, they escape through a small opening at the back of the cave and dance southwards.

At the start of this journey, the Pitjantjatjara artist Niningka Lewis has beautifully illustrated the Seven Sisters as a row of river red gums (*E. camaldulensis*) lining the creek at Irawa bore.[50] Nearby a Wati Nyiru spirit man has also become a tree, ever watching. The Sisters morph into humans and move on southwest, camp and sleep, then turn into granite boulders to escape the Nyiru. The river red gums at Irawa forever mark a women's place, where young women are taught the many lessons arising from the adventures of the Seven Sisters.

Having explored aspects of the rich diversity of Aboriginal cultural perspectives on eucalypts on the mainland, the next two chapters explore further insights gained from Southwest Noongar people and those from Tasmania. With the richest concentration of eucalypts on the continent, Southwest Australia has an extraordinary Noongar Aboriginal oral tradition pertaining to eucalypts, and this deserves special treatment.

two

Noongar Sacred Cosmology and Eucalypts in Southwest Australia

✻❈✻

Noongar/Nyungar is a collective noun that has been adopted for the people who occupy most of Southwest Australia.[1] This region is a global biodiversity hotspot endowed with large numbers of threatened endemic species, and contains the richest concentration of native eucalypt species on Earth (see illus. 4). This richness is a heritage that the Noongar people deeply appreciate and integrate into their Dreaming. In the early twentieth century Ngilgian, a Noongar woman from the Busselton area south of Perth, articulated this responsibility specifically in relation to trees and other plants as:

> *Marri* and *jerrail, kolyung* and *mungaitch* [*Corymbia calophylla,*
> *Eucalyptus marginata, Acacia saligna, Banksia grandis*], and all the
> trees and plants and roots are our '*moorurt*' [relations, family],
> and many of them are our totem fathers and brothers, and
> they give us gum to eat, and honey [nectar], and '*marrain*' [all
> vegetable food].[2]

Many Noongar uses of eucalypts match those already described for people from other parts of Australia. For example, the importance of bloodwoods (*Corymbia*) as medicinal plants was recognized early, and similar use made of them by early settlers:

> farm women . . . concocted family health remedies [including]
> stewed eucalyptus leaves as an asthma inhalation, boiled red

gum bark [of *marri*, C. *calophylla*; see illus. 16–20] and strained and bottled it for stomach upsets (an Aboriginal remedy) . . . and took finely powdered charcoal for biliousness.[3]

A beverage, *numbrid*, was made from the nectar of the flowers of *marri* by soaking and partially fermenting them in fresh water held in paper-bark containers (*Melaleuca* spp.). Trees were scarred when used to make various implements (illus. 33), as well as to mark burial sites. Hunting in eucalypt vegetation was highly developed. A special favourite in *muert* (mallee) vegetation were the eggs of the *gnow*, the mallee fowl, which are incubated in large mounds up to 6 metres (20 ft) across (illus. 34). This megapode is widespread across semi-arid southern

33 Scarred trees, mainly caused by Noongar activity. *E. gomphocephala*, Kings Park, Perth.

34 Mallee vegetation from semi-arid Southwest Australia across to northwestern Victoria is home to this mound-nesting megapode, the mallee fowl, known as *gnow* to the Noongar people. Its eggs are a prized delicacy.

Australia. It is now vulnerable to predation by introduced foxes and cats, and habitat loss caused by clearing for broadacre agriculture and associated infrastructure. Its eggs are rarely eaten by people these days.

Trees are included in the Noongar creation story *Moondang-ak Kaaradjiny*, the Carers of Everything, by Noel Nannup Karda and family.[4] This tale relates that tree spirits formed with other plant, animal and people spirits at the end of the Nytting (ancient cold period), before the land and sky had separated and formed.

[There were] countless tree spirits and they were the most powerful of all. The Trees declared that there should be a carer of everything. And so a process of elimination began.

The tree spirits said, 'When we become real we will only grow in one place, which means we won't be able to look after anything else. It doesn't stop us, however, from making this promise: that we will provide whatever we can to help whoever wins the right to look after us and everything else. All we ask is that we are not used until there is none of us left'. Once the tree spirits made this promise they all moved to one side.[5]

Burls on eucalypts are interpreted by the Nannup family as signifying places for female business.[6] For example, a special open-mouthed cave on Hyden's Kaata gidj granite outcrop has York gums (*E. loxophleba* subsp. *loxophleba*) by its entrance, each with several burls resembling *boodjari yog* (pregnant women). This is the birthplace of the Noongar people, where they became real, and is thus an ancient cathedral of inestimable spiritual value.[7] Ignominiously, it is marketed as Hippo's Yawn by tourist operators unaware of its cultural significance.

Mallet, Maarlak, Moort, Muert, Wwyal (Mallee) and *Martilgarrang*

There are many small trees in Southwest Australia, and some with unique habits are known as *mallet*, *maarlak* (little hand, for the finger-like buds) and *moort* (family) to the Noongar people. *Mallets* include *E. astringens*, *E. gardneri* and *E. clivicola*. *Maarlak* and *marlock* embrace *E. conferruminata*, *E. utilis* and *E. macrandra*, while *moort* includes *E. platypus*, *E. vesiculosa* and *E. nutans*. All are killed by fire, regenerating from copious seed stores borne in the canopy. Typically, they form dense thickets that are impenetrable to people on horseback, as early European explorers quickly discovered.[8] Some of these trees are used for spears, since juvenile plants after fire grow tall and straight, and are of a suitable thickness. Indeed, the town of Merredin is reportedly named after the use of a local *mallet* as a source of spears, known as *merrit*.[9]

Some *maarlak* and *moort* species are associated with stories of evil spirits that entrap and eat any children or women who venture into

35 Illustration of *martilgarrang* (*Eucalyptus macrocarpa*), the largest-flowered eucalypt, a mallee from Southwest Australia with large silvery leaves.

their uniform stands.[10] Brown *mallet* (*E. astringens*) is known to the Noongar people from southeast of Kojonup as *wonnerak*, alluding to its preference as a source of women's *wanna* (digging sticks).[11] Today, the species continues to support a small industry involving the manufacture of wooden handles for tools.

A mallee or *muert* (multi-stemmed) eucalypt with bright silvery leaves from the *kwongkan* (sandplain) areas of Southwest Australia has names or stories that indicate its special importance. This spectacular species, with the largest flowers and nuts of any eucalypt, is *martilgarrang* (mottlecah, *E. macrocarpa*; illus. 35). The species is found in semi-arid wheatbelt country ranging from the central wheatbelt up to the *kwongkan* regions inland from Dongara and Geraldton on the west coast of Southwest Australia. The Noongar name for this species has been recorded variously as *matilgarring* in 1842, *mottelcah* in the early 1900s, *muttlegar* in 1928, *martilgarrang* in 1976 and, most recently, *marukaa* or *maruka* by Quairading Noongar Elders a few years ago.[12] The meaning of this name is literally derived from *maar* (hand or cloud, wind), *dilbi* (leaf) and *garrang* (anger, angry, fighting). The explorer and politician George Grey provided additional insight into the use of . . . *ang* by Noongars: '*angur* is used as a compound in words denoting some result of terror,' for example, '*kidjenangur* = to kill, to rend with the spear'; '*goortangur* = to howl with fear'; '*meerangwin* = crying'; '*ngoontoongur* = to dream [possibly nightmare]'; '*koondurnangur* = to thunder or rend the clouds'; '*moordabalangur* = to be firm, immovable'; '*morangur* = sick, unwell, having the cholic'; '*mannangur* = to hang down, to be pendant'.[13] Thus a translation of *martilgarrang* replete with references to powerful Dreaming might be the 'angry, enspirited plant with hand-sized leaves'.

The Nannup's story of the Carers of Everything has the original spirit woman Djindalade/Joondal/Woorjalluk (illus. 36) wandering

36 *Left: The Charnock Woman*, mosaic of Djindalade/Joondal Woorjalluk, the spirit women involved in creating Noongar *boodja* (country in Southwest Australia), by Jenny Dawson, Miv Egan and Sandra Hill, 1996, Claisebrook Cove, East Perth. Banished from walking on Earth for her role with spirit man Mulka in removing spirit babies from their place in the country, Djindalade (Jindalee)/Spirit Woman trampolined into the sky at Kaata gidj/Wave Rock and became the Milky Way. Spirit babies on the ground used eucalypt trees to make a scaffold to hold up the sky, then turned into *coolbardies* (Australian magpies) to peck children from her hair.
37 *Right:* Some of Southwest Australia's Noongar people see eucalypts like this *E. utilis* as the upside-down embodiment of Djindalade. When on Earth, she must stand on her head with feet aloft.

country in search of spirit man Mulka, picking up spirit baby stones on the way and placing them in her long grey hair. Djindalade realizes that her behaviour is improper and also is distraught when she discovers her husband eating spirit babies. She walks to Kaata gidj/Wave Rock near Hyden, which is still soft, and trampolines off the rock like a spear into the sky to seek atonement. She becomes the Milky Way and is banished from walking on Earth again. However, she returns upside down in the form of eucalypts like *E. utilis* (illus. 37) with two trunks (her legs) and short bole (abdomen), with the roots (her hair) clinging to the soil.

Old-Growth Eucalypt *Wiernyert* (Dreaming) of the Merningar Bardok Knapp Family

The Merningar Bardok dialect group of Noongar people ranged from Israelite Bay to Denmark along the south coast of Western Australia, with rights along sacred paths further west to the Warren River. One Merningar Bardok family who retain continuous oral history are the Knapps.[14]

At a critical period in the 1960s, two family members escaped the stolen generations – being incarcerated in missions where Western culture and the English language were enforced on children who had been stolen from their parents by official government policy. Dr Lynette Knapp is the one surviving member of her family to escape this persecution; because she contracted childhood meningitis in the first week of her captivity, the authorities chose not to care for a sick child and returned her to her parents. Subsequently brought up by her father, Alf, and other family members, Lynette learned about her family's culture in bush camps listening to full language speakers, while her father worked on farms and as a dingo hunter in the Albany region close to his birthplace.

Here we focus on the family's old-growth eucalypt Dreaming stories as taught to Lynette and her son Dion Cummings by Alf and other family members of his generation. The stories range from the parts of the south coast with the highest rainfall, supporting such giant eucalypts as *karri* (*E. diversicolor*) and red tingle (*E. jacksonii*), to the richly endowed mallee communities of Fitzgerald River National Park and Cape Arid National Park further east, including the most diverse eucalypt stands known.

Warrumbup: where the karri *trees gave birth to the rocks*

Warrumbup is a hill on the northern shore of Wilson Inlet, today part of the site of Denmark town. Its name was conveyed from nearby Albany's Resident Colonel Barker by his young Noongar guide Mokary/Mokare on an exploration trip in February 1830, and passed down through the generations by oral history. Here Lynette Knapp presents the story in three versions at different times and places. Three examples are necessary to highlight the richness and diversity of Meningar storytelling. Depending on context – including location, time of year and audience – different aspects of the *wiernyert* (Dreaming) are emphasized in these examples of recorded oral history:

> In 1974 I lived with my husband Bruce Cummings on Ocean Beach Road, Denmark, and my father [Alf Knapp] used to visit us. We'd pick Alf up from Albany and bring him here to stay with us. A lot of his stories came from Denmark. Denmark was the birthplace of the rocks that formed the hills and mountains around this way, and more importantly, the Borongorup [Porongurup] where those rocks are sacred. It is a part of this place as well. The place is behind us [where the birthplace lies]. That's what I've learned when I lived here. Warrumbup [Weedon Hill]. It's a place because of its sacredness that you don't go near. Even so, I've been up there many years ago. The same place where the rocks are, where the trees look like they are giving birth to the rocks. The Indigenous emphasis put on it is for all the rocks in this area. All

38 Warrumbup/Weedon Hill, Denmark, Western Australia,
where trees gave birth to rocks: *karri* (*Eucalyptus diversicolor*).

the *kaarts*, yeah, all the big hills. That hill, the sacredness of
it, is something to behold. It's the beginning of everything.

LYNETTE KNAPP,

20 February 2018, Denmark

Warrumbup is where I was told that the trees gave birth to
the rocks. Those rocks are sacred to us because they're our
keepers, our spiritual keepers. The importance of rocks in
and around this area and the birth of them in that birthplace is because we've got two totems. All Aboriginal people
have two totems, one of an animal and the other of a plant.
When we die we believe that our spirits go back into our
totems to replenish them and keep them going. When they
die, when the totems die, they become totemic spirits, and
all our totemic spirits go back into the rocks. The birth of the
rocks started in Denmark. The totem spirits go into the rocks

of Borongorup, or what they [white people] call the Poron-
gurups. So borongor, if what I said to you totem you'd understand what I mean. If you said to me what's your borongor,
well that's my totem. Borongor means totem. Borongorup is
the place of our totemic spirits. And Warrumbup is where
those rocks started from, and travelled to all the places where
rocks are, and rested. The Borongorup was the first place they
travelled to from Denmark. That is my great-grandmother
Jackbam's story passed down. Warrambup — Waar means
female kangaroo, so it's a female area. To prove it, if you go to
a certain area on the top of that *kaart* [hill] you'll see a place
where rocks were created from trees. Trees are birthing
rocks.

LYNETTE KNAPP,
22 April 2019, Goode Beach

This is a women's place. It's one of our creation stories here.
That's very important to us because we belong to the Earth

39 Warrumbup/Weedon Hill, Denmark, Western Australia,
slopes with *marri* (*Corymbia calophylla*) giving birth to granite rocks.

and the Earth belongs to us. But the Earth tells us what it is and where it is, whatever the story is. We have the same DNA as what you see growing around us [*karri* forest, *E. diversicolor*]. This place isn't really cared for now is it? The people over this side of the [Denmark] River had ways of clearing all the leaves [away from big *karri* trees]. Therefore, if it was a bushfire, a big bushfire [the fire could not run up shedding bark on *karri* trunks]. The main thing you have to care for is the beautiful old-growth forest. If there's dry wood on the ground, that will go up [in flames] like nobody's business. In the time when Aboriginal people managed this forest, and were free to do so, it definitely was not like [it is] today. From a traditional viewpoint, all trees belong to our totems and tell us where we come from. Consequences of burning would be very hard. It would kill the old growth. That'll all disappear. For the people that belonged to these totems it'd be a different way of looking at things altogether. People who relate to these trees belong to them. That's the *karri* people. Fire brings up certain fungi that they eat. But fire that destroyed the place where trees gave birth to the rocks would see the creation Dreaming story disappear altogether. Imagine if someone went there and all the trees were burned down and they were all missing. It just wouldn't tell the same story, would it? That would break down and ruin a bit of our [*wiernyert*] Dreamtime legends. Annihilate it. Women do most of the burning. My aunties used to do so. It would be women who looked after this site, and the blokes would know. This was definitely a no-go area for men. The site should be preserved, and possibly cleaned out with small, cool fires and litter removal. I remember just raking and raking, pulling out all the litter away from the trees and burning the dead wood safely. Never leave the dead wood in a heap. You'd get into a lot of trouble. They would form harbours for snakes. Trees are living creatures. This is a travesty. This is wrong [pointing to present vegetation understorey]. Needs to be brought back to traditional ways of burning. Elders need to be heard.

LYNETTE KNAPP,
16 October 2020, summit of Warrumbup

These three renditions of the same creation story powerfully illustrate oral traditions among First Nations. This simple story connects eucalypt trees as fundamental givers of life (oxygen), granite hills or *kaart* (the same word as is used for 'head', the hills being places where the all-seeing spirits overlook the land and ensure that people behave according to the law) and females – *waar* is the female western grey kangaroo, and places using her name, such as Waarumbup and Waariup to the northeast of Albany, are women's places. Hence Waarumbup is an allusion to the Earth Mother.

Presumably, the trees that form plates atop granite boulders with their roots going down through cracks in the rock on Warrumbup are also evidence to the Noongars of the eucalypts giving birth to the rocks (illus. 38, 39). This phenomenon is not expressed so prominently anywhere else on the south coast as it is at Waarumbup.

Kornt boorna: *ancient red tingle from the Walpole region*

There are three species of tall tingle tree confined to the higher rainfall parts of the south coast. Red tingles (*E. jacksonii*) are the most distinctive because of their enormous bulk and their tendency to buttress at the base. Lynette Knapp eloquently described their traditional and contemporary significance to Noongars/Merningar Bardok people while sitting beside one tree that is known to *nydiyang* (white people) as the Pleated Lady (illus. 40, 41), west of Bow Bridge.

We are among these beautiful living beings [red tingle trees]. It feels pretty safe. You know that you are among fellow creatures like your own. Like when I talk about my DNA haplotype, with 75,000 years' connection to the south coast, this one here [indicating the Pleated Lady] is probably not far off that.

My people, if they were walking through here, we'd note the [the tree] resembles a *kornt* [a hut made of sticks and bark]. When the people walked through here, and I'm talking about the jarrah people because from the Denmark River east of here, that's our boundary line, but we [Merningars] were allowed to walk right through this place to the Warren River. [We could] have our say over this Country, and I know

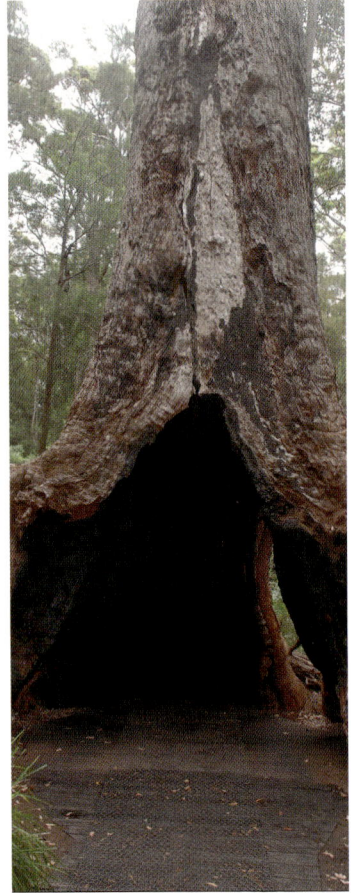

40, 41 *Kornt boorna* (ancient red tingle, *Eucalyptus jacksonii*) from the Walpole region (*right*), including the Pleated Lady (*left*).

because I'm doing that now. I know that this place belonged to the jarrah people from west of the Denmark River. We are all part of the Bibbulmun race. The Bibbulmun go as far east as the Phillips River [in Fitzgerald River National Park], this side of Ravensthorpe. They're all Bibbul to there, and we're known as the East Bibbulmun, so I'm also part of that group by birth, that's what I've inherited.

If they were passing by this tree they'd call it a *kornt boorna* because it resembles a *kornt*, which is shelter for blackfellas to sleep in or live in when they move from one place to the other, so this would have been a huge marker at one stage. Many many years ago you wouldn't be able to see all this [under-storey] regrowth growing through here. It would have been clear as [the eye could see], all part of a walkway to go from one part of the Country to the other.

The trees are all part of our beautiful moieties, of the jarrah people, they belong to the jarrah people, like we're taalyaraak [*E. pleurocarpa*] people over the other side [further east] The trees belong to their totems. When you're totemic people you don't own this, nor do you own anything else growing on your Country. You belong to it, and it belongs to you. That's the way that a lot of people don't get across [this relationship]. Some people put ownership on it. You don't own it. You belong to it.

They'd also have animal totems. When you belong to trees that big you must have the top animals as your totem too. That would be the *waalitch* [wedge-tailed eagle], the things that soar above, and look [at] how big these [trees] are. Burn-ing – this would have been like parkland. It would be con-trolled by fire, and it wouldn't be heavy fire. You wouldn't find all these horrible limbs lying around [dead dry wood], because they'd all be burnt. All burnt up and everything cleared. You'd be able to see way in the distance looking at this bush. You'd see right through it, and movement of animals etc.

This today is death on Earth. It would be the worst kind of bushfire you could meet. So what do you think they'd feel seeing these most beautiful trees destroyed by fire? This is hot fire, this is fire that would kill everything. Kill all the animals and slow-moving creatures. It would definitely kill these poor trees. They're not managed properly. It's misman-agement. Traditionally the old people would have created a lot of space for walking across Country. In my lifetime we didn't keep to paths or *maart*. It was straight to the point. Look at this. It's a death trap. And not just a death trap for people, it's a death trap for everything that's precious to this land. All the animals you need to survive here would be wiped out. Ground creatures would be gone. One day you'd look around and nothing would be left. You can't just keep burning like people have been burning.

Waalitch would love this because people can't get to his nest. But you imagine if there's a big fire then his nest would be wiped out too. He'd be all right but the nest would be gone. They live at the top of the tier of our totems and gov-ern our customs and law practices and marriage practices. Those blokes and the *djillian* or sea eagle are the top two ani-mals. He'd love this because no one is interfering with him in his life.

LYNETTE KNAPP,
24 May 2022, west of Bow Bridge

The great reverence felt by Noongar people for these majestic tingle trees is evident in this story. Every individual tree is valued and pro-vides a home for creatures that need to be cared for. Lynette Knapp makes it clear that this can't happen unless the forest is managed carefully, like a parkland, not burned to foster dense understorey, as happens under present-day management regimes. She is heartbroken to see old-growth trees killed by fire, and strongly urges a return to traditional ways of caring for country in old-growth forests.

Gnaama boorna: *sacred medicinal and water trees*
(marri (Corymbia calophylla))

We have become aware of *gnaama boorna* only through collaborative research commencing in 2016 with the Knapp family. These medicinal and spiritual water-holding trees are priceless living relics, and relatively few survive to the present day, owing to old age and mismanagement. They deserve protection wherever they occur, and celebration as reminders of 50,000 years of Noongar custodianship of the lands on which we live. Simply raking away flammable litter and vegetation from their bases is a vital first step in protecting them from fire. Lynette and Dion take up their story:

> This is a *gnaama boorna*. *Boorna* is tree or wood. *Gnaama* is pool. The women used to fashion this kind of thing. Sometimes they'd let it grow so high, then burn the centre and clean it out and create that space. They'd put in little [vertical] channels in the bark. So when the rain hits the tree it just comes down and runs into the hole. The majority of times it's full. You can come here on a really warm day and put your hand in and it's freezing. When we were kids we used to always use it for drinking because we used to live up the end of the road there and this was on our path to school. The adults also used to use that.
>
> LYNETTE KNAPP,
> 5 April 2018, Mt Melville

This was mainly used for men's business. This *gnaama* tree was usually used for men's water. That there [pointing east] was the old *corroboree* ground where it's dug out [as a sand pit]. They used to do the *corroboree* so that this tree could be healthy and safe. They used to look after this tree so that it would be plenty full of water for their ceremonies. They used to dance an old *corroboree* and keep this tree. My Pop, Alfie Knapp, told me this. This was a sacred tree to the Aboriginal people. They used to look after it. Do their *corroborees*. Dance around. Make sure the water comes up from out of the ground so they believed. Only men. The other one [on Mt Clarence, near the water tank] had the old fire bloke and old lady to look after it. That was their tree. At the Upper Kalgan River crossing, an old boss man was in charge there. He sat there forever because he was the guardian for that crossing. They had nowhere but there to go to if people came from different Country. They were told where the two rivers meet [salt- and freshwater] you'll see that old bloke and he'll direct you along the way. The *gnaama boorna* there was his water source. In summertime he could make tools with the water. With the freshwater side and the saltwater side, most people think that us Aboriginals just go there and do things, but it was pretty sacred. You didn't go and use the waters unless it was the right time and someone had the right song for the place. Then they could use it. That old bloke, he had the song to cross that water at Upper Kalgan. So that's how the people from Esperance, and then going back that way, that's how they'd cross over, using that old bloke. If you weren't meant to cross over he'd probably knock them in the head. If you weren't part of that tribe that come down for their Dreamtime. He was the Guardian – he looked after who'd come in and who'd stay out. He knew them because they would be marked up from their tribes. That's how they knew each other. The people from Esperance were still Noongars. Young River was basically the home of the grey kangaroo. From Ongerup to Young River they'd go around, but they weren't able to meet with people until they get to Whudjerup [Wheejarup/East Mt Barren] in Hopetoun. If they wanted to get into the hill people they'd have to go and do a ceremony on top of Whudjerup. The Whudjari land. That's a ceremonial hill for the sea people down the bottom. Mum has the story of royal hakeas [*Hakea victoriae*] there. Pop just told me Albany stories. How far you go, how far you come. Certain rocks in places. Alf said that through his mother, Lily Bevan, we are Bardok people. Wudjari/ Whujarup is actually an echidna, chasing white ants. When the emu stepped along the coast, he turned them into stone. The white ants are on the west side of Wudjari. The sacred *waarkarl* come out from Cocanarup [and] made it all the way down to the reef at Hopetoun. That's where he's resting.

DION CUMMINGS,

17 May 2019, Mt Melville

Another name for a water tree is *wiernyert*. *Wiern* is for spirit, to do with law stuff. That shows you how important these trees are to our customs and traditions. I'm just amazed at all these beautiful trees that you've found [in Denmark, northeast of Poison Point] right next to a track where trees were knocked over. It's an amazing thing. It is important to have people to keep an eye on these beautiful artefacts. My recognition of *gnaama boorna* comes from the teachings and learnings of my immediate family. I can only speak for them. Life skills. It's all about the importance of surviving. This [tree] is for us, medicinal. That's where the real name for *wiernyet* comes from. *Wiern* is spirit. This is very medicinal. So going in the *gnaama boorna* we can access that and keep our spirit healthy.

Looking around us, all this undergrowth or overgrowth I call it, is dangerous. When our oldies walked the Country they'd know where every *gnaama boorna* was, because first of all they would create them. Then they would have kept them cleaned out and going. It was mainly life skills, about survival. Everything was about survival. When they came along and these were full of water, the oldies would pick leaves. They'd cover that hole and they'd push it down. Then drink from that. It had all its medicinal properties to keep our spirits going.

It was highly sought after by Aboriginal people. To make them they'd pick a tree that was growing and take the main branch off. They would have ensured that at least two shoots were on that tree to enable it to grow when the leader was removed. They would fashion that into this [pointing to the *gnaama boorna*]. If anything in the middle grew back they'd fire it. Then line it with a bit of ochre or clay, even blackboy [*Xanthorrhoea*] gum. Powder it, spread [it] around and fire it. If you burn it too hot, it'd be all the same as separate little balls. So you have to watch it. It added taste and flavour to the water. Yummy.

This is all women's stuff. The men had little to do with it. Lizard traps are the same. The women would provide meat for their kids and water for their kids. When you get things like this [*gnaama boorna*], when they grow especially in rocky places they grow a little bit differently. They would be put there for ceremonial purposes. Sorry. I was knockin' the blokes but a lot of these would be used by blokes.

I've heard stories that people said that the *gnaama boorna* was built for giving birth. My family's story is that no, you might lean up against a tree when giving birth, but they are for medicinal purposes and water. And the adjacent rocks here. Rocks aren't dead things. They're alive, and form natural communities of plants. They've got powers, launching powers. Sometimes you can rest on a rock and feel its power coming up. Amazing. So when giving birth you wouldn't be right on a rock.

We do need to keep the *gnaama boorna* clean. We need to scrape away litter from the trunk to prevent fire taking hold. Mulch and roots will burn for ages. Fire will definitely kill the tree. My father told me that trees and plants have got a root growth that spreads out to hang on to the spinning world. The tree hangs on to the living world by its root system, and fire can spread through the root system.

The trees here are in a line along a walk path. They're always thus, but a little bit off the path itself.

LYNETTE KNAPP,

5 April 2023, south Denmark

These three expositions reinforce the spiritual significance of *gnaama boorna* to Noongar men, women and children. Generation after generation, families invested time in their care and maintenance, displaying rational reverence for the longevity and life-giving attributes of trees.[15]

Historical records of *gnaama boorna* outside the Knapp family's oral history include an early description by Surveyor-General John Septimus Roe, who was travelling north of Albany near the source of the Napier River on 12 February 1835:

> Our native companions shortly after stopt at a gum tree in which, at the height of 9 or 10 ft from the ground, where it branched off into 4 forks, there was found excellent water about 3 ft in depth, which our sable friends [Noongar guides] informed us was one of several reservoirs of the kind to which their Countrymen resorted for supplies during the absence of water on the surface of the ground. The existence of several notches in the bark which were used as steps, corroborated the statement and bespoke its having been frequently visited.[16]

Further east and north, the water in *gnaama boorna* was of increasing importance in its own right as drinkable fluid in an often dry land. The Ngadju Schultz family based in Norseman emphasize this for what are called *wanyar* trees (salmon gums, *E. salmonophloia*; illus. 42) placed strategically between large granite outcrops where the only other readily available source of fresh water is to be found.[17] *Wanyaar* is also the Ngadju term for young unmarried women, affirming the femininity of these important life-giving trees. Salmon gums are

42 Sacred *gnaama boorna* (water trees) occur across Southwest Australia. Here, a *wanyar* pool occurs in salmon gum (*E. salmonophloia*), Norseman, Western Australia.

widespread in semi-arid Southwest Australia and beyond, into the heart of the desert. Water pools constructed in salmon gums and adjacent black *morrel* (*E. longicornis*) also occur to the northeast, near Mukinbudin.

Yardie *trees on Princess Royal Harbour*

Ceremony is a fundamental part of Noongar life. Women's dance grounds and the ceremonies performed on them are called *yardie* in the Merningar Bardok dialect. The shores of Princess Royal Harbour, on which today's town of Albany is located, has fertile alluvial flats supporting large *karri* (*E. diversicolor*) and *moin* (*E. cornuta*) trees. Here, at the aptly named Big Grove on the western shore, *karri* trees have been manipulated horticulturally for generations to surround an oval *yardie* ground. Paired trunks are a feature of this horticultural practice. This can be achieved by pinching out the seedling's lead shoot and constraining subsequent resprouts to just two trunks. The trees typically

70

display no marks of chainsaw or axe, so the creation of the double trunks by *nydiyang* (white men) can be discounted. It is difficult to determine the age of *karri* trees, but the size of the *yardie* trees at Big Grove suggests that several human generations have to pass before they mature. This is long-term horticulture being applied.

There are *wiernyert* (Dreaming) stories of ancestral women banished from walking on Earth because of serious misdemeanours against children or their community. Such women could return from banishment, fixed to the Earth upside down as a tree, their hair forming the roots and their legs the soaring trunks, if paired (see illus. 36, 37). This is what you see at Big Grove, as Lynette Knapp explains:

> Most of these trees have been fashioned I'd say from when they were little ones. This is a huge campground. It's a really big one. Merningar people camped all the way round this harbour. This place here in particular was a pretty heavy [important] campground where they moved to and from. Looking at the trees, to me, it's woman's business, woman's business, just by the way that the trees are shaped. If you have a look at their shape, it would take on the shape of a woman. That's the way they would have been grown, for women to recognize. It was a big camp. Upside-down women. It's amazing. Absolutely amazing. This oval incorporates a *gnaama boorna* [water tree], and you can see that the majority of the trees were fashioned to be a *gnaama* but only one or two worked out. Aboriginal women would have shaped these. It's woman's lore. To me they're built for a *gnaama*. They've been trained for a *gnaama* tree, because these trees don't just grow like this [double-trunked]. They grow tall [and single-trunked]. They grow really, really big. And look at it. They're amazing. On shallow ground. This tree, on the other side, looks proper woman [with breasts and pregnant belly]. Just imagine the business of this place, the women and young girls being taught about womanhood. It's very important. The plants,

landform, just over 100 metres from the water. Ideal for ceremonial stuff. Ideal because they are not dirtying the water, are they?

LYNETTE KNAPP,
16 February 2023, Big Grove

The care and attention to detail shown over the generations by women in creating this *yardie* encircled by paired-trunked trees display the maxim that the people belong to the trees, rather than owning them. This was reinforced at birth when Merningar babies were covered with ash of the bark of *moin* trees (*E. cornuta*) rather than washed in water.

Kylie *(boomerang) manufacture at Boyankaartup/ Little Beach, Two Peoples Bay*

Wiernyert stories often involve ancestral beings capable of morphing from human to animal to spiritual, who can appear like everyday mortals involved in daily routines. Often, the stories have a moral component as well. Someone did something, consequences followed and lessons were learned. Such a saga is involved in the men's Dreaming story about two brothers who fought over a woman, with dire consequences and ongoing relevance to understanding relationships of neighbouring groups in the Albany region. Eucalypts are involved in part of this yarn.[18]

The big story involves the Seven Sisters following their dingo from New South Wales to Albany. They were warned by an ancestral man that, when at Albany, they must not look at the waters of Princess Royal Harbour because they contained black magic of the *waitch* (emu). The oldest Sister, pregnant, ignored this advice and immediately turned to stone. Her body stretched along the Torndirrup Peninsula, her baby is in rock at the Sand Patch and her pregnant belly eventually lay at The Gap. Djimaalap, the ancestral *bordier* (boss man) at Albany, retrieved her baby son, Boyankaartup, from her stomach and took him northeast to the Two Peoples Bay region, where Djimaalap's daughter Tandara and biological son Yilbarup lived. Tandara was promised to Yilbarup, but she fell in love with the adopted orphan Boyankaartup from The Gap. Tandara became pregnant and the two brothers did not know who was the father. Yilbarup killed the baby after birth, and Tandara was so distraught that she tore out her heart and placed it near Yiilangarup/Boulder Hill. The two brothers fought initially with stones, creating patches of bare sand in Two Peoples Bay Nature Reserve and at the foot of Yilbarup/Mt Manypeaks near Boulder Hill. When stones failed to kill either brother, Yilbarup threw his Number 7 *kylie* (boomerang) and at the same time Boyankaartup threw a spear in retaliation. Both weapons found their mark. Boyankaartup collapsed with the *kylie* in his back, like a shark's fin, as still seen today atop Maardjit Gulin/Mt Gardner in Two Peoples Bay Nature Reserve. The spear struck Yilbarup in the stomach and trailed behind his body, looking like a stingray in profile, which Mt Manypeaks resembles today. Thus, ever since, the totem of Two Peoples Bay people is the boomerang and that for Yilbarup is the spear. Dion heard the following story from his Pop, Alf Knapp, regarding the source of wood used by Noongars to make boomerangs in the vicinity:

> This place [Waterfall Beach at Two Peoples Bay Nature Reserve, just south of Little Beach] is one of the main spots when we were kids that we went swimming. Boyankaartup – there's a story about how he got hit in the back with a boomerang. Just at the foot of the hill that is Boyankaartup's head in stone, there's a eucalypt above the beach that is one of the main trees used to make boomerangs. When Boyankaartup got hit by the boomerang and became part of a shark is part of the stories of boomerang making and all that in that corner of the beach. [*Quararl* (*E. angulosa*) is the species used; see illus. 43] Nice big thick hardwood is carved right down and dried out. You'd wet both ends and burn them and the two

ends would draw the water into the middle. This makes it heavy and balanced in the middle and makes it go round and come back. It makes the two outside bits light and the water-logged middle makes the centre heavier. From here Boyankaartup threw a spear east across the bay at Yilbarup and hit him in the stomach. Where the rock is on top of the highest peak, that's the end of the spear. Yilbarup turned into a stingray. At the bottom of the hill there are many spear-making trees [*Taxandria juniperina*]. When he got speared Yilbarup took the spears and that's where the spears got made. Vice versa, Boyankaartup got hit by the boomerang here, so that's where the boomerangs were made ever after. So shark mob here. Stingray mob at Manypeaks.

DION CUMMINGS,
15 December 2022, Little Beach,
Two Peoples Bay Nature Reserve

This story of the two brothers fighting over a woman and ending up as shark and stingray is presented on signage at The Gap in Torndirrup National Park, south of Albany. Lynette Knapp provided the information, with her brothers' permission. She says that having the events occur at two different places reinforces the importance of the story and asserts rights along the South Coast for Merningar Bardok people. She also recalled that for recreation, mallee stems and small round lignotubers of *quararl* were used for games of hockey.

Gardidi boorn *(weeping gum,* Eucalyptus sepulcralis*), the beautiful, tall, wispy trees of Fitzgerald River National Park*

'Yongerap' was a story published by Lynette Knapp in her book *Mirnang Waangkaniny*.[19] A marriage was arranged between the Elders of the Emu people (Ngadju) of the Fraser Range near Balladonia, and

43 *Kylie* (boomerang) manufacture at Boyankaartup/Little Beach, Two Peoples Bay, was undertaken using *quararl* (*Eucalyptus angulosa*), the coastal mallee illustrated here.

44 Clouds of spears thrown by the Yonga/Kangaroo Noongar people of the Stirling Range killed two young Waitch/Emu men from the Ngadju people of the inland Fraser Range who had run away from an arranged marriage. Blood turned the ground red in patches, and the two young men transformed into two hills, today's spiritual home on the south coast for Waitch people. Spears became the distinctive *gardidi boorn* (weeping gum, *Eucalyptus sepulcralis*) of the eastern Fitzgerald River National Park. In the foreground, a rescue party of Waitch warriors, too late, were caught in the open and crouched to hide, morphing into rounded granite outcrops at Bald Rock Creek near the north boundary of the park – a place known to Noongars as Waitch Noolar/emu back. From Lynette Knapp's *Mirnang Waangkaniny* (2011), illustration by Karl Brand.

the Kangaroo people (Goreng) of the Stirling Range. A young man of the Emu people travelled with a companion east to the Stirling Range to meet his intended wife, but felt something was wrong. After sending a message home for help, the two men ran southeast to the Barren Ranges of Fitzgerald River National Park, chased by angry Kangaroo people, shamed by the rejection of the marriage proposal, who threw spears (illus. 44, 45):

> The spears were landing upright in the ground where they transformed into beautiful, tall, wispy trees. The wispy trees can still be seen across the ranges, tall and thin, just like the spears that landed there in the days of our ancestors. The Emu men could not escape and were hit by many spears. As they ran wounded and bleeding across the Country, their blood soaked the soil turning the ground red. As they fell to the ground dying from their wounds, they transformed into

two hills. Today you can see the Emu men's spiritual home in the ranges. In the late afternoon you can clearly see their faces in the two hills. One young man is lying peacefully looking to the north towards his Country. The other is lying with his mouth open.[20]

Intriguingly, the Latin name given to the tall, wispy trees of the Eyre Range in the southeast of Fitzgerald River National Park is *Eucalyptus sepulcralis*. The specific name *sepulcralis* means 'burial place' or 'of the tomb', an allusion to the weeping, wispy habit that makes the tree suitable for planting in cemeteries. Some aspects of the appearance of eucalypts seemingly evoke similar responses across cultures. Noongar people would say that this was a case of country speaking subconsciously to the taxonomist who named these evocative eucalypts. The

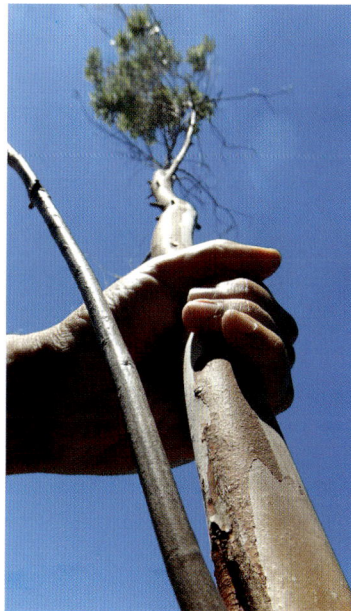

45 *Left*: *Gardidi boorn* (weeping gum, *Eucalyptus sepulcralis*).
46 *Right*: Spearwood mallee (*Eucalyptus doratoxylon*), known to Noongar people as *kiitjmaund* or *geitch-gmunt*, meaning 'spears all together'. The species ranges from near the town of Denmark eastwards along the south coast of Western Australia to Cape Arid National Park.

ancestral story of young men speared to death was irrepressible, so of course *E. sepulcralis* was chosen as an apposite name.

Several other mallees from Southwest Australia were used for making spears, among them the spearwood mallee (*E. doratoxylon*; illus. 46). The Noongar name for this species, *kiitjmaund* or *geitch-gmunt*, means 'spears all together', alluding to the many straight stems that arise from the lignotuber; they are just the right size for spears if carefully managed through fire regimes.

Taalyaraak *and the tree marking original Noongar* boodjar

A silver-leaved species is *taalyaraak* (tallerack) or blue mallee (*E. pleurocarpa*; illus. 47), which ranges across the south coast of Western Australia between the Stirling Range and the Esperance area, extending inland to the southern wheatbelt, with a few isolated populations on the west coast inland of Jurien Bay, north of Perth. Today some Merningar/Minang and Whudjari Noongar people regard *taalyaraak* as a marker of their *boodjar* (country), beyond which they would not stray in traditional times unless formally invited to do so by their neighbours. A similar observation was made by Augustus Oldfield in 1865.[21]

Esperance Noongar people have named their newly incorporated organization registered under the Corporations (Aboriginal and Torres Strait Islander) Act 2006 the 'Esperance Tjaltjraak Native Title Aboriginal Corporation'. *Taalyaraak* (*tjaltjraak*) was and is of great cultural significance.

The sister species to the blue mallee is *E. extrica*, the green (*pirrung*) *taalyaraak*. This species ranges from Cape Le Grand National Park eastwards to Israelite Bay. It is the marker for what is regarded as the original Noongar country. Strictly, Noongars are Merningar Bardok warriors who have gone through two sets of law, inland and coastal.[22] So women can't be Noongars. Instead, families – such as the Knapps – use 'Bibbulmun' or 'East Bibbulmun' as the collective descriptor of their Merningar people and adjacent groups, such as the Wudjari.

47 A cultural boundary marker is illustrated by *tjaltjraak/talyaraak* (tallerack) or blue mallee (*Eucalyptus pleurocarpa*) from southern Southwest Australia, demarcating Merningar *boodjar* (country).

Tasmania is another place where Aboriginal cosmology of eucalypts has been documented, albeit patchily. Moreover, this is the place where the first herbarium specimens of *Eucalyptus* were collected, heralding more than two centuries of Western scientific investigation. Let's now turn to the island state for a detailed look at its significance across cultures for human interaction with eucalypts.

E U C A L Y P T U S obliqua.

48 *Eucalyptus obliqua* L'Herit.', plate engraving by Pierre-Joseph Redouté, accompanying
the original description of the genus *Eucalyptus* by Charles L'Héritier de Brutelle
in his self-published book *Sertum Anglicum* (An English Wreath, 1788).

three

Tasmania, the European Naming of *Eucalyptus* and Palawa People

※❀※

T his chapter examines early interaction between European botanists and the Tasmanian Palawa Aboriginal people, in the context of the discovery and naming of the genus *Eucalyptus*. In so doing we learn of the tragic suppression of the only Indigenous culture of Aboriginal people that had existed in isolation for more than 10,000 years, at a time when European scientific knowledge was expanding rapidly.

The scientific naming of eucalypts has a rich, colourful – and ongoing – history, peppered with personalities, events and unexpected encounters large and small.[1] This is illustrated very well by the nomenclatural birth of *Eucalyptus*. It arose from the intrigues of cross-national European competition and collaboration to advance botanical knowledge. *Eucalyptus* was first published in 1788 by the wealthy, self-taught French botanist and magistrate Charles L'Héritier de Brutelle with a single species, *E. obliqua* from Tasmania, the first to be named.[2]

Specimens of *E. obliqua* (illus. 48) were collected during British exploratory work on Captain James Cook's third expedition to the Pacific Ocean (1776–80). Failing to achieve its mission of locating a northwest passage from the Pacific to the Atlantic Ocean through Arctic seas, and with Cook losing his life in Hawaii on the return trip, the expedition brought back to Britain a wealth of scientific collections and observations, including those destined to introduce *Eucalyptus* as a new genus of plants to European Enlightenment savants and horticulturists. How did a Frenchman end up trumping the British with this most valuable early contribution to taxonomic botany?

Charles L'Héritier de Brutelle

In 1772 L'Héritier (1746–1800) was appointed Superintendent of Parisian Waters and Forests at the age of 26, becoming interested in the botany of trees both native and exotic. Philosophically, he was a follower of the practical Linnaean sexual system of classification, rather than the now widely adopted natural system advocated by some of his more academic French contemporaries. The natural system embraces the investigation of as many characters as possible to identify and classify taxonomic and evolutionary relationships, rather than intuitively picking a few key characters that enable ready identification, as Carl Linnaeus did for the number of male stamens and female chambers in flowers in his sexual system. Some acrimony developed in pre-revolutionary France and other European nations around these opposing views of how best to classify nature. Similar arguments prevail today with respect to proposals to recognize *Eucalyptus* and *Corymbia* as separate genera or the same genus, for example.

With considerable zeal, from 1785 onwards L'Héritier self-published plant species that were new to science in a series prosaically named *Stirpes Novae* (New Plants). They came primarily from gardens, since L'Héritier was too busy to collect in the wild. Instead, he paid young men to help him identify flowers of potentially new species appearing in the gardens of Paris. Each species from the second volume of *Stirpes Novae* (1786) onwards was illustrated from live garden material by the then relatively unknown but skilled botanical artist and L'Héritier's good friend, Pierre-Joseph Redouté.

This approach to the classification of living plants aided by beautiful botanical art was far-sighted and has proved particularly apposite for the study of the diverse and complex genus *Eucalyptus*, which offers much more to the botanist working with living plants than to those who confine their attention to dried and flattened specimens preserved in herbaria. L'Héritier had the meticulous zeal and personal wealth to forge ahead with the naming of new species during an exceptional pioneering period of the Enlightenment.

In 1786 L'Héritier travelled in haste from Paris to London, taking with him a collection he had received of South American plants from a Spanish/French-funded expedition of the French explorer Joseph Dombey. Naming new plants in this collection was claimed by Spain as a contractual right, and the French government had agreed to return the specimens to Spanish officials. L'Héritier was so keen to name the new species that, rather than hand the collection back to the Spanish, he chose botanical exile in London. With appropriate introductions from French botanists and cordial correspondence with the British in advance of his visit, he was granted access to the collections and library of Sir Joseph Banks in Soho Square, London. However, the welcome was soon worn out to the extent that Banks wrote to his librarian, the Swedish botanist Jonas Carlsson Dryander, that 'of all the impudent Frenchmen in the whole world he [L'Héritier] is the most impertinent and dangerous.'[3]

The brusque L'Héritier had used Banks's name without approval to get the Dombey collection through British customs, and had also asked permission to name new species of *Pelargonium* in Banks's collections. This interest extended to describing new plants in the Royal Gardens at Kew and elsewhere, rather than solely those in the Dombey collection and in the genus *Pelargonium*.

Banks's initial concerns about L'Héritier were echoed by some of his French contemporaries. L'Héritier's publications and parsimony, for example, were described by the naturalist and zoologist Georges Cuvier: 'His works were superb, but his table frugal and his clothes simple. He spent 20,000 francs a year on botany, but went about on foot.'[4] L'Héritier was both generous and behaviourally complex with the Swiss botanist Augustin Pyramus de Candolle, whom he mentored. L'Héritier – whose life ended with his murder by an unknown assailant near his home – was summarized by a modern biographer and botanist as an aristocrat who had so eagerly adopted the principles of the French revolution, the straight-forward and honest magistrate of both the old and new regimes, the fervent Linnean botanist, who as an amateur and self-made scientist had found his way to the highest ranks of the French Academy of Sciences. Even now . . . it is extremely difficult to judge the man L'Héritier. He consistently refused to have his portrait made. In his extensive correspondence there are rarely remarks of a personal nature. Even in his public quarrels, L'Héritier showed great restraint and reserve and seldom betrayed human emotion. As a judge he was well known for this attitude of strict and almost impersonal correctitude. As a botanist he was an ardent Linnean disciple . . . and primarily concerned with classification rather than understanding.[5]

L'Héritier slowly won over Banks and other English botanists, however, through his diligence, scientific rigour, open sharing and discussion of the new species he proposed to name, his engagement of James Sowerby to illustrate his monograph *Geranologia* and his decision to name genera of plants after several British botanists: *Boltonia*, *Dicksonia*, *Lightfootia*, *Pitcairnia*, *Relhania*, *Stokesia* and *Witheringia*. Consequently, on his return to Paris, and with the acknowledged assistance of English botanists, he self-published a new book, *Sertum Anglicum* (An English Wreath; 1788). Self-effacingly, he described 'this little work' in a brief preface as 'a gift [to English botanists], not unwelcome I hope, nor insignificant'. Indeed, it was neither.

It was in this book that L'Héritier described the genus *Eucalyptus* in a brief entry, here translated from Latin:

Plants with flowers with twenty or more stamens

EUCALYPTUS

PERIANTH: *Operculum* on top, entire [undivided, simple, without teeth or lobes or notches], truncate [ending very

abruptly, as if cut straight across]. *Petals: Calyptra* [bud cap]
hemispherical and broader towards the top than the base,
the margins of the calyx separating in front before flowering.
Filaments numerous, inserted into the calyx. *Ovary* inferior,
turbinate. *Style* singular. *Capsule* subquadriloculate [with
four chambers or fewer], the apex dehiscing exactly/evenly.
Seed very much angulate.
EUCALYPTUS *obliqua*. Plate 20.
Native of New South Wales. [Specimens collected by]
Nelson [and] Wm. Anderson. A woody plant.

Tasmanian Collections of the Type Species of *Eucalyptus*

The specimens on which L'Héritier's description was based came
from collections made south of present-day Hobart at Adventure Bay
on the east coast of Bruny Island. Captain Cook's third expedition
landed there on 26 January 1777 to obtain fresh water, wood, grass
for onboard stock and natural history specimens. Cook was aware of
this watering point from the log of Captain Tobias Furneaux, who –
having become separated from Cook's ship *Resolution* on the second
voyage to the Pacific – had stayed there for five days in March 1773
and named the bay after his own ship, *Adventure*.

Furneaux wrote: 'There are a great many gum trees and of a vast
thickness and height, one of which measured in circumference 26 feet
[8 metres] and the height under the branches was 20 feet [6 metres].'[6]
This reference to such large, thick-based, straight-boled trees undoubtedly whetted the botanical appetites of the third expedition's surgeon-
naturalist, William Anderson, and gardener-botanist, David Nelson.
What could the trees be? Cook's decision to anchor at Adventure Bay
led to Nelson and Anderson making collections of pressed specimens
and the seed of a brown stringybarked eucalypt that is still to be seen
along the shoreline and in the adjacent forest.

Anderson examined the trees expertly, using all his senses, producing a description that bears full quotation as the first published

scientific field observations of the type species (*obliqua*) of *Eucalyptus* and of other plants with which it grew:

> The forest trees are all of one sort [genus], growing to a great height, and in general quite straight, branching but little till towards the top. The bark is white, which makes them appear, at a distance, as if they had been peeled; it is also thick; and within it are sometimes collected pieces of a reddish trans-parent gum or resin, which has an astringent taste. The leaves of this tree are long, narrow and pointed; and it bears clusters of small white flowers, whose cups were, at this time, plenti-fully scattered about the ground, with another sort resembling them somewhat in shape, but much larger, which makes it probable that there are two *species* of this tree. The bark of the smaller branches, fruit, and leaves, have an agreeable pungent taste, and aromatic smell, not unlike peppermint; and in its nature, it has some affinity to the *myrtus* of the botanists.[7]

It appears that Anderson here described the peeled white bark of *E. globulus* (illus. 49, 50), rather than the brown, stringy bark of *E. obliqua* (see illus. 48). Undoubtedly, these are the two species that he deduced were present based on two different nut sizes evident on the forest floor. Both species still grow together along the shoreline. Anderson correctly ascertained an 'affinity to the *myrtus*' of the Mediterranean for these lofty eucalypts. They have been unequivocally placed in the family Myrtaceae ever since his pioneering observation.

What is not widely known is that Anderson coined a generic name for the two eucalypts – *Aromadendrum*, meaning 'aromatic tree' – and wrote it in pencil on the herbarium sheet of his specimens.[8] However, this name was never published, and Anderson's potentially significant role in the systematics of *Eucalyptus* has been relegated to the above published notes in Cook's journal.[9] Many plants and names have gone this way as botanists became distracted or were unable to see their field observations worked up into scientific print.

49 George Tobin, 'In Adventure Bay, Van Dieman's Land . . .', 1792, watercolour. Sketched at Two Tree Point beside Resolution Creek at Adventure Bay on Bruny Island, Tasmania, during William Bligh's expedition on HMS *Providence*, it is one of the earliest European depictions of *Eucalyptus*, showing the Tasmanian blue gum (*E. globulus*).

Ever the pragmatist, Captain Cook – having seen eucalypts at Botany Bay and further north on the mainland in 1770, and having at first dismissed their wood as 'too hard and ponderous for the most common uses' – changed his tune at Adventure Bay. He wrote that

> the tall straight forest trees . . . are of a different sort to those found on more northern parts of this coast. The wood is very long and close grained; extremely tough; fit for spars, oars, and many other uses; and would, on occasion, make good masts (perhaps none better), if a method could be found to lighten the timber.[10]

This was high praise indeed from the normally circumspect Yorkshire mariner, and it anticipates future commercial logging of such magnificent eucalypts.

Following Cook's death in Hawaii, the expedition made its way back to England. Nelson and Anderson's Tasmanian collections, among

50 Still standing in 2014, the two Tasmanian blue gums (*Eucalyptus globulus*) that were sketched by George Tobin in 1792 at Adventure Bay on Bruny Island, Tasmania. Penguin Island on the lower right horizon marks the southern tip of Adventure Bay, 3.2 kilometres (2 mi.) away. Perhaps owing to soil enriched by guano, it yielded the best grass Captain Cook's party found to provision the animals aboard the *Resolution* and *Discovery* in 1777. The tall eucalypt forests had little grass, save on the hills, where the soil was poor, the trees thin and open patches in evidence, possibly from Aboriginal burning to maintain forage for wallabies.

many others, were diligently delivered to Sir Joseph Banks, and the new genus described by L'Héritier and illustrated by Redouté while he was in London in 1786. It may have been that immature plants of the eucalypt yet to flower were probably at the Royal Gardens at Kew at the time, grown under glass because the species is sensitive to cold, so L'Héritier had to rely on specimens in Banks's herbarium to draft the description of the new genus and species.[11] He did not choose to use Anderson's *Aromadendrum*, perhaps wisely, since *Eucalyptus* more aptly focuses on a character of the bud (the calyptra) that has indeed endured as diagnostic of all members of the genus (see illus. 5, 9–13).

Labillardière Names the Tasmanian Blue Gum and Other Species

The Tasmanian blue gum (*E. globulus*), also growing at Adventure Bay, was well illustrated on William Bligh's expedition in 1792 by ship's artist George Tobin at Two Tree Point beside Resolution Creek (see illus. 49, 50). However, the species escaped collection or subsequent survival as herbarium specimens of Nelson and Anderson on Cook's third voyage. The French again beat the English in the naming of this most famous and widely planted of eucalypts. The honour fell to Jacques-Julien Houton de Labillardière, naturalist on Antoine Raymond Joseph de Bruni d'Entrecasteaux's expedition of 1792 in search of the missing naval explorer Jean-François de Galaup, comte de La Pérouse.

Admiral d'Entrecasteaux anchored his ships *La Recherche* and *L'Espérance* in Recherche Bay to the southwest of Bruny Island on 23 April 1792 and again on 20 January 1793, and stayed each time for several weeks. These visits gave Labillardière and other naturalists ample time to collect plants, including what became the type specimens of *E. globulus*, which was described in Labillardière's *Relation du voyage à la recherche de La Pérouse* and again in *Novae Hollandiae plantarum specimen*.[12] The latter is one of the first treatments of the Australian flora to be published. D'Entrecasteaux's expedition took Cook's

advice and used the timber of Tasmanian blue gums to repair their oared boats, setting a precedent for generations of use in the production of fine wood products and artwork from the sometimes massive trunks.

Labillardière published several new species of eucalypt from Tasmania – *E. globulus*, *E. viminalis*, *E. ovata*, *E. amygdalina*, *E. cordata* – and also collected the type specimen of *E. pulchella*. Most were gathered on his first walk ashore at Recherche Bay in 1792. His record-keeping was not meticulous, however. For example, he listed the southeast Australian endemic swamp gum (*E. ovata*; illus. 51) as coming from the south coast of Western Australia when he published the name in 1806. At Recherche Bay he initially confused *E. globulus* with *E. resinifera*, the latter described in 1790 from Port Jackson and not occurring in Tasmania. Nevertheless, he was eloquent in his commendation of the lofty giant eucalypts he first saw in 1792:

The finest trees in this country are the different species of *eucalyptus*. Their ordinary thickness is about eighteen feet: I have measured some that were twenty-five in circumference. The spongy bark of the *eucalyptus resinifera*, becoming slippery in consequence of the moisture that constantly prevails in the heart of these thick forests, renders it still more difficult to penetrate into them. This bark very readily peels off into pieces that have a great degree of flexibility, and are used by the natives for covering their huts. They often find long stripes [strips] of it about a foot in breadth which spontaneously shell themselves off from the lower part of the trunk. They might easily peel it off in pieces of twenty-five or thirty feet in length.[13]

51 Swamp gum (*Eucalyptus ovata*) near Kingston, Tasmania. This species, which is also found on the adjacent mainland of Victoria, southeastern New South Wales and southeastern South Australia, was one of five new eucalypts to be named by Jacques-Julien Houton de Labillardière in 1806 from collections made in 1792 and 1793 south of Hobart.

52 `Eucalyptus globulus`, plate engraving by Pierre-Joseph Redouté in Jacques-Julien Houton de Labillardière, *Voyage in Search of La Pérouse*, vol. 1 (1800), as part of the original description of the species.

He also gave an account of an effectively built windbreak:

> We found on the skirts of the forest a fence constructed by
> the natives against the winds from the bay. It consisted of
> stripes [strips] of the bark of the *eucalyptus resinifera* interwoven
> between stakes – fixed perpendicularly into the ground,
> forming an arch, of about a third of the circumference of a
> circle, nine feet in length and three in height, with its convex
> side turned toward the bay.[14]

The bark of E. *globulus* was clearly of significant value, especially since
the great long peels shed from the lower trunks of these large trees.

On 6 May 1792, after felling a tree and inspecting its buds and
fruits, Labillardière realized that he had mistaken a new species for
E. *resinifera*, and provided a comprehensive account of the species he
resolved to name E. *globulus* in reference to its 'coat-button' fruits
(illus. 52).

Abel Tasman and Aboriginal Tasmanian Tree Climbing

European reference to the giant trees of southern Tasmania dates back
to the Dutch seafarer Abel Tasman's expedition of discovery in 1642.
On 2 December Pilot-Major Franchoijs Jacobz Visscher, commander
of the *Zeehan*, sent out two exploratory boats to the northwestern
shore of Storm Bay. The crews reported

> two trees about two to two and a half fathoms thick and
> measuring 60 to 65 [Dutch] feet [about 40 imperial feet] to
> the lowest branches and the bark of these trees was peeled
> off and they were notched with flint stones (to climb up and
> rob the nests of birds above) to form steps five [Dutch] feet
> apart [3½ imperial feet], so that our men presumed that the
> people here must be very big or that they avail themselves
> of some practical means to climb the trees. In one of the

trees these carved steps were very fresh and green as if they had been cut less than four days before.[15]

We now know that the tallest flowering plants on Earth are included in the exceptional forests of Tasmania, including specimens of *E. regnans* (up to 92 metres/302 ft; see illus. 1), *E. delegatensis* (88 metres/289 ft), *E. obliqua* (84 metres/276 ft) and *E. globulus* (60 metres/197 ft).[16]

Tasman's journal highlights the long association between these giant eucalypts and Aboriginal Australians. Rather than the Tasmanians being giants themselves, they were adept at ascending straight-boled eucalypts with the simple help of a stone axe to cut toeholds and

53 Aboriginal tree-climber, Atherton Tablelands, north Queensland, *c.* 1890, using the rope and toehold method recorded for Tasmanian people climbing giant eucalypts by Abel Tasman and subsequent mariners and colonists.

a piece of rope around the trunk (illus. 53). Accounts of women ascending as high as 60 metres (200 ft), primarily for possums, are vividly conveyed by Tasmanian colonial observers. The naturalist and missionary James Backhouse, for example, observed in 1832:

> the climbing of the lofty, smooth-trunked gum trees, by the women, to obtain opossums, which lodge in the hollows of decayed branches, is one of the most remarkable feats I ever witnessed. This is effected without making any holes for the thumbs or great toes, as is common among the natives of New South Wales, except where the bark is rough and loose, at the base of the tree. In this a few notches are cut by means of a sharp flint or hatchet; the latter being preferred. A rope, twice as long as is necessary to encompass the tree, is then thrown around it. In former times this was made of tough grass [wire grass], or strips of kangaroo skin, but one of hemp is more generally used . . . By this means the woman will ascend a lofty tree, with a smooth trunk [often a blue gum], almost as quickly as a man would go up a ladder.[17]

When she reached the appropriate branch, the woman would walk out on to it, grab the possum by the tail from its hole, bash its head against the branch and hurl the animal to the eager team below, who would catch and immediately dispatch the possum if it were not already dead. Even when a possum ran for the tip of the branch, it was shaken out by the seemingly fearless climber, who then returned to the main trunk for a quick descent, using the encircling rope for support.

Sheds, Hollow-Butted Tree Caves and Fire-Managed Coastal Forests

The practical use of eucalypts by Indigenous Tasmanians for other purposes was evident to early European explorers. Cook observed at Adventure Bay in 1777: 'There were little sheds or hovels built of sticks, and covered with bark. We could also perceive evident signs of their sometimes taking up their abode in the trunks of large trees, which had been hollowed out by fire, most probably for this very purpose."[18] This was a novel use of fire for constructing shelter as tree caves (illus. 40, 41), eminently sensible in a cold southern climate exposed to the roaring forties. Anderson elaborated:

> What the ancient Poets tell us of *Fauns* and *Satyrs* living in hollow trees, is here realized. Some wretched constructions of sticks, covered with bark, which do not even deserve the name of huts, were indeed found near the shore of the bay; but these seem to have been only erected for temporary purposes; and many of their larger trees were converted into more comfortable habitations. These had their trunks hollowed out by fire, to the height of six or seven feet; and that they took up their abode in them sometimes, was evident from the hearths, made of clay, to contain the fire in the middle, leaving room for four or five persons to fit around it. At the same time, these places of shelter are durable; for they take care to leave one side of the tree sound, which is sufficient to keep it growing as luxuriantly as those which remain untouched.[19]

Similarly, Labillardière, D'Entrecasteaux and others on the expedition at Recherche Bay in 1792 observed that many of the large eucalypts near and inland from the shore had been hollowed out at the base by fire on their eastern sides, opposite the prevailing southwesterlies that brought rain. The conclusion seemed obvious: that these hollows were created as shelters by Aboriginal people. D'Entrecasteaux recorded:

> I had one of these trees measured at the level of a man's head, and its circumference was twenty-five feet, eight inches. It was completely hollow, and there was a small part of the

exterior trunk left, which was broken at a height of thirty
feet. Several men could stretch their whole length in there
very comfortably.[20]

Anderson added an eloquent description of the vegetation and
landscapes immediately inland and north of the beach of Adventure
Bay, typical of many well-watered parts of southern Australia:

> parts of the country adjoining the bay are quite hilly; and
> both those and the flat are an entire forest of very tall trees,
> rendered almost impassable by shrubs, brakes of fern and
> fallen trees; except on the sides of some of the hills, where
> the trees are but thin, and a coarse grass is the only inter-
> ruption.[21]

Undoubtedly, the vegetation he observed was a product of sophisticated Aboriginal burning to create a mosaic habitat for macropods of
forest and thicket for shelter, and open grassy woodland for forage.[22]
Anderson was unaware of this form of animal husbandry and did not
comment on it, but he did note:

> The *kangooroo* . . . without all doubt, also inhabits here, as the
> natives we met with had some pieces of their skins, and we
> several times saw animals, though indistinctly, run from the
> thickets when we walked in the woods, which, from the size,
> could be no other. It would seem, also, that they are in consid-
> erable numbers, from the dung we saw almost every where,
> and from the narrow tracks or paths they have made amongst
> the shrubbery.[23]

These macropods were likely to be Bennett's wallabies (*Macropus
rufogriseus* subsp. *rufogriseus*) or smaller Tasmanian pademelons (*Thylogale
billardierii*), rather than kangaroos.[24] The protection of shrubs from
fire to create shelter thickets for wallabies near more frequently

burned eucalypt woodlands suitable for grazing is a recurrent theme of traditional Aboriginal land management across Australia.[25]

Anderson was perceptive of the underlying soils, which the Nuenonne Palawa people had observed over generations and used to their advantage in constructing vegetation mosaic, applying fire to the nutrient-deficient hills but less to the lowland forest. For the hilly soils, Anderson noted: 'where there are few trees, it is of a tough, grey cast, to appearance very poor', compared to the tall forest soil, which was 'either sandy, or consists of a yellowish mould [soil], and, in some places, of a reddish clay'.[26] Here was an early European description of the local mosaic of soils so typical of Australian landscapes: some highly infertile and deeply weathered, others bioengineered into peaty sands or ferruginous clays and laterites by the specialized roots of dominant plants from the families Myrtaceae and Proteaceae mining essential nutrients from these phosphorus-deficient substrates.[27]

Anderson was also astute in noting the closer resemblance of the hydrological regime enjoyed by Adventure Bay's eucalypts to the Mediterranean climate of South Africa (winter wet, summer dry) – the landscape yielding only small ephemeral creeks issuing on the beach – than to that of well-watered New Zealand to the east:

> Upon the whole, it has many marks of being a very dry country, and perhaps might (independent of its wood) be compared to Africa, about the Cape of Good Hope, though that lies ten degrees farther Northward, rather than to New Zealand, on its other side, in the same latitude, where we find every valley, however small, furnished with a considerable stream of water.[28]

The cultural adaptations of the Nuenonne Palawa people to such an unusual mix of climate, landscape, soil and, above all, eucalypt-dominated vegetation were profound, but only briefly glimpsed and understood by this globally experienced scientist.

Tasmanian Aboriginal Eucalypt Names, Creation Stories and *Awara* (Totems)

Understandably, given their intimacy with the natural world, Tasmanian Aboriginal people had names for different species of eucalypt. Labillardière observed in Leillateah/Recherche Bay in May 1792 (illus. 54) that the Lyluequonny Palawa Aboriginal people

> have given particular names to every vegetable. We assured
> ourselves that their botanical knowledge was unequivocal,
> by asking several of them, at different times, the names of the
> same plants. In this interview we had an opportunity of add-
> ing considerably to the vocabulary of their language, which
> we had before begun to collect, and which will be found at
> the end of this work.[29]

This attention to botanical classification was affirmed after settlement by Joseph Milligan, who as Superintendent and Medical Officer of the Aboriginals 1843–55 compiled 'A Vocabulary of the Dialects of Some of the Aboriginal Tribes of Tasmania' (1859), in which he noted that 'for each variety of gum tree and wattle tree, etc., etc., they had a name.'[30]

Unfortunately the native names of eucalypts were not recorded for posterity by these authors, save Labillardière's short 'Vocabulaire de la langue des sauvages du cap de Diemen' giving the word *tara* for trees of the genus *Eucalyptus*.[31] Milligan gives the Southeast language words *tarra wayleh*, meaning to 'weep'.[32] Perhaps *tara* for eucalypt alludes to the trees' weeping gum, weeping bark or weeping foliage? Regrettably and inexplicably, Labillardière's records of other Aboriginal plant names were not published.

Labillardière's 'Vocabulaire' of 73 words is one of 44 known word lists of Tasmanian people to have been recorded between 1777 and 1847.[33] These lists were opportunistic records consisting of between one single word and 1,040 entries. Once again, the surgeon-naturalist

Anderson was a pioneer in this field, recording ten words of the Nuenonne people at Adventure Bay on Bruny Island from a few brief meetings by various expedition members.[34]

No reference to the majestic trees forming a backdrop to these early cross-cultural meetings is found here. In silent witness, the eucalypts – some of massive basal girth and burned to form cave-like shelters – were central and totemic to the world view of the Nuenonne Palawa, but not regarded by the British as being of prime importance to the understanding of their local names. This tradition of plant blindness and indifference or hostility to Aboriginal culture would persist following colonization for all but a few of the newcomers for almost two centuries.

Despite the paucity of word lists and the variation in rigour employed by recorders, scholars have been able to document twelve languages in five language families across Tasmania (illus. 55).[35] Thus variation in names for the same eucalypt species was and is undoubtedly

54 'Savages of Van Diemen's Land, preparing their Repast', plate engraving by Jacques-Louis Copia, after a sketch by Jean Prion on the Bruni d'Entrecasteaux expedition in Recherche Bay, southern Tasmania, 1793. It depicts a beach scene involving friendly cross-cultural interaction, with tall forests of giant eucalypts depicted in the background like European oaks. Such interaction led to the compilation of a short vocabulary of the Lyluequonny Palawa language by the naturalist Jacques-Julien Houton de Labillardière, including the word *tara* for *Eucalyptus* trees.

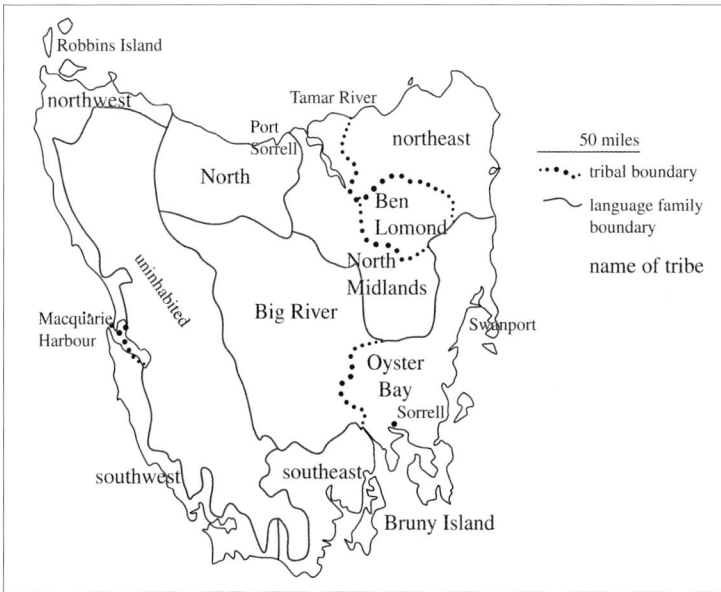

55 Map of Tasmania, with tribal/nation boundaries inferred from ethnographic literature (including Lyndall Ryan, *The Aboriginal Tasmanians*, 1981) and language family boundaries determined from multivariate analyses of word lists.

present. Published names remain meagre, however, only confirming that *Eucalyptus* trees were and still are known in native Tasmanian dialects as *tara, moonah* and *lotte* or *lote* (Southeast language), *lottah* or *loatta* (Oyster Bay language) and *loyke* (Northwest language).[36]

For individual eucalypt species, *poericker* from an undisclosed location and *toilena* have been recorded in the Oyster Bay language for stringybark trees (*E. obliqua*).[37] *Lenna* (Oyster Bay language) or *line* (Southeast language) means 'house, hut', and *toline* was recorded as meaning 'bark of a tree' at Recherche Bay (Southeast language), perhaps alluding to the utility of *toilena* in providing sticks and bark for the construction of huts. *Toienook boorack* means 'to hear' (Oyster Bay), the only use of *toi/toy* written down by Milligan.[38] This is also consistent with a house or hut as a place for conversation in shelter.

Another possible meaning alludes to cross-cultural misunderstanding or joking. *Leenny/leena/leenai* means 'penis' in the Southeast language, and *leieena* may also mean 'fundament, backside' in the Oyster

Bay language.[39] So, when asked the name of the stringybark, possibly after several attempts at getting the white person to pronounce it correctly, the Aboriginal teacher may have been saying 'listen, willy' or 'listen, arse' in modern vernacular. Such wordplay across linguistic divides is not unknown, especially given the sense of humour evinced by Aboriginal people.

The Tasmanian blue gum is known as *tara monadro* to contemporary Nuenonne people of Lunnawanna-alonnah/Bruny Island.[40] *Monodadro/monouadra* is the name in the Southeast language for the seeds of *E. globulus*, so perhaps *tara monadro* is a name with the second word shortened, alluding to the tree with prominent seeds or gum nuts, given that blue gums have the largest fruits of any Tasmanian eucalypt species.[41]

The importance of blue gum seeds to the continuation of Tasmanian life was highlighted in a recently published Dreaming story as follows: in the creation of Trowenna/Tasmania, the Nuenonne people tell of the sun (Punywin) and his wife the moon (Venna) travelling across the sky, creating life, commencing with dropping seeds of the great gum tree *tara monadro* and 'all the plants that grow on *Trowenna* today . . . All throughout the Dreamtime, the seeds sprouted and became trees and other plants. The leaves fell down from the trees and plants of *Trowenna* and mixed with the sand and became the soil.'[42]

An east coast story from Drayter/Great Oyster Bay explains how the blue wren *Luina* and the blue gum each received their striking colours during the Dreaming.[43] When the spirit son Dromerdene (the star Canopus) of Punywin (the sun) and his wife Venna (the moon) first came to Earth, the *wurrawena corinna* (ghost or spirit) Thylacines (Tasmanian tigers) attacked Dromerdene, and he fell exhausted at the base of *tara*, the great gum tree. A tiny grey bird flew down from the branches to defend Dromerdene. A tiny star blinded the *wurrawena corinna*, and *tara* threw *imbe* (gum nuts) at Dromerdene's assailants before lifting him to safety. The *wurrawena corinna* clawed in anger at the base of *tara*, which to this day has rough ribbons of bark near ground level. Dromerdene rewarded his allies, making the star brighter as Elary Romtena (the evening star), giving *tara* a mantle of blue and naming him *tara luina*, the blue gum, and crowning the small bird with heavenly blue atop a black head, naming it *luina*, the blue one.

These creation stories affirm the fundamental importance accorded to eucalypts by Aboriginal Tasmanians. Indeed, according to one account, Tasmania itself was called Mara Tara Lupari, the island of blue gum trees in the Oyster Bay language.[44] Unsurprisingly, blue gums were noted by the same author as significant totems: *lottah* (gum tree), *tuli-ana* (plant spirits), *awara* (totem).[45]

This record of the blue gum as a totem for the Oyster Bay people was affirmed independently by the preacher and public servant George Augustus Robinson, who recorded in 1831:

> the natives make small spears which they throw at and stick into different trees. Those of Great Oyster Bay/Drayter spear the stringy bark trees/*toilena, poericker* – *Eucalyptus obliqua*, peppermint trees/*E. amygdalina*, honeysuckle trees/*Banksia marginata*, known as *myore* to Oyster Bay people and *tangan* in the Macquarie Harbour language of the west coast.[46] The gum trees/*E. globulus* they claim as theirs and call them countrymen. The stringy bark trees the *Brune* [the Neunonne people of Lunnawanna-alonnah] call theirs, as being their country-men, the peppermint the Cape Portland [the people of Lumaranatana, the northeastern tip of Tasmania] call theirs, and the Swanport claim the honeysuckle. Thus if the natives of Oyster Bay spear the trees of another native they are much annoyed and go and pull them out.[47]

Throwing spears 'into trees with great dexterity and a good deal of strength' was also noted by d'Entrecasteaux in 1792 at Leillateah.[48]

It is a remarkable coincidence that the tree the Neunone people of Lunnawanna-alonnah call 'their countrymen', their totemic family, *toílena* (*E. obliqua*), is the same species that Nelson and Anderson collected in 1777 at Adventure Bay on the island, and that L'Héritier made the type of the genus. My Noongar Aboriginal teachers from Southwest Australia would ascribe this not to coincidence, but to country (*boodjar*) speaking to all people, irrespective of cultural origin. *E. obliqua* is unquestionably a species of powerful influence on the thinking of all who encounter, know, use and revere eucalypts. Fortunately, such an important species is widespread, now known from five Australian states, common in Tasmania, Victoria and New South Wales, and extending to the Mt Lofty Range and Kangaroo Island in South Australia, and to just southwest of Brisbane in southeastern Queensland.[49]

Equally telling for the importance and conservation of eucalypts is the Tasmanian Aboriginal use of individual trees as totems. In 1832 the missionary George Washington Walker accompanied fellow Quaker James Backhouse on a visit to the Aboriginal settlement at the Lagoons, on Flinders Island in Bass Strait. The small number of Aboriginal people there had been rounded up across Tasmania by Robinson at the end of the Black War, and moved voluntarily (for self-protection) to the Flinders Island group a few months before the Quakers visited. Walker observed:

> A married woman had selected a certain tree, according to their practice when in the bush, which tree, in such case, is considered the representative of the person who makes choice of it, and is regarded as their inviolable property, at all times to be held sacred. Through some accident this tree, which had been selected by *Roomtyenna* [the woman], was pulled down or mutilated by a party of her countrymen, which she so violently resented that, snatching up a firebrand, she ran in amongst them and dealt her blows very freely around. Her husband, who was of the party, at length struck her on the head with his waddy [hitting stick], and drew blood. When he saw that she bled, he was apparently

as disconcerted as she was, and would have gladly made it up;
but the lady was not so easily appeased, and it was some time
before *Trygoomy-poonauh* could regain his wife's smiles.[50]

We have here a practice of choosing individual trees as personal
totems, to be cared for with reverence and fierce protection by
their Aboriginal custodians. This was emulated elsewhere, such as
for totem trees at birth sites by the Noongar people of Southwest
Australia.[51] In this way Aboriginal people are spiritually connected to,
and care for and nurture, eucalypts across Australia.

four

Modern Species, Subspecies and Hybrids

❁

Western scientific knowledge of the diversity and biology of eucalypts has progressed significantly since the first European encounters with the stately trees of Tasmania in 1642. We now turn to aspects of the science and art of taxonomy, and examine how botanists have gone about naming and classifying eucalypt species, subspecies and hybrids.[1]

We've already learned that approximately nine hundred species of eucalypt are now known. It is important first to consider what is meant today by the word 'species' in this context. Are all nine hundred eucalypt species equivalent in terms of biological character and relative distinctiveness? If not, how do today's taxonomists grapple with natural variation and enable some consensus on that basic question of how many species of eucalypt there are?

Although this philosophical question has attracted controversy and debate for many years, there are two main theoretical approaches that underlie the bulk of eucalypts that are described as new species, subspecies and hybrids. I categorize these two schools of thought with reference to the names of the two British historical figures who played pivotal roles in the relevant scientific advances: Sir Joseph Dalton Hooker (1817–1911) and Charles Darwin (1809–1882).[2]

Perhaps surprisingly, despite constant reference to taxonomy as a science, relatively few eucalypt taxonomists publish definitions of the categories of species, subspecies and hybrid when they apply names at these ranks. Without clear definitions provided as falsifiable hypotheses, readers have no way of evaluating whether the available evidence supports or falsifies the erection of a new species, or the submerging of two named species or of supposed hybrids into one. To understand why this is so, a little history is needed.

Much of modern taxonomy – including that used to describe eucalypt species, subspecies and hybrids – draws its intellectual origins and traditions from the emergence of the Royal Botanic Gardens at Kew in southwest London as an instrument of British empire in the nineteenth century. Kew flourished under the honorary leadership of Sir Joseph Banks, the celebrated botanically inclined, self-funded gentleman who accompanied Captain James Cook on his first global circumnavigation. Being the first Europeans to visit Australia's east coast in 1770, Cook and Banks were both celebrated on their return to the United Kingdom, including by King George III, who had agricultural interests and a small royal garden at Kew Palace. Banks volunteered to turn the latter into the leading institution for botanical discovery and the use of economically valuable plants. This strategy worked well for more than forty years. However, the death of both Banks and the king in 1820 led to the gardens at Kew falling into slow decline and disarray, to the point at which their dismemberment was proposed by agencies of government.

Following pressure from Britain's scientific elite, a Committee of Enquiry was appointed and recommended to Parliament that Kew become the nation's centre for botanical science. Moreover, a paid director was to be appointed to lead this new initiative. Sir William Jackson Hooker took up the post in 1841, bringing with him a very large private herbarium and library, as well as a formidable network of correspondents and collectors from around the world. His energy and diplomacy achieved remarkable advances for the now Royal Botanic Gardens, Kew. He mentored his son Joseph, who travelled widely on voyages of exploration to the Antarctic, Australia, oceanic islands and the Himalayas. Joseph secured the job of deputy director at Kew in the 1850s, and succeeded his father as director in 1865, ultimately becoming Kew's most decorated scientist. Both Hookers, father and son, saw Kew as central to British imperialism, arguing convincingly – as Banks had done – that the discovery and description of new plants from the colonies would ensure the ongoing expansion of agricultural crops and bring other economic benefits for the empire.

To achieve this, a series of descriptive colonial floras was initiated. This involved the rapid description of thousands of plants, many of which were new to science, and their placement in a global system of classification that was worked up in a partnership between Joseph Hooker and Kew's other writer of colonial floras, the biologist George Bentham. Such outcomes could be achieved only by applying a broad species concept, not spending too much time on developing a detailed understanding of patterns of variation in often far distant lands. This set up a degree of conflict between the central hub of Kew and botanists in the colonies, the latter having the benefit of observing plants in the wild, seeing obvious differences that did not appear in the dried herbarium specimens shipped back to London.

Joseph Hooker's solution was to advocate the primacy of broad species concepts and the necessity of examining large transnational herbarium collections associated with big libraries and living specimens in botanic gardens, such as Kew. Only with such resources, he argued, could a comprehensive overview of variation patterns be obtained. Conveniently, he also suggested (rather than proved) that many characters discernible in the field were highly variable and environmentally induced, so they should be ignored in favour of the more constant floral differences on herbarium sheets that Linnaeus had focused on in his 'sexual' system for classifying plants (counting the numbers of male and female parts as primary organizing characters for all plants). Further, Hooker maintained that the existence of any intermediates between otherwise clearly distinct plant populations meant that one variable species should be named, rather than two or more species and their occasional hybrids. Trivial variation within such broad species was of little interest, attracting Hooker's attention only when other botanists he termed 'hair-splitters' or 'species mongers' tried to elevate varieties to species against the views of central command at Kew. This line of argument meant that colonial botanists should leave the naming of plants to those experts in the big European herbaria, and preferably to Kew staff in most circumstances.

While such autocratic control of naming ensured a degree of constancy in approach, and enabled colonial floras to be written expeditiously, it stifled enquiry by field botanists in the colonies. It constrained thinking as to which characters would be most important for identifying species in any given group, and left unresolved many distinctive plants that were buried within concepts of broad variable species. It also consigned the study of natural hybridization to obscurity, to the point where many herbarium-based botanists – even up to the present day – disregard hybrids as being of no merit in taxonomic enquiry and classification. Modern whole-genome genetics has called for a drastic rethink on this matter.

Hooker's approach to defining species intuitively and broadly from an examination of herbarium specimens has been called the 'taxonomic species concept' (a species being defined as such by a herbarium-based taxonomist, based on characters discernible from the comparative study of dried herbarium specimens). To ensure the understanding of historical origins, I prefer to call this concept the 'Hookerian species concept'. With no clear criteria articulated as to the limits of such a species (or subspecies or hybrid), it remains a classic example of the abandonment of evidence-based scientific hypothesis-testing, except within the narrow confines of the comparative examination of herbarium specimens. One person's variety or subspecies is another's species, depending on how narrowly or broadly they wish to include specimen variation under the one name. Moreover, each view is perfectly legitimate and untestable in terms of evidence. Expert opinion prevails, and where two experts disagree, users of taxonomy have to choose which to follow, rather than consider what the available evidence indicates within the framework of an explicit definition of a species or other rank. Joseph Hooker himself indicated in correspondence to Darwin that at times he ceased caring about what was called a species, so problematic were some variation patterns in herbarium material.

In these circumstances there are two great historical ironies that bear upon the question of species concepts right up to modern times. Firstly, in Hooker's working life he became Darwin's primary scientific confidant, especially during the critical decade of the 1850s, when Darwin was producing his most significant work, *On the Origin of Species*, establishing the principle of evolution through natural selection. Darwin's scientific theory of biological evolution shone a new light on the question of how new species evolve, an issue that had been dispensed with for generations by creationists as having only one answer (special creation by a deity). *On the Origin of Species* elevated the importance of understanding variation within species, and of the process of hybridization, matters that Hooker regarded as trivial.

Darwin also made a major methodological contribution through his meticulous, self-critical attention to the scientific method. He acquired detailed evidence through experimentation bearing on evolutionary questions, readily discarding hypotheses if the evidence falsified their premises. He tried whenever possible to avoid intuitive judgement, by contrast with the practice of Hookerian taxonomists when they decided upon naming species, subspecies or varieties and hybrids.

Darwin defined species as transitional forms, but importantly where reproductive barriers to further hybridization had undergone natural selection to the point where hybrids if produced were almost sterile. In a masterful exposition of this new concept, he marshalled experimental evidence beyond that observed in dried herbarium specimens to demonstrate convincingly that European primroses and cowslips were distinct, reproductively isolated and true-breeding biological entities that occasionally hybridized (producing the rare infertile oxlip).[3] In Darwin's mind, the evidence was compelling that primroses and cowslips were best ranked as species, not varieties as some influential Hookerian taxonomists had argued for generations.

Darwin's approach to combining the study of specimens and experimental testing for reproductive barriers to mating became a mainstream interest in the twentieth century, an approach that I refer to as embodying the 'Darwinian biological species' concept. The second great irony, however, was that advocates of the Hookerian species concept in herbaria did not change their views or practices, even when claiming that they had accepted evolution by natural selection as the major biological law operating in nature. This anomaly may have been caused by ongoing pressure to name species quickly for the production of floras and monographs in a world in which so many species were still undescribed. Herbarium botanists continued to name new species from herbarium collections, primarily for an audience of other herbarium botanists, while the rest of the botanical world diverged into experimental botany pioneered in an evolutionary context by Darwin.

Modern Species Concepts Applied to Eucalypts

Turning, then, to the question of the nature of eucalypt species, subspecies and hybrids, the historical record suggests that we remain in a predominantly Hookerian world, or perhaps a time of transition from Hookerian to Darwinian perspectives on eucalypts. Intuitive decisions about characters and their variation underlie many described species. Such decisions were predominantly made by major contributors to the early description and classification of eucalypts from the limited material provided by herbarium specimens. George Bentham of Kew, for example, published the first overview of eucalypts in 1867 in his monumental seven-volume *Flora Australiensis* (1863–78), without visiting the continent or seeing a single eucalypt in the wild. At the time approximately 150 eucalypts were recognized, applying a very broad species concept.

Unless collectors record on their specimen labels sufficient information about the whole tree – its size, shape, bark, colour of leaves and flowers, aroma (and taste if the botanist is as assiduous as William Anderson at Adventure Bay) – as well as the abundance of plants and their variation, ecology, associated species and so on, the herbarium botanist has a limited view of the plant from small herbarium sheets with a few leaves, buds, flowers and fruits (see illus. 48, 52). The process of drying herbarium specimens causes plant organs to shrink and change colour, and their chemicals, including DNA, may denature and not be amenable to subsequent analysis. Such constraints clearly limited the evidence that was available to herbarium botanists like Bentham when describing and classifying new eucalypt species. Indeed, in 1857 Ferdinand von Mueller, the state of Victoria's first colonial botanist, with a fascination for eucalypts and with experience of field collecting across the nation, observed in relation to recent fieldwork:

> I found it necessary, for the sake of satisfactory distinctions, to describe all the tropical Eucalypti (nearly thirty species) on the spot, and I was never at a loss how to discriminate between variety and species, by considering all the characters of the trees collectively, and by paying due attention to the soil, structure and texture of the bark.[4]

The emphasis on field characters, such as bark attributes (see illus. 5–8), by both George Caley in Sydney and von Mueller in the tropics was ignored by Bentham at Kew because it was not consistently recorded on all herbarium specimens available to him. Consequently, Bentham often combined under one name several Darwinian species that differed in a range of readily discernible characters in the field, and were reproductively isolated by variation in habitat, flowering time or genetic incompatibility. Such was the power and influence of Kew over the botanical world, however, that Bentham's Hookerian approach to classifying Australian eucalypts prevailed, and still does across the continent, despite the more biological Darwinian approach of Lindsay Pryor and Lawrie Johnson becoming more widely adopted from the 1970s onwards.[5] Regrettably, Hookerian views drawing from Bentham's work became further entrenched in the literature with the publication in 1988 of a book on eucalypts as part of the *Flora of Australia* series.[6] This was after a latent period of the description of new species since the 1940s, wrongly interpreted as a conclusion of species-level work in such statements as: 'It is likely that relatively few taxa still await discovery as a result of exploration in botanically little-known areas.'[7]

History has now shown that one of the three regions richest in eucalypt species, Southwest Australia, was just such a 'botanically little-known area', containing an exceptional number of new locally endemic species and broadly conceived Hookerian species requiring

56, 57 *Eucalyptus* series *Levispermae* is a taxonomically challenging group endemic to Southwest Australia. The seedling leaves offer the best way of distinguishing between the sister species *wandoo* (*E. wandoo*), with its large, green, heart-shaped seedling leaves lacking hairs, and inland *wandoo* (*E. capillosa*), which has smaller, more slender, blue-green, hairy seedling leaves. The new bark also differs in colour, being yellow and orange respectively.

58 Typical habitat of *Eucalyptus caesia*, seen sprawling atop a massive granite inselberg at Boyagin Rock, Western Australia.

comprehensive field studies to reveal many new entities. For more than a century the hub of eucalypt taxonomic work had been Sydney, and none of the leading lights of the day had spent sufficient time in Southwest Australia to understand its hidden riches adequately.

On top of this, an exciting modern trend, underpinning the most recent acceleration in recognizing new eucalypts, has been the use of DNA sequencing to distinguish species, subspecies and hybrids. However, we are only at the beginning of this process, since DNA markers have mainly proven useful at levels above the species in helping to resolve eucalypt classification. Only very recently has there been adequate and consistent discrimination among closely related eucalypts and hybrids using genomic DNA approaches.[8] Examples include extensive work on species in *Eucalyptus* series *Levispermae* (illus. 56, 57) and on subspecies in *E. caesia* (illus. 58).[9]

Identifying Natural Hybrids and Their Evolutionary Significance in Eucalypts

Natural hybridization involves the mating of individuals from distinguishable populations, usually of distinct taxa, and the production of later-generation progeny from such mating.[10] Evidence predicted from this process includes:

· morphological intermediacy between parental taxa
  (illus. 59, 60);
· the relative rarity of such intermediates compared
  with parental taxa in the wild;
· pollinators observed to move between parental taxa;
· partial or full sterility of the intermediates;
· additive inheritance in the intermediates of
  distinguishing biochemical and DNA markers from
  both parental taxa;
· a close match of the characters of wild intermediates
  compared with experimentally produced hybrids of
  parental taxa;
· segregation in the progeny of the wild intermediates
  towards either parental form.

Hookerian taxonomists using only herbarium collections are usually limited in their identification of hybrids to evidence of morphological intermediacy. This has the pitfall that intermediate characters can arise either from natural hybridization or from natural selection working on characters along an environmental gradient (called primary intergradation or clinal variation by evolutionary biologists). There is no way of distinguishing hybrids from primary intergrades in the herbarium. Darwinian taxonomists, on the other hand, including Darwin himself in the case of primulas described earlier, turn their hands to experimental testing for evidence of hybridization across the full range of phenomena listed above.

An example concerns an inference from herbarium specimens that the critically endangered rose mallee (*E. rhodantha*; illus. 61) of Southwest Australia was a hybrid between *martilgarrang* (*E. macrocarpa*) and the Dowerin rose (*E. pyriformis*).[11] Extensive field surveys, population sampling and measurements, and reproductive and genetic studies established that *E. rhodantha* was in fact a true-breeding species in its own right, easily distinguishable from hybrids of *E. macrocarpa* and *E. pyriformis* (see illus. 61).[12]

59, 60   Natural hybrids are often rare in the wild and are usually found with their parental taxa. Morphological intermediacy of rare individuals offers the first clue that species may be hybridizing, as here seen in *Eucalyptus arborella × brandiana* in Fitzgerald River National Park, Southwest Australia. The top image illustrates flowers and buds of the hybrid and the bottom image a leaf and fruit(s) of both parents (*E. brandiana* to the left), with the hybrid in the middle.

61 A bud, flower, leaf and fruit of the critically endangered rose mallee (*E. rhodantha*, top centre), and the hybrid with which it was mistaken (centre bottom column) of *martilgarrang* (*E. macrocarpa*, left column) and the Dowerin rose (*E. pyriformis*, right column). Note the classical intermediacy of the hybrid between its two parents (especially in leaves and fruits) and the more divergent features of the rose mallee.

A recent case established interspecific hybridization as a threat to the reproductive security of the endangered Badgingarra box (*E. absita*).[13] Some 19 per cent of the seedlings *E. absita* produces are hybrids with other species. Similar Darwinian approaches have enabled compelling evidence to be marshalled that intermediates between silver-leaved ironbark (*E. melanophloia*) and White's ironbark (*E. whitei*) in central Queensland are not hybrids. Rather they are primary intergrades along a cline/transitional gradation arising from natural selection on leaf characters correlated with a transition in rainfall.[14] Conversely, a transition from alpine yellow gums (*E. subcrenulata*) into the shrubby alpine varnished gum (*E. vernicosa*) over a distance of 1.5 kilometres (just under 1 mi.) on Mt Arrowsmith in Tasmania was first inferred to be a broad hybrid zone. Instead, it proved to be primary intergradation along an altitudinal gradient (illus. 62). More recently a complex system has been inferred whereby each 'parental' taxon upslope and downslope varies towards a *subcrenulata*

117

62 The continuous variation that occurs over 1.5 kilometres (1 mi.) on Mt Arrowsmith, from Tasmanian alpine yellow gum trees (*E. subcrenulata*, pictured) down to shrubby varnished gum (*E. vernicosa*), was originally thought to be primary intergradation caused by a response to altitude. However, DNA and measurement studies of other mixed populations on two nearby mountains showed no such intergradations, with complete separation of DNA markers between the two species, establishing that the Mt Arrowsmith population was of hybrid origin involving extensive backcrossing to both parental species. Only a Darwinian approach to identifying hybrids affords such conclusive evidence. Hookerian taxonomists can only guess as to the causes of intermediacy in herbarium specimens.

form at intermediate altitudes, with no apparent hybridization involved.[15]

Natural hybridization may have positive evolutionary consequences, leading to the origin of new kinds of eucalypt. Populations of river red gum (*E. camaldulensis* subsp. *arida*) – known as *collaílle* to the Watchandie Nanda people of the lower Murchison River area, Western Australia, and further south – are a genetically stabilized hybrid of *E. camaldulensis* × *E. rudis* parentage (illus. 63).[16]

Across the continent, other DNA studies, especially those carried out by Tasmanian workers, have afforded precise genetic markers demonstrating that natural hybridization and the associated introgression of genes into participating species is extensive in eucalypts,

63 Natural hybridization may have positive evolutionary consequences, leading
to the origin of new eucalypts. *Collaille* (westernmost river red gum, placed within
Eucalyptus camaldulensis subsp. *arida*) is a genetically stabilized intergrade of *E. camaldulensis*
× *E. rudis* parentage, on the way to becoming a new kind of eucalypt. Murchison River,
Kalbarri National Park, Western Australia (see also illus. 32).

although constrained by evolutionary relationships and various permeable isolating barriers.[17] Indeed, it is evident that a hybrid origin occurred for southeastern Tasmanian populations of *E. globulus* subsp. *globulus* centred on Hobart, including those giant trees first seen by European naturalists on voyages of exploration.

Moreover, now that the whole genome of flooded gum (*E. grandis*) has been sequenced, we know that a whole genome duplication occurred in the ancestors of eucalypts some 110 million years ago, probably owing to chromosome doubling as a result of interspecific natural hybridization.[18] The disdain or lack of interest that many Hookerian taxonomists have shown towards the collecting and recognition of natural hybrids is ever more regrettable given that the pre-eminent evolutionary role hybrids play has been increasingly elucidated by modern field and molecular studies.

Conclusion

About nine hundred species of eucalypt are currently recognized. Darwinian analysis of the *Eucalyptus* series *Levispermae* indicates that the upward trend in naming new eucalypts from among the legacy of Hookerian-defined broad species has some way to go. It seems reasonable to predict that there may well be more than 1,000 Darwinian species of eucalypt.

There is a clear need for taxonomists to be explicit about the concepts of species, subspecies and hybrids they are applying in their work, be they broadly Hookerian or Darwinian.[19] This will clarify, but not stop, ongoing taxonomic debate about species, subspecies and hybrids in the eucalypts. As Lawrie Johnson famously wrote, the ideal consensus classification is like a rainbow's end — seemingly within our reach but never quite attainable.[20] Science is about successive approximations to the truth, not absolute truth.

five
Distribution and Habitats

❋

Eucalypts are ubiquitous across Australia, with just twelve species found to the north on the Malesian islands of the Indonesian archipelago and Papua New Guinea (illus. 64). Fossil eucalypts are found in New Zealand, Argentina and probably India, but wild eucalypts are no longer extant in these countries.[1]

The general features of the geographical distribution of Australian plants, including eucalypts, were first articulated by the Scottish biologist Robert Brown, the naturalist aboard Matthew Flinders's ship *Investigator* when it circumnavigated the continent in the first years of the nineteenth century.[2] Brown identified southwest, desert, east coast and tropical floristic regions of Australia. Subsequent exploration and analysis by many authors have broadly affirmed and elaborated Brown's scheme.

We now know that most species of eucalypt are found in southern Australia, where the greatest concentration of geographically restricted local endemic species occurs (see illus. 65, 66). Six of the ten richest places are found in southern coastal Western Australia, where 86–116 eucalypts per 10,000 square kilometres (3,860 sq. mi.) grid are found. The other four places richest in eucalypts (86–92 per grid) occur in the Sydney region and in the border region of northern coastal New South Wales and Queensland.

These concentrations of eucalypts are associated with old, climatically buffered, infertile landscapes (OCBILs) – upland landscapes that, in global terms, are tens of millions of years old. They are climatically buffered by prolonged oceanic influence and are especially low in phosphorus, owing to millions of years of weathering by rainfall.[3] OCBILs occur predominantly in the southern hemisphere and are proving to be exciting landscapes for novel biological discovery and challenging conservation issues. The eucalypts exemplify this pattern.

Fourteen centres of species found nowhere else (endemics) or eucalypts with narrow geographical ranges have been identified, the richest being from Southwest Australia (illus. 65) and the east coast

64 Rainbow gum (*Eucalyptus deglupta*) in plantations on Maui, Hawaii, one of the four eucalypts not native to Australia and among twelve found in the tropics on the Malesian islands of the Indonesian archipelago and Papua New Guinea. It is the only eucalypt that occurs in the wild north of the Equator and was the first eucalypt to be described by Europeans as a polynomial in 1743.

65 *Muert* (mallee), *marlaq* and *moort* eucalypt vegetation in the Fitzgerald River Biosphere of south coastal Western Australia, the richest in species (116 in this 100 × 100-kilometre 62 × 62-mi. grid square) and in local endemic eucalypts, thanks to fine-scale soil mosaics on old, climatically buffered infertile landscapes.

66 The Blue Mountains World Heritage Area flanking the Sydney Basin is the second major centre of eucalypt richness and endemism, here seen from Evans Lookout, Blackheath, looking north to Mt Banks. Following surveys up to 2010, the World Heritage Area contained 96 eucalypts, with Sydney peppermint (*Eucalyptus piperita*) shown here in the foreground.

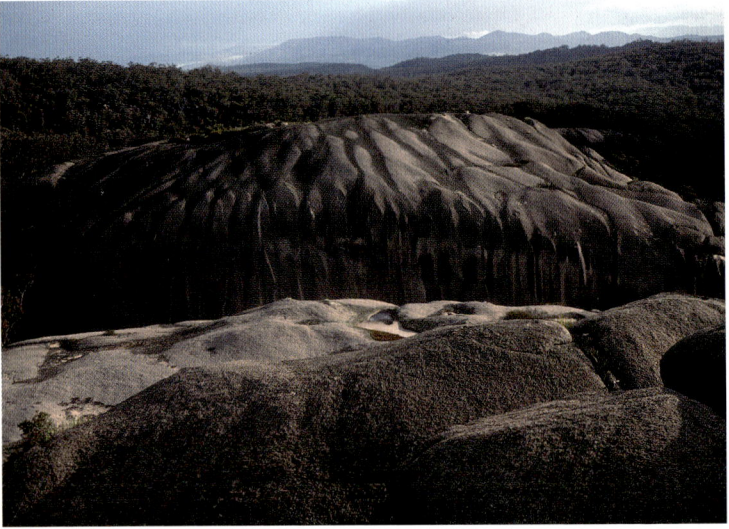

67 The third-richest centre of eucalypt endemism is centred on the Border Ranges
of north coastal New South Wales and southeastern Southern Queensland.
Here a local endemic, Wallangara white gum (*Eucalyptus scoparia*), is embedded
in shallow soils beneath a large granite outcrop.

in the Sydney region (illus. 66) and in the northern coastal New
South Wales/Queensland Border Ranges region (illus. 67).[4]

However, six, not four, major regions of eucalypts across Australia
are now known: the southwest, southeast, southern semi-arid, central desert, monsoonal north and tropical/subtropical east coast. The
most distinctive eucalypt assemblage is in the region of Southeast
Australia, characterized by mountains and hills covered in snow in
winter. The Southeast Australian eucalypt region is subdivided into
alpine (Great Dividing Range), Tasmanian and Victorian subregions,
each having its own range of eucalypts. The region includes the spectacular Greater Blue Mountains World Heritage Area to the west of
Sydney; 96 eucalypts had been found there by 2010, of which 54 were
widespread and 42 of more restricted geographical distribution.[5]
Southeast Australia displays little congruence between species richness and centres of endemism, implying that there are many widespread species overlapping in distribution and actively diverging,
rather than concentrations of narrow-range eucalypt endemics.

The remaining parts of Australia divide into southern and central/northern regions. The most distinctive eucalypt region of this remaining group of five is coastal Southwest Australia (illus. 68), which enjoys a Mediterranean climate (winter wet, summer dry). The most colourful eucalypts in terms of flowers, buds, fruits and bark are concentrated there (see illus. 4–12). There are three subregions: southeast, north and south. The richness of the eucalypt vegetation is exemplified by such local Noongar Aboriginal terms as *muert* (mallee), *maarlak* and *moort* for various eucalypt thicket formations.

There is a much closer correspondence in coastal Southwest Australia than in Southeast Australia between places rich in species and rich in endemism. Subtle climatic variation and a mosaic of soil types are strongly correlated with the Southwest, which is rich in endemic eucalypts.[6] Hence many localized species and subspecies are found, rapidly turning over across Southwest landscapes. In contrast to the rich aggregations of more widespread species found in Southeast

68 The Southwest Australian coastal region has exceptional diversity and local endemism in its eucalypts. Here, *E.* × *tetragona* sits adjacent to Lucky Bay in Cape Le Grand National Park. This species was collected by Robert Brown in 1802 on the Flinders *Investigator* expedition and subsequently selected as the type species for a new genus, *Eudesmia*, which is today regarded as a subgenus of *Eucalyptus*. Moreover, the species is a transitional form, intergrading between *E. pleurocarpa* to the west and *E. extrica* to the east. All three species are known to Noongar people as *tjaltjraak/taalyaraak* (tallerack).

Australia, the Southwest has an ever-changing occurrence of many eucalypts over short distances.

A large southern semi-arid to desert region (Eremaean South) extends from the eucalypt-rich Southwest (illus. 68) to the southeast. It has four subregions, corresponding to the Great Western Woodlands of Western Australia (illus. 69), the Nullarbor Plain, the southern Murray-Darling Basin mallee and woodlands and a subregion flanking the deserts of central Australia. Some trees of exceptional size are found there growing under conditions that, on other continents, are occupied by barren deserts. All these southern Australian eucalypt regions are strongly correlated with high winter rainfall, compared with the summer rainfall experienced in northern Australia.

Looking north, the most distinctive eucalypt region runs up the east coast from subtropical New South Wales north of Sydney

69 *Opposite*: The Great Western Woodlands of semi-arid to desert country in southern Western Australia are part of a broad Eremaean South region here exemplified by the large tree *woorac* (salmon gum, *Eucalyptus salmonophloia*) near Geelabbing/Mt Churchman.
70 The tropical/subtropical region that runs up the east coast of Australia from north of Sydney to Cape York has giant eucalypts emergent from rainforest, as seen here in a *benaroon* (blackbutt, *Eucalyptus pilularis*) 70 metres (230 ft) tall on the slopes of Middle Brother Mountain in New South Wales.

(illus. 70) into southern Queensland to tropical Queensland, culminating in the Cape York Peninsula subregion. Throughout this tropical/subtropical coastal region, eucalypts vie with rainforest and intermix on the margins. Some of these eucalypts are essentially rainforest trees, capable of regenerating after major events, such as landslide, fire, flood or damage from strong winds, and attaining substantial height and size. Of course, the region is diverse in its vegetation, which is not merely tropical/subtropical rainforest. It includes the Border Ranges centre of high eucalypt species endemism, including those found on granite outcrops in shallow infertile soils – classic OCBILs (see illus. 67).

The monsoonal eucalypt region is primarily occupied by species of savanna communities (illus. 71), with east–west subregions occupying the Top End of the Northern Territory and offshore into Malesia, the tropical savanna of northern Queensland, that of the north-central semi-arid Northern Territory and the Kimberley region of far north Western Australia.

71 Savanna vegetation is the home of most eucalypts of the monsoon region, which extends from Western Australia's Kimberley through tropical Northern Territory to northwestern Queensland. Here a silver box (*Eucalyptus pruinosa*), which ranges across the region, flanks a track running towards the sandstone beehive hills of Purnululu National Park (Bungle Bungles) in tropical Western Australia.

72 A small number of eucalypts occupy the snowy tops and flanks of mountains in southeastern Australia. Pictured is the Smithton peppermint (*Eucalyptus nitida*) in Cradle Mountain National Park, Tasmania.

Lastly, the central and western Australian deserts (Eremacan North) have a distinctive eucalypt flora of relatively few species (see illus. 31). Here again are four subregions, trending east–west, from southern central Queensland and adjacent northwestern New South Wales to central Australia across the Northern Territory into Western Australia, culminating in the Pilbara of arid northwestern Western Australia and the arid to semi-arid central coast of that state, ranging from Exmouth Gulf to Shark Bay and south almost to Jurien Bay. By and large, eucalypts are sparse and stunted across the central Australian deserts, except where they flank permanent waterholes or other wetlands.

Indeed, the vast majority of eucalypts occupy well-drained soils on plains, slopes and rugged terrain in both temperate and tropical climates. A few, including Australia's most widespread species, *E. cama-ldulensis* (see illus. 63), favour the seasonally flooded banks of creeks, rivers, lakes and ephemeral swamps. Some occupy the margins of inland salt lakes and coasts. Several occur where it snows in the mainland alps and highlands of Tasmania (illus. 72).

Permanently wet swamp margins are preferred by a few species, such as Western Australia's *E. patens*, and one (*E. aquatica*, regarded by some as a subspecies or variant of *E. camphora*) inhabits a single hanging swamp in the eastern coastal highlands south of Sydney. Many species are specialists of shallow soils on rock outcrop OCBILs (see illus. 58, 67), often growing as small, sinuous-trunked trees or mallees. Upright trees are most commonly seen, growing on deeper soils. Where rainfall is sufficient, these will form forest or even tall forest, whereas semi-arid to arid communities tend to be the realm of spreading woodland trees or mallees. Eucalypts are absent from only the harshest deserts, save those species that are capable of tracking the rivers, creeks, lakes, ridges and dunes.

Across this broad range of habitats, environmental circumstances and major disturbance regimes vary significantly.[7] The eucalypts share a number of life-history attributes that enable their persistence and proliferation across the continent. The next chapter outlines such attributes.

six

The Eucalypt Life Cycle

✳

Eucalypts have a diverse array of life cycles.[1] From the giants of the tall forests to the diminutive coastal mallees less than 1 metre (3¼ ft) tall, these iconic plants have evolved sometimes surprising ways of coping with disturbance and varying habitats.

Pollination and Fertilization

To conceive new life, eucalypts depend on transferring male pollen from the numerous anthers of a flower to the receptive female stigma on the tip of the centrally located style or pistil. The anthers are golden-yellow vessels less than 1 millimetre long, each one perched on a firm, thread-like filament standing in a colourful mass of others around the rim of the flower (see illus. 9–12). An anther and its supporting filament are known together as a stamen.

In many eucalypts, the stamens are doubled over in the bud so that pollen could conceivably be placed on the stigma as the filaments straighten up when the bud cap (operculum) falls off. Such self-pollination is averted, however, because the female stigma does not become receptive and sticky until between one and seven days after the flower opens (illus. 73), a process known as protandry (male first).

Eucalypts consequently need an agent to move pollen from a fresh flower to an older flower with a receptive stigma. Wind or rain could do this, but microscopically triangular eucalypt pollen is a little sticky and is not shed in fine clouds like that of sheoaks, oaks, conifers or grasses. Rather, animals are the preferred pollinating agents of eucalypts. They are usually attracted to the flowers by sugary nectar secreted around the base of the style in the cup of the flower (illus. 74). Some animals also consume the anthers and pollen, which are rich in protein.

Eucalypt flowers attract a broad range of animal pollinators (illus. 74, 75). These include diverse insect groups (wasps, bees, flies, moths, butterflies, beetles, ants, thrips), some birds (honeyeaters,

73 Protandry evident in sectioned half-flowers of *E. caesia* subsp. *magna*. The flower on top has fresh anthers shedding pollen, and the green top (stigma) of the central style is dry and non-receptive. A week later, the older flower below has shed most of its stamens, but the stigma is noticeably shiny with sticky exudates that retain pollen and stimulate germination of the pollen grains.

74 A red wattlebird feeds on nectar at the base of the style of *yorgum* (red-flowering gum, *Corymbia ficifolia*) in south coastal Western Australia.

lorikeets, cockatoos, other parrots, silvereyes and occasional kurra-wongs and ravens) and mammals (possums, flying foxes, rodents).

Most eucalypts typically attract a broad array of animals with cream or white stamens up to 1 centimetre (⅓ in.) long, massed in floral clusters across and inside the canopy. Such mass flowering means that animals foraging on nectar and pollen can readily move among adjacent flowers. However, moving pollen among flowers on the same plant results in self-pollination. Only animals flying in from another tree are likely to place outcross pollen on stigmas.

Self-pollen and outcross pollen grains germinate on sticky recep-tive stigmas (see illus. 73), each grain producing a tube that grows down the style to fertilize the female ovules at the well-protected base (hypanthium) of the flower. Following fertilization, the hypanthium,

75 Western Australian insects, birds and mammals are all attracted to the abundant pollen and nectar of eucalypt flowers, cream-coloured and red. Pictured here is the western pygmy possum (*Cercartetus concinnus*) taking nectar from *E. caesia*.

which encases the ovules and placenta, grows into the woody gum nut over several months of maturation.

The pollen tube, a large cell, carries the male nucleus full of paternal DNA ready to fertilize the female ovule. If, on fertilization, the pollen has come from the mother's flowers, most self-pollinated seed routinely either aborts to form the woody dross or chaff so common in gum nuts (illus. 76) or performs poorly in germinating and subsequent growth as seedlings. Seed derived from the cross-pollination of flowers on genetically different trees performs much better. The eucalypts have a mating system, consequently, described as preferentially outcrossing, in which maternal plant tissue can biochemically recognize pollen from other plants and give it a better chance of siring seed than its own pollen.

As a general rule, larger animals need more food than smaller animals, and will move further to find it. If they are warm-blooded, they will also feed in cold weather. Larger animals are thus more likely to move between trees when feeding, and would make better pollinators, being more reliable as such in cold, wet conditions if warm-blooded. Hence, some eucalypts, especially in the Southwest Australian Floristic Region (SWAFR) and other parts of seasonally cold southern Australia, have flowers that favour large pollinators, such as birds and mammals, over smaller, less mobile insects.[2]

A simple way to achieve pollination by large pollinators is to spread the anthers and elevate the stigma away from the nectar source. Small-bodied insects can crawl to the nectar right past the stigma if it is held far enough above the bowl of the flower, whereas the larger head of a bird or mammal will not avoid contact with the stigma (see illus. 74, 75). Eucalypts with large flowers (see illus. 9–12) include *martilgarrang* (*E. macrocarpa*; see illus. 35, 61), bushy yate (*E. lehmannii*; see illus. 9–12), bell-fruited mallee (*E. preissiana*), Talyuberlup mallee (*E. talyuberlup*), purple mallee (*E. pluricaulis* subsp. *porphyrea*), illyarrie (*E. erythrocorys*), cup gum (*E. cosmophylla*) and Tasmanian blue gum (*E. globulus*; see illus. 70). Except for the last two species, which are from eastern Australia, these are all from the Southwest and have colourful stamens, either red or yellow, rather than the white or cream of most eucalypts (see illus. 9–12). Red flowers are known to be difficult for insects to see and conspicuous to birds and mammals

76 Plump round seeds and withered angular chaff (aborted ovules or seeds) from within the gum nuts of blue mallet (*Eucalyptus gardneri*).

(including humans). Rather than evolving to please people as desirable horticultural subjects, several SWAFR eucalypts with spectacular large red flowers and yellow stamens evolved more for self-interest in attracting vertebrate pollinators.

There is another feature of many large-flowered eucalypts that encourages pollinators to move between plants: producing few flowers per tree (less than one hundred, or far fewer in the case of four-winged mallee, *E. tetraptera*; see illus. 11) compared with the thousands seen on most small-flowered species. For an adequate feed of nectar, a honeyeater, parrot or possum must move between at least a few plants, ensuring cross-pollination.

Ridge-fruited mallee (*E. incrassata*) and caesia (*E. caesia* subsp. *caesia*; see illus. 13, 58, 75) have a more subtle way of discriminating in favour of birds and mammals. They flower during the cold winters of southern Australia and secrete nectar mainly overnight. Warm-blooded vertebrates begin feeding on nectar before dawn, a few hours before nectar-feeding insects become active, forcing the insects to look for other nectar sources.

Scarlet pear gum (*E. stoatei*; illus. 77) and its near relatives flower in the late summer, and have evolved essentially tubular flowers in

77 Southwest Australia's scarlet pear gum (*E. stoatei*) buds and a flower, illustrating the rare evolution of functionally tubular flowers in eucalypts.

78 A ringneck parrot (*Barnardius zonarius*) feeds destructively
on flowers of a river red gum (*Eucalyptus camaldulensis*).

which the stamens do not spread when the operculum falls off.
They remain tightly bent inwards, as if in the enclosed bud, forming
a narrow tube lined with opening anthers that release pollen and
through which only a long-billed honeyeater or narrow-snouted
honey possum (*Tarsipes rostratus*) can push past the stigma to get at the
copious nectar on offer.

Even in species that are predominantly pollinated by birds and
mammals, most pollen nonetheless is transferred among flowers on
the same plant. It is not a perfect outcrossing system. Also, far more
flowers, pollen and ovules are produced by most eucalypts than are
required to achieve successful seed production. There is a lot of
apparent waste. However, many animals eat flowers or nectar without pollinating them. Ringneck parrots (*Barnardius zonarius*; illus. 78),
for instance, bite off eucalypt flowers, chew them to extract nectar
and possibly pollen and spit them to the ground. The apparently
excess reproductive bounty of eucalypts may also serve other evolutionary functions, including forming visual clues to attract incoming
flying animals, and enabling intense maternal selection pressure on

developing seeds so that only the few strong outcrossed seeds are preferentially nurtured, rather than the vast majority of self-pollinated
seeds that the system delivers. The latter maternal controls are so far
poorly researched.

Seeds

Over a period of some months, fertilized ovaries swell and their
encasing hypanthium hardens to produce the characteristic gum
nuts or fruits of eucalypts. Each usually contains a few seeds where
gum nuts are small, but there are up to several hundred seeds in the
largest-fruited species, such as the four-winged mallee (*E. tetraptera*;
see illus. 11). The seeds are often very distinctive in shape, colour, surface texture and size, enabling a trained eye to recognize species or
groups of species at a glance (compare illus. 19 and 76).[3]

The largest seeds are those of *marri* (*Corymbia calophylla*) from the
SWAFR forest regions. They are black and about 1 centimetre (⅓ in.)
long (see illus. 16–19). Only a few seeds can fit in the large fruits that
May Gibbs made famous in her illustrations for children's books.[4]
The seeds are so nutritious that *djarayilbardang* (red-capped parrots,
Purpureicephalus spurius) have evolved an elongated upper jaw that enables them to scoop out the seed feast as a staple of their diet. Other
parrots are expert at crushing the green fruits of many eucalypts across
Australia to feed on seeds. The seeds usually remain in the fruits on
the tree for several years, or until the branch is killed by fire, drought
or other damage.

Actual seed production per plant varies enormously in eucalypts,
although it has yet to be quantified in detail. Forest trees produce
seeds in the millions over their lifetime, compared with hundreds or
at the most thousands in small mallees, such as *E. tetraptera* and its
close relatives.

Any fruits that do open and shed their seeds prematurely have
little hope of contributing to the next generation. Ants constantly
patrol the litter layer beneath eucalypts and gather seeds to eat. The

79 Indehiscent fruits of *Eucalyptus caesia* subsp. *magna*, typical of most eucalypts.

few seeds that do germinate endure a similar fate; herbivorous invertebrates dine on the actively growing seed leaves, or the roots of
mature trees deplete moisture and the seedlings die from drought
stress. That is why it is rare to see eucalypts regenerating from seed in
undisturbed habitats.

Exceptions, however, include the groups of eucalypts (some
Blakella and coolabah *Eucalyptus*) that have small, thin-walled, fragile
fruits that dehisce (burst open) as soon as they mature. For example,
smooth-barked or western coolibah (*E. victrix*), the tough stalwart of
desert watercourses and occasionally flooded flats, drops its seeds in
the tens of thousands from minuscule fruits (2–4 millimetres wide),
a strategy that makes sense when seeds germinate after unpredictable
rainfall events. Most eucalypts, however, have fruits that remain tightly

closed (indehiscent) until a disturbance, such as fire or wind damage, causes the death of the branch (illus. 79).

Fire and Other Disturbances

Fire – whether initiated by lightning or by human activity – is a common disturbance that is important in the life history of eucalypts.[5] If it is severe enough it will kill adult plants, although most species resprout from the basal or underground lignotuber and from vegetative buds beneath thick bark on trunks and branches (illus. 80). Prolific recruitment through seeds released by adult trees is another coping strategy (illus. 81). However, other disturbances have been shown to be as important for similar behaviours as fire for some eucalypts: flooding regimes, the windthrow of entire trees during storms, grazing by animals (illus. 82–4), the deposition of dust and sand by strong winds, earth movements and landslides, to name just a few.

Eucalypt biologists vary in their recognition of the importance of fire regimes (that is, the season, frequency, area and intensity of fires). Some see fire as so all-pervasive that, they argue, eucalypt responses to it must have evolved as adaptations to cope.[6] Others are more cautious, urging the need for research in specific circumstances and for each species of interest before it is assumed that fire has been the singular and driving evolutionary force favouring traits that help plants to cope with the disturbance it brings.[7]

Obviously, if all eucalypts are adapted to fire, managers of wildfire and prescribed burning need not pay attention to when, how and why they burn or control fire. If fire is just one of many disturbance regimes that may have influenced the evolutionary adaptation of eucalypts, a better understanding of and greater caution in fire management for eucalypts would be the wise course to avoid unexpected results.

Fire sensitivity occurs in 10 per cent of eucalypts.[8] These are called obligate seeders. Adults are routinely killed by fire or other disturbance, so that regeneration is achieved only by the release of

80 Some eucalypts cope with fire by resprouting from a basal woody lignotuber, as seen here in *Eucalyptus caesia* subsp. *magna* on Chutawalakin Hill, Southwest Australia.

seed and subsequent germination. Most obligate seeders (78 species) are found in the SWAFR, while nine are found in eastern Australia.

Fire and other disturbances assist regeneration by temporarily removing most of the seed and seedling predators and pathogens. The canopy is opened so that sunlight bathes the soil and there is less competition with adults for moisture. Fire also provides ashbeds (see illus. 81), clears the ground facilitating flooding and dust storms and fertilizes topsoil in which nutrients are concentrated in otherwise nutrient-poor soils. Branch death through fire, drought, storm damage, rainfall and landslide stimulates the drying out of fruits and the release of seed.

The synchronized opening of fruits and subsequent rain of seed upon the ground may occur within a day or two of disturbance. The density of seeds shed on the ground varies by species and the patchiness and intensity of the disturbance. Many mallees have only a light

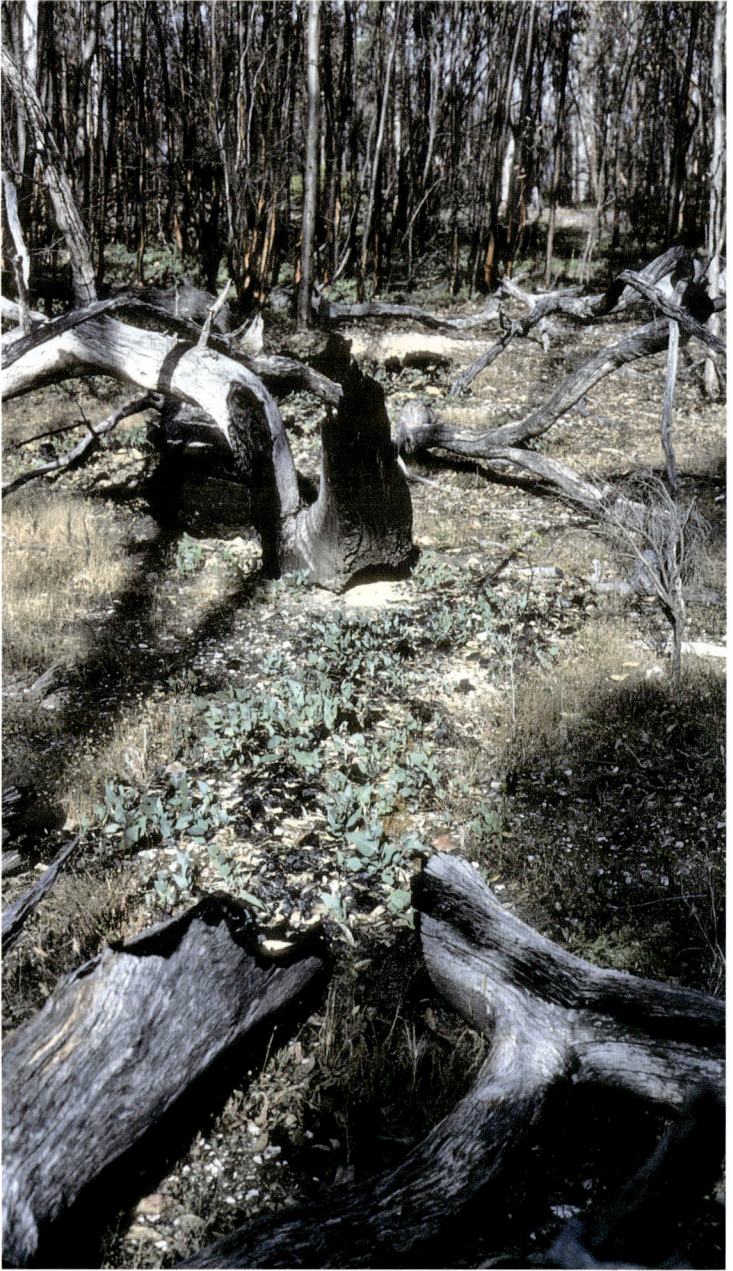

81 The ashbed effect in *Eucalyptus wandoo*, Southwest Australia. A section of a burnt log has prolific seed germination (blue leaves) localized on top of the nutrient-enriched ash.

seed rain and regenerate predominantly from the underground tuber. At the other extreme, obligate seeders carpet the ground with a few thousand seed per square metre.

An obvious risk associated with climate change is that eucalypt vegetation in southern Australia is receiving less rainfall and becoming exceptionally prone to fire. Moist places, such as wetlands, rivers, creeks,

82–4 Common eucalypt herbivores include gumleaf grasshopper nymphs (*Goniaea australasiae*, *bottom*), which favour seedlings of *Eucalyptus marginata*, the nymph here seen near Brisbane, Queensland; processionary sawfly larvae/'spitfires' (*Perga affinis*, *top right*), seen here on *E.* × *missilis* in Torndirrup National Park, Southwest Australia; and koalas (*Phascolarctos cinereus*, *top left*) in southeast Australia.

85 This white-tailed black cockatoo in flight may be
dispersing seed in a nut of *marri* (*Corymbia calophylla*).

peat swamps and natural springs, are drying out more frequently. This is shortening the intervals between fires to the point where obligate seeders, such as *mallets* and *maarlaks*, do not have time to recover enough seed to survive the next fire. Mallees, although seemingly indestructible, can also be killed by two fires in quick succession over a few years. The dramatic fires that occurred across southern Australia over the black summer of 2019/20 may well be a portent of a warming world. This calls for a significant rethink of approaches to the use of large-scale prescribed burning where vulnerable eucalypt populations are at risk.

The vast majority of eucalypts have no obvious means of seed dispersal other than gravity, and the assistance of wind in the case of some bloodwoods with winged seed (see illus. 16–19). Consequently, the overwhelming majority of seed falls directly below or close to the mother tree, usually being dispersed over a distance less than twice the height of the tree. However, very rarely, fruits are carried for several kilometres by parrots (illus. 85) or by fire storm updraughts.

One remarkable exception to the lack of obvious and frequent seed dispersal is found in *cadaghi* (*Blakella torelliana*; illus. 86), from the coastal ranges and hills between Ingham and Cooktown in tropical northern Queensland. Stingless social bees (*Tetragonula carbonaria*) harvest a resin that *cadaghi* secretes within its fruit. As they do so, they inadvertently transport the seeds stuck in the sticky resin as far as 300 metres (980 ft) to their nests.[9]

86 *Cadaghi* (*Blakella torelliana*) from the tropical coastal hills of northern Queensland, with its characteristic green bark. This species exhudes a sticky resin inside its fruits that is collected by native bees, which also pick up seeds attached to the resin and disperse them.

Germination

Eucalypt seeds are relatively easy to germinate. All that is needed is appropriate moisture, temperature and light. Germination usually begins a couple of weeks after rain in seasonal environments.

The tolerance of young germinants to waterlogging and salinity varies by species. Some, such as the salt river gum (*E. sargentii*), from the SWAFR are exceptionally tolerant of such stresses. Most species are not. For example, many mallees (see illus. 2) grow only in dry, exposed, well-drained sites in semi-arid or montane Australia. Some, including a mallee subspecies of *E. sargentii*, can persist in wet saline habitats.

Eucalypts grow through three stages of leaf formation (see illus. 16–19). The germinating seedling first produces a pair of cotyledons (seed leaves). These vary in size and shape, and may be diagnostic of groups of species. In the SWAFR, forest species that grow in well-watered sites, such as *jarrah* (*E. marginata*) and *marri* (*Corymbia calophylla*), have large cotyledons more than 1 centimetre (⅓ in.) square. They are usually dark green above and maroon below, the latter caused by a light-sensitive pigment that is helpful for photosynthesizing in low ambient light. These pigments presumably give the germinants a quick start in life, turning on the photosynthetic machinery so that they can shade out competitors. At the same time, the tiny seedlings are invaded by fungi that live in their roots and further stimulate growth in a symbiotic partnership. The seed leaves of many mallees and woodland trees of semi-arid country are not as large as those of forest trees and bloodwoods, since competition for light in these harsher environments is less of a problem early in life.

Seedling density varies enormously, matching that for seeds shed from dead or resprouting parent trees. I have counted up to 2,000 seedlings per square metre (nearly 11 sq. ft) for southern brown *mallet* (*E. astringens* subsp. *redacta*) in the Stirling Range National Park following a wildfire. After the same fire, common trees and mallees, such as *wandoo/wornt* (*E. wandoo* subsp. *wandoo*), *jarrah* and *taalyaraak* (blue mallee,

E. pleurocarpa), produced much lower seedling densities. At the other end of the spectrum, many populations of several mallee species yielded scarcely a single seedling per hectare (2½ ac). *Jarrah*, growing as a stunted mallee upslope on rocky soils of the Stirling Range, produced abundant fruits, but only a handful of seedlings were recorded. The reason for this remains a subject for further research.

Environmental conditions are critical for the survival and growth of eucalypt seedlings. Sufficient moisture, nutrients, light and freedom from predators and pathogens are needed. If the seedlings survive beyond producing their seed leaves, they produce several pairs of juvenile leaves that are usually broader than the adult foliage. Often, the juvenile leaves are diagnostic of species or species groups, providing, for example, the most reliable discrimination between *wandoo* and inland *wandoo* (*E. capillosa*; see illus. 56, 57).

After fire, for such species as *wandoo*, ashbeds have a significant effect on seedling growth (see illus. 81). The linear charcoal and ashbeds where logs have been incinerated are easy to identify, since they have greater densities of germinants and healthier, faster-growing seedlings. A similar pattern is often seen on arid or semi-arid floodplains, where accumulated lines of debris and litter from receding water often support lines of seedlings of the river red gum (*E. camaldulensis*). Species that favour water-retaining sites may germinate on adjacent well-drained soil during the wet season, but the seedlings soon persist only along moisture-retaining creeklines and flats as seasonal drought occurs.

Juvenile Growth

The first few years after eucalypts germinate are critical for their survival. As the plant community regenerates following fire or other disturbance, there may be intense competition among seedlings and resprouting adults. The eucalypts have to compete among themselves and with other fast-growing plants, such as wattles (*Acacia*), that dominate for several years following disturbance.

In this phase of juvenile growth, the importance of outcrossing comes to the fore. The intermixed planting of self-pollinated and outcrossed eucalypt seedlings in experimental trials has shown that the outcrossed group comes to dominate the canopy as the plants mature. This superior growth of outcrossed individuals is known as hybrid vigour.

Genetic studies undertaken using DNA markers routinely show that mother trees display more average genetic variation than their seedlings. Genes come in double doses, one from the mother and the other paternal. With outcrossing, there is a higher probability that the parental forms of a gene (alleles) will be different. Surviving juvenile plants and ultimately mature maternal trees, therefore, tend by and large to have more alleles than their progeny, which routinely include many self-pollinated inbred individuals. Self-pollination and inbreeding reduce such genetic variation.

The seasonal summer drought in southern Australia presents another challenge to the survival of eucalypt seedlings. Even where good germination occurs following winter rains, the seedlings' ultimate survival will depend on how quickly they can develop a root system that is able to sustain the plant over the summer. Often summer rainfall makes or breaks the plants' survival over this critical period.

Most seedlings die during the summer after germination, as the weaker, slower-growing or inappropriately placed seedlings are thinned out. On granite outcrops inland from Perth, it is several years before survival to maturity is guaranteed. Seedlings that may grow to 1 metre (3¼ ft) or more tall over a couple of good rainfall years may be killed if a harsh summer follows. Over the long lifetimes of adult eucalypts capable of resprouting, a rare sequence of events is needed to successfully recruit surviving progeny: the right disturbance regime and sufficient seeds, followed by a run of favourable seasons and the suppression of pathogens and herbivores.

Grazing increases as the animal community recovers after fire and other disturbance. Kangaroos and herbivorous insects (see illus.

82—4), which favour green regenerating plants during the first growing season after disturbance, may cause local patches of mortality. The spatial array of the disturbance events is critical here.[10] Small fires may allow animals to wipe out all seedlings, whereas large fires may keep the insects in particular at bay long enough for juvenile trees to get a head start. Pathogens may also influence the outcome, increasing in virulence as other stresses mount on seedlings.

It is little wonder, then, that most eucalypts produce such an abundance of reproductive material. Successful recruitment seems to be exceptionally rare, especially in mallee communities in the absence of fire or other disturbance. Indeed, under global warming climatic regimes, some mallees have almost no chance of successfully recruiting from seed. It will be important to improve our understanding of their seedling biology and actively intervene if extinction seems likely.

Maturity

The time it takes to reach reproductive maturity varies considerably in eucalypts. As might be expected, obligate seeders should mature and start producing faster than resprouters to ensure that some seed is available should the return interval of fire or other disturbance be short. However, in one study of forty obligate seeders from Western Australia matched against forty resprouters in a common garden, both groups reached reproductive maturity in four to eight years.[11]

It is clear that the eucalypts that grow to maturity are an elite few. Moreover, their development is a very individual process, as in humans. Differences in size, trunk form, canopy and health of foliage occur.

The adult appearance of each eucalypt is determined by its inherited genetic features interacting with environmental conditions. The growth of new shoots may be terminated by herbivores, drought, storm damage or fire. Some branches may escape damage long enough to take the lead in canopy development, so their trunk and branches become larger.

The location of adjacent trees and competition for light may also determine which branches will grow. Laterals are inhibited in dense forest, and upward growth is favoured.[12] In open paddocks or on rock outcrops, a swelling canopy growing outwards as much as upwards may occur, albeit in diminished form. Mallees do similar things.

Herbivores include mammals, such as the koala, as well as a range of invertebrates (see illus. 82–4). Trees are rarely defoliated, since the leaves are packed with oil glands that may not be palatable. However, stressed trees seem particularly susceptible to herbivore attack.

The bark of eucalypts is highly variable (see illus. 5–8). Smooth-barked species shed their bark annually, often revealing brightly coloured new bark beneath. Rough-barked species hold on to their outer layers. Some species have a rough-barked stocking giving way to smooth bark above. Little experimental work has been done on eucalypt bark to discover the functions of the various types. An intriguing example is the bubbling of bark in rain as soapy chemicals

87 This Stirling Range mallee (*E. × erectifolia*), of possible hybrid origin, forms a circular doughnut 20 metres (66 ft) in diameter. Its individuality is indicated by a uniform yellow-green canopy and confirmed through genetic analysis of leaf samples from around the circle. Given that mallees grow outwards at 1–2 centimetres (¹⁄₃–³⁄₄ in.) per year, the size of the plant exemplifies the age of some mallees, which may be thousands of years old.

are released. This may soften water-shedding soils and allow the rain to penetrate the soil more deeply, recharging local aquifers.

The age attained by eucalypts has been estimated, with upper limits ranging from a few hundred years for obligate seeders to more than 10,000 years for some clonal mallees (illus. 87).[13] Over such periods, eucalypts provide habitat for and facilitate the growth and reproduction of animals, plants and fungi alike. They endure fire and other disturbance in complex ways that vary in space and time. Understanding their evolution, ecology and conservation is therefore, not surprisingly, a challenge.

seven

How Australia Made the Eucalypts

❄

Significant advances in the study of fossils, the formation and movement of continental masses (plate tectonics) and landscape evolution over the past three decades have generated fresh insights into the origins of the eucalypts and the Australian biota more generally. Take, for example, the marsupials (see illus. 75, 82–4). These are today the dominant mammals on the continent, with a much smaller representation in South and North America. Understandably, based on that biogeographical pattern, early views were that marsupials originated in Australia. However, fossil studies have now established unequivocally that marsupial ancestors arose in the northern hemisphere, most probably North America, more than 120 million years ago (Ma).[1] They had spread to China/Eurasia by 100 Ma and South America by 70 Ma.

Gondwanan Heritage: Plate Tectonics and Marsupials

The earliest known Australian fossil marsupial, *Djarthia murgonensis*, discovered in southeastern Queensland, has been dated to 55 Ma.[2] *Djarthia* belonged to a lineage that was pan-Gondwanan, extending across the great southern hemisphere supercontinent from Australia to South America. It was probably a small, insect-eating mammal that lived in trees. Its marsupial credentials appear impeccable, making *Djarthia* one of the earliest fossils now known for this group. It is an early form of marsupial, outside any extant group found today in Australia.

The ancestors of *Djarthia* and other Australian marsupial lineages have been aged to 65–75 Ma. Fossils of extant Australian carnivorous dasyurid (of the family Dasyuridae) marsupials, such as Tasmanian devils (*Sarcophilus harrisii*), appeared much later, about 30 Ma, and those of living South American lineages some 20 Ma. What we see today in marsupials, then, belies a much more complex evolutionary and biogeographic pattern in the past.

At the time of the emergence of true marsupials, the world's continents were in flux. Gondwana was still rending apart. This had begun as early as 180 Ma, with the initiation of the separation of Madagascar from Africa and the subsequent rift of India from East Antarctica and Southwest Australia by 150 Ma.[3] South America and Africa began separating in the South Atlantic about 138 Ma.

By 100 Ma, when marsupial ancestors had spread from North America to Eurasia on the northern supercontinent Laurasia, South America and Australia remained connected through Antarctica in the southern hemisphere. This prevailed until 49 Ma, when a seaway first appeared below what is today Tasmania.[4] However, it was not until 30 Ma that the Antarctic Circumpolar Current was established through the Tasmanian Gateway. This was a critically important time for environmental change and the evolution of biodiversity on the Australian continent. Marsupials and eucalypts flourished and diversified as more arid conditions prevailed.

It is posited that all Australian marsupials share a common ancestor, one presumed to have migrated from South America to Australia through long-distance dispersal.[5] Alternatively, the antiquity of the earliest Australian marsupial fossils now known suggests that an Australian origin is likely, with one lineage subsequently migrating back to South America.[6] At present, we can't be sure which way it went.

The marsupial story is relevant to that of the eucalypts because fossil eucalypts have been located in Australia and South America too, as well as in New Zealand and India. Intriguingly, similar controversy to that for marsupials prevails for eucalypts over the details of their origins. Were eucalypts born of volcanic fire in ancient South

American or Australasian lowland rainforests, on fertile soils, or did they arise in Australia in ancient, infertile, infrequently disturbed uplands that are still evident today?

The Formation of Australia's Landscape, Climate and Habitats

Australia has an arid core, first established at 30 Ma, which extends to the coast in northwestern Australia and to the Nullarbor Plain in the south. Surprisingly, much of this desert region is well vegetated with woody perennials tapping underground water, and massive eruptions of annuals occur when occasional rains drench the red sands and rocky ranges.

To the north, east, southeast and southwest of this Arid Zone are climatically diverse regions of higher rainfall. Tropical savanna dominates northern Australia (see illus. 25–7, 71) and extends down through Queensland. Subtropical forest and woodland (see illus. 70) extend further south until they are replaced by temperate forest, woodland and heath in Victoria, Tasmania, parts of South Australia and the Mediterranean climate region of Southwest Australia. Snow-capped peaks are limited to the Australian Alps and a few mountains in Tasmania (see illus. 72). Rainforest – tropical in the north and temperate in the southeast – occupies less than 1 per cent of the continent (see illus. 70, 86). None is found today in the Southwest, but fossils tell us that diverse rainforest plants occurred in the region until about 2.6 Ma.

Australia is the most topographically subdued continent. The Great Dividing Range forms a spine down the east coast, with the tallest peak, Tarangal/Mt Kosciusko, a mere 2,228 metres (7,310 ft) above sea level. Short coastal rivers run eastwards. Inland of the Great Dividing Range, country slopes down towards the Lake Eyre Basin, occupying one-sixth of the continent. The Murray-Darling Basin has Australia's largest river drainage, one-seventh of the nation's area. The western two-thirds of the country is a subdued ancient plateau dominated by inactive palaeo-rivers that today form chains of salt lakes. There are short coastal rivers in the Southwest and tropical Top End. Uplands are scattered. Summer monsoonal rainfall occurs in the north, winter rainfall in the south and aseasonal rainfall across the vast Arid Zone.

A striking feature of Australia is that most of the country's landscapes are depositional, meaning that they weather very slowly in global terms.[7] Subdued uplands of laterite, sandstone and granite, such as Uluru, represent the more resistant residues of ancient mountain systems thrust up by major geological events as the continent has moved slowly across the Earth and tectonic plates have collided. Erosional surfaces with nutrient-rich soils are confined to rivers, lakes and coastal regions, and to steep upland slopes. Such slopes erode more rapidly in regions of higher rainfall.

Active mountain-building over the past 40 million years has been confined largely to the path of a volcanic hotspot that has moved down the Great Dividing Range from Queensland to the western plains of Victoria as Australia has drifted north at 6–8 centimetres (about 2–3 in.) per year.[8] Thus the mountains from the Hillsborough volcano south to Buckland in central Queensland range in age from 33 to 25 Ma; those from the Glass House Mountains in Queensland south to Mt Canobolas in New South Wales from 27 to 13–11 Ma; and Mt Macedon in Victoria is 6 Ma. Even younger volcanic mountains are found in North Queensland's Atherton Tableland (3 Ma to 10,000 years ago), Undara National Park (2.7 Ma to 10,000 years ago) and the Great Basalt Wall National Park west of Townsville in Queensland (5 Ma to 13,000 years ago). In the volcanic plains northwest of Melbourne, such mountains as Mt Napier and Mt Eccles last erupted 5,000–6,000 years ago. The youngest volcanic feature in Australia is found at Mt Gambier in South Australia, parts of which erupted 4,500 years ago.

Most Australian uplands are much older than this and more stable, weathered by rainfall for tens of millions of years. These venerable hills and isolated mountains have been leached of nutrients, yielding phosphorus-deficient soils that are highly infertile.[9] Across the nation, farmers have to load their wheatbelt soils with superphosphate fertilizers; nitrogenous fertilizers, on the other hand, are scarcely needed. Curiously, these poor soils are demonstrably richest in biodiversity of all but the most mobile organisms. Think of the richness – especially in terms of plants – of Sydney and its hinterland perched atop the Hawkesbury sandstones (see illus. 66) and Perth in the Southwest extending on to ancient granites. Kakadu National Park in the Northern Territory and Gariwerd/Grampians National Park in Victoria offer other examples of plant-rich ancient landscapes.

A final factor that has had a significant impact on the history of Australia's landscapes and biodiversity is found in coastal dynamism and oceanic currents. The Great Barrier Reef running down the east coast is deservedly celebrated as a UNESCO World Heritage Site. Less well known are the remarkably biodiverse inshore kelp reefs of the south coast. Again, there is a striking difference between the east and north coasts and that of the Southwest. East and north are closer to the leading edge of the Australian continental plate's inexorable journey north and east. These are dynamic coastlines.

In the Southwest are coastlines that have been in existence for more than 100 million years, at the tail end of the continental plate, although still tectonically active with many minor earthquakes as the tail flexes up and down. The west coast is globally unique in having the inshore Leeuwin Current, a warm, tropical, infertile, clear-water drift running down from the north. All other continental west coasts have cold, polar, nutrient-rich oceanic currents. The Leeuwin Current originates in the tropical Pacific Ocean, and comes via the Indonesian Throughflow east to west across the north of Australia. It bends southwest then south down the coast of Western Australia before turning east to dissipate along the south coast near the Great Australian Bight, south of the Nullarbor Plain.

Because the Southwest coastline has been relatively stable, with fluctuations associated with sea-level change on gently sloping coastal shelves, the Leeuwin Current is estimated to have persisted for more than 40 million years.[10] This consistent oceanic influence has buffered the climate of the Southwest from the dramatic fluctuations experienced elsewhere on Earth over tens of millions of years.

OCBILs and YODFELs:
The Big Duality in Landscape Evolution

Southwest Australia has globally unusual landscapes characterized by three attributes: old age, climatically buffered disturbance regimes and infertile soils. As we saw in Chapter Five, such landscapes have been called OCBILs (old, climatically buffered, infertile landscapes; illus. 88–91).[11] They include granite outcrops, sandstone and quartzite ranges, lateritic mesas and high sandplains. OCBILs are found elsewhere in Australia, including the Grampians in Victoria, quartzite ranges in western Tasmania, Hawkesbury sandstone plateau in New South Wales, isolated sandstone mesas in Queensland and sandstone uplands of the Northern Territory and Western Australia's Top End.

OCBILs grade into younger, often-disturbed, fertile lowlands in the Southwest and elsewhere. Called YODFELs, these lowland environments offer some of the few fertile enclaves in the Southwest, and have active disturbance regimes typical of alluvial soils along rivers, around lakes, on steep slopes and along coasts. YODFELs are more common in eastern Australia (illus. 92).

OCBILs can be converted to YODFELs by major disturbance events that rejuvenate the fertility of the soil, such as glaciations, volcanic eruptions, inundation by water, dust storms and earthquakes. Consequently, OCBILs are found elsewhere on Earth where such disturbances have been subdued for tens of millions of years, mainly in the southern hemisphere. OCBILs are rare or absent in the northern hemisphere and relatively recently formed mountains in the south because of the impact in particular of Pleistocene glacial cycles.

Glaciers smother landscapes and grind up bedrock, releasing minerals and creating fertile soils. Periglacial landscapes are consequently richly fertile. They favour plants and animals that are capable

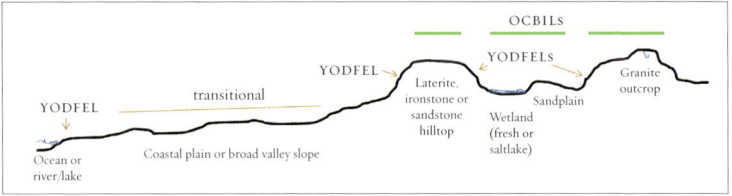

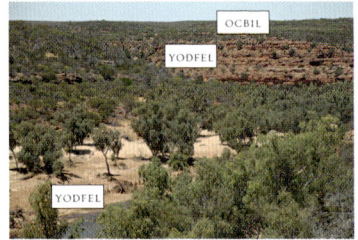

88–91 Photos and a schematic profile illustrating the juxtaposition of old, climatically buffered infertile landscapes (OCBILs) and young, often disturbed fertile landscapes (YODFELs) within Southwest Australia. *Top*: OCBILs in the form of the tops of lateritic mesas and high sandplain, with YODFELs represented by eroding scree slopes or breakaways of the mesas, Moresby Range, north of Geraldton. *Centre*: Schematic profile from a coastal/valley floor wetland dominated by YODFELs to OCBIL uplands with eroding YODFEL slopes. *Bottom left*: OCBIL granite outcrop uplands, running down to lacustrine and coastal dune YODFELs, on the Vancouver Peninsula south of Albany. *Bottom right*: Murchison River alluvial YODFELs often disturbed by flooding, with the OCBIL Kalbarri sandplains atop ancient sandstone cliffs, Kalbarri National Park.

of rapid dispersal and extensive colonization. OCBILs represent the direct opposite. They favour plants and animals that disperse poorly. Essentially, moving even short distances away from home base places OCBIL organisms in direct competition with other species that have become adapted to their site through tens of millions of years of largely uninterrupted evolution. A much safer bet on OCBILs is to limit your dispersal to the immediate vicinity of the family home. Then, when mother dies, if you are a plant, you have a high probability of establishing at the same site. An outcome of such a strategy is natural selection limiting dispersal, with prolonged persistence in small areas, leading to endemic speciation and pronounced genetic divergence across short distances from OCBIL upland to upland.

OCBILs are renowned for their species and genetic richness and high endemism. The Southwest Australian flora, for example, is celebrated for its globally significant richness (8,500 species) and high levels of endemism (49 per cent).[12] Similarly, in the fauna, high richness and endemism are seen in diverse groups of less mobile animals. More broadly, OCBILs have now been discovered in 12 of the world's 35 global biodiversity hotspots (places on Earth that are richest in endemic species under threat). The vast majority of these are in the southern hemisphere, including Australia, Madagascar, South Africa, New Caledonia and parts of Brazil.

Low phosphorous levels on OCBILs come about primarily through leaching by rainfall over tens of millions of years. This has prompted plants and animals to evolve a diverse range of strategies to acquire nutrients.[13] Cluster roots, for example, found in the genera *Banksia* and

92 Widespread species on YODFELs display relatively little genetic divergence among populations, with evidence of long-distance seed dispersal up to 300 kilometres (185 mi.) now available for yellow box (*Eucalyptus melliodora*), seen here in Terrick Terrick National Park and on Mt Hope, adjacent to the Murray River plains of northern Victoria.

93 Bald Island *marlock* (*Eucalyptus conferruminata*), a small tree from granite OCBILs,
exemplifies the large, colourful flowers of many Southwest Australian eucalypts
that attract vertebrates, especially birds, as pollinators. In this species many flowers
are aggregated into a cricket ball-sized cluster, and the fruits are tightly packed in
a dense head on a decurved stalk. Similar aggregated features in the related mallee
bushy *yate* (*E. lehmannii*) led the German botanist Johann Schauer to name a new genus
of eucalypt in 1844, *Symphyomyrtus*, now the largest subgenus of *Eucalyptus*. Various
transitional species, with flowers and fruits ranging from aggregated to free and
solitary, were subsequently discovered, so the key generic characters of *Symphyomyrtus*
that he identified were not sufficient to maintain a distinct genus.

Grevillea (family Proteaceae), are produced each year for several weeks
during the wet season. They exude chemicals that essentially mine
phosphorous that is otherwise unavailable for plant growth. Sand-
binding roots are another probable adaptation to phosphorous
deficiency. An alternative to securing sufficient nutrients is to form

partnerships with underground fungi that live in roots (mycorrhizae). This is the primary eucalypt strategy.[14]

Another nutrient-limited strategy that makes a lot of sense in OCBILs is the production of low-cost floral nectar to attract pollinators. Nectar is basically water containing sugars and a limited number of other chemicals. Mass flowering is a feature of OCBIL floras, ensuring that at least some pollinators will be attracted to guarantee some seed set. Moreover, dilute nectar features in flowers that are pollinated by vertebrates (birds or mammals). The Southwest Australian flora is the richest on Earth in bird- and mammal-pollinated flowers (15 per cent of the flora), even more so (40 per cent) among rare plants that predominate on subdued OCBIL uplands. The eucalypts exemplify this pattern (see illus. 9–12, 74–5, 93–4). Indeed, there are more eucalypts with large, colourful flowers attracting birds and mammals as pollinators in the Southwest than there are anywhere else in Australia.

94 *Yorgum* or red-flowering gum (*Corymbia ficifolia*) is a small tree endemic to OCBILs of deep sand and granite outcrops near the south coast of Southwest Australia. It is pollinated predominantly by birds, such as the *wooreng* (New Holland honeyeater, *Phylidonyris novaehollandiae*), a common, fast-flying, sometimes gregarious, often territorial nectar-feeder ranging across southern Australia and up to the central east coast. *Yorgum* is Southwest Australia's most widely cultivated eucalypt, and is seen in gardens and as street trees from Cape Town to Los Angeles.

95 Salmon gum (*Eucalyptus salmonophloia*) on deep red earth at Geelabbing/
Mt Churchman attains a great size under what is essentially a desert climate regime.

96 Salt salmon gum (*Eucalyptus salicola*) by a salt lake in the Great Western Woodlands, the world's largest intact temperate semi-arid forest, west of Balladonia in Western Australia.

Eucalypts of OCBIL uplands display other unusual attributes: gigantism as very tall trees (illus. 95); large clones more than 20 metres (66 ft) across with underground rootstocks (illus. 87); diverse mechanisms for rapid recovery from events that remove all aboveground vegetation; and rare old natural hybrids (illus. 87) rather than extensive hybrid swarms, to name but a few examples. We are just learning that some eucalypts from isolated rock outcrops have devised ways of persisting in very small populations, overcoming the usual effects of inbreeding (illus. 58). Complex relationships with gall-forming parasitic insects and other parasites, such as mistletoes, are known. Ancient salt-lake systems forming OCBILs along old palaeodrainage lines have specialized, salt-tolerant eucalypts (illus. 96). Not all eucalypts cope well with fire, however.[15] Even tough old mallees with underground lignotubers for resprouting may be killed outright by two fires in quick succession.

Eucalypt Evolution

Traditionally, it has been assumed that eucalypts originated in or adjacent to tropical rainforests on fertile lowlands, born of fire.[16] This inference is drawn from observations that sister genera to the eucalypts are tropical, that fossil eucalypts from South America are from volcanic lands rich in lowland rainforest species, and that eucalypts are able to tolerate fire through various coping strategies inferred as fire adaptations. Essentially, then, it is posited that eucalypts are from young, often disturbed, fertile landscape origins, with diversification driven by increasing aridity and fire frequencies.

An alternative hypothesis is that eucalypts are born from ancient infertile uplands – OCBILs. Eucalypts are essentially of Australian origin, having first evolved as lignotuberous mallees on nutrient-deficient soils on subdued ancient uplands under prolonged influence of oceanic climatic buffering. The capacity to cope with fire may be more of an adaptation of early eucalypts in response to factors that remove above-ground vegetation, such as grazing, flooding, storm damage, fire and frost, rather than an adaptation to fire specifically. Biological mysteries abound in the study of eucalypts. Perhaps fresh eyes from a novel theoretical perspective would help to unravel such mysteries (illus. 97, 98). Indeed, a formative start at investigating the origins of the Sydney Basin eucalypts shows considerable promise in helping us to understand eucalypt evolution in one of the three epicentres of eucalypt diversification.[17]

Overall data point towards an OCBIL origin for eucalypts, rather than one in volcanic lands adjacent to or embedded in lowland tropical rainforest.[18] However, more research is needed if we are to examine this intriguing question fully.

97, 98 Biological mysteries abound in the study of eucalypts. OCBIL theory may provide a useful framework to investigate these wonders. The first rains after a dry summer spell cause soap-like chemicals (saponins) to bubble and cascade down the trunks of yellow tingle (*Eucalyptus guilfoylei*) near Walpole, Western Australia (*left*); and the main tap root of *marri* (*Corymbia calophylla*) penetrates massive laterite near Perth (*right*), unlike the extensive lateral roots of such rock outcrop OCBIL species as *E. caesia* (illus. 58).

Understanding the precise mechanisms of genetic diversification in eucalypts similarly is at an exciting stage as modern genomic studies enable deeper understanding. Speciation occurs frequently when populations are divided up into separate island-like habitats such as OCBILs, but reproductive isolation often appears to involve changes in chromosome structure that promotes divergence.[19]

eight
Cultivating Eucalypts Abroad and Modern Uses

❉

E ucalypts are relatively easy to grow. The seed of most species requires no pretreatment and can simply be placed in a free-draining soil just below the surface and given water. It can be difficult if fungal diseases attack germinants or young seedlings, but, given hygienic growing conditions and plenty of sunlight, most eucalypts will reward the grower (illus. 99).

Today *Eucalyptus* is the most widely grown hardwood on Earth. This came about in stages.[1] It began with the transmission of seed to Kew Gardens near London from Adventure Bay, Bruny Island, Tasmania, collected by Captain Tobias Furneaux on Cook's second expedition in 1773. In 1774 Kew's head gardener, William Aiton, named Furneaux as the supplier of seed of the messmate or stringy-bark tree (*Eucalyptus obliqua*), grown for the first time that year, as reported in the second edition of *Hortus Kewensis* in 1789. The plant was labelled as a greenhouse bush ('G.H.B.'). In May 1788 Captain Arthur Phillip sent seeds of red mahogany (*E. resinifera*) from Sydney to Sir Joseph Banks.

The earliest horticultural record of *Eucalyptus* outside the United Kingdom is from Java in 1790, when the Dutch gathered seed of the Timor white gum or Timor mountain gum (*E. urophylla*) for planting in Bogor and Jakarta. In 1800 *E. globulus* from Tasmania was also planted in Java, probably from the expeditionary seed sources of Jacques-Julien Houton de Labillardière, who was imprisoned there in 1794 with other crew members on Antoine d'Entrecasteaux's return voyage to Europe.

Tipu Sultan (born Sultan Fateh Ali Sahab Tipu) first introduced eucalypts to India when on the throne of Mysore (now Karnataka) in about 1790. He grew them in his palace garden in the granitic Nandi Hills, 65 kilometres (40 mi.) from Bangalore. Reportedly, he introduced some sixteen species as ornamentals. They were given to him by French friends, and the first species was presumably from seed originating from the d'Entrecasteaux expedition, collected by Labillardière and others. Thereafter seed from Sydney collected for Phillip, Banks and the French slowly made their way as far afield as Mysore – if the figure of sixteen species grown for Tipu Sultan is accurate.

In 1745 the Scottish nurserymen James Lee and Lewis Kennedy formed a partnership in Hammersmith, west London. Lee sent out a collector to Sydney in 1790, as a result of which he undoubtedly offered eucalypts to his clients, although that has not been recorded.

The first outdoor planting of a eucalypt in mainland Europe was of *E. robusta* at the royal palace of the king and queen of Naples in Caserta in 1792, by the German horticulturist Johann Andreas Graefer, probably with seed obtained from Banks.[2] Graefer had long experience in England as a nurseryman and was employed at Caserta

99 River red gum (*Eucalyptus camaldulensis*) germinated and grown in Namaacha Province at the Forest Seed Centre, Maputo, Mozambique, 2009.

under Banks's patronage. However, the English garden he established there at the behest of Queen Maria Carolina fell out of favour with the Italian public and the Neapolitan royals, and – with its eucalypts – was abandoned.

In March 1792 Sydney was visited by the Spanish expedition led by the Tuscan explorer Alejandro Malaspina. On board were the French-born botanist Luis Née and the Czech Thaddeus Xaverius Peregrinus Haenke, who collected plants from as far afield as Botany Bay and Parramatta. Specimens ended up in the hands of Née's friend the first director of Madrid's botanic garden, Antonio José Cavanilles, who named three eucalypts. The sowing book at Madrid recorded seed of a eucalypt from Botany Bay received from 'the Lady Ambassador to London', recorded as 'ignota' (unnamed) and sown on 26 April 1797. Later notes indicate that Botany Bay seeds, presumably collected by Banks, were planted on several occasions at Madrid, and the genus *Eucalyptus* was mentioned specifically in the garden's seed list of 1800.[3]

E. robusta was reportedly growing on Mauritius by 1800 and was listed in a British catalogue of Mauritian flora in 1810. Seedlings of eucalypts made their way from Mauritius to Cape Town, South Africa, possibly as early as 1807, and probably in the case of *E. globulus* by 1828.

The French also began growing eucalypts, especially owing to the patronage of Napoleon Bonaparte's wife, Empress Joséphine, who was building a collection of exotic plants at Malmaison around the turn of the nineteenth century. *E. diversifolia*, a mallee of coastal limestones of the southern Nullarbor region, was described in 1814 by the explorer and botanist Aimé Bonpland, the specimens listed as 'cultivated at Malmaison, Jan 1809' and 'cultivated at Jardin Botanique de Toulon, 1813'. The seed came from collections made on the Baudin expedition of 1800–1804.

Italian records indicate a gradual accumulation of eucalypt species, beginning with *E. robusta* (introduced in 1803 in Caserta), *E. capitellata* (1805), *E. aromatica* (syn. *E. piperita* subsp. *piperita*, 1810), *E. resinifera* (1812) and *E. saligna* (1812). These species were probably planted several years before the dates noted.[4]

It is ironic that Australia's most widespread eucalypt, *E. camaldu-lensis* (see illus. 63), was named by the German gardener and bota-nist Frederick Dehnhardt in 1832 after an order of Tuscan monks, the Camaldolese. The eucalypt – which at the time of its scientific descrip-tion was 5.4 metres (nearly 18 ft) high and ten years old – was growing in a hermitage built in the mountains east of Naples in the sixteenth century.[5] The garden of the Camaldolese (Hortus Camaldulensis) was then a Neapolitan garden belonging to Francesco Ricciardi, count of Camaldoli. Dehnhardt, its chief gardener, probably received seed via England from that collected by the botanists Charles Fraser and Allan Cunningham in April 1817 along the Lachlan River near Condobolin in New South Wales.[6] There has been tortuous debate over the taxonomy of this species, but the name persists – which is fortunate, because it is the most commonly referred to of all eucalypts in literature, and is now grown in seventy countries across more than 500,000 hectares (more than 1.2 million ac) of plantation.

Eucalypts were first planted in Crimean Russia (where they failed) in 1816, in Chile in 1823 with *E. globulus*, in Brazil with *E. robusta* and *E. tereticornis* at the Rio de Janeiro botanic garden in 1825, and in Portugal with *E. globulus* at Porto in 1829. In that same year, euca-lypts were planted south of Vila Nova de Gaia in northern Portugal, and these produced what may have been the first eucalypt timber in Europe. There are suggestions of much older trees in Portugal, per-haps derived from secret early explorations of Australia, but defini-tive evidence remains elusive on this matter. In 1852 the Marquis de Massarelos planted *E. globulus*, *E. obliqua*, *E. viminalis* and *E. pulchella* on his estate, Quinta da Formiga, south of Porto. Some of these early trees survive today.

Plantations

The utility of eucalypts beyond ornamental horticulture soon became apparent. It was fortuitous that the earliest eucalypts described by Western scientists, such as *E. globulus* and *E. obliqua*, grew as massive straight trees in cool temperate climates. Their immediate use for firewood and as hardwood timber appeared self-evident. Moreover, they were fast-growing and few animals ate their leaves. The first plantations of *E. globulus* in Mysore displayed spectacular growth rates, reaching 6–7.5 metres (20–25 ft) in eighteen months, exceeding 'that of any tree indigenous or introduced', and 'four times as fast as the teak-tree'.[7] They could also tolerate water stress, affording shelter and shade in regions where trees were scarce or absent (illus. 100). In addition, Aboriginal people had long established that the volatile oils of eucalypt leaves had medicinal properties. Honey was another abundant by-product.

Taking advantage of such uses through plantations in new countries spread slowly. There were many scientific questions to be answered about the trees' preferred growing conditions; temperature, altitude, soil moisture and soil type all needed consideration. Moreover, the taxonomic exploration of the eucalypts was piecemeal and lagged for half a century following the first descriptions. The greatest early contribution – from Robert Brown, the botanist on Matthew Flinders's circumnavigation of Australia on the *Investigator* in 1801–5 (see Chapter Five) – was not published. Brown was disappointed at the lack of interest in the first volume of his flora of Australia, self-published in 1810 under the Latin title *Prodromus florae Novae Hollandiae et Insulae Van Diemen* (Prodromus of the Flora of New Holland and Van Diemen's Land). He had collected more than 64 species of eucalypt on the voyage, from coastal Southwest Australia, South Australia, Tasmania, New South Wales, Queensland and the Northern Territory.[8] He had developed critical insights not only at species level, but into major groups that are today recognized as subgenera and genera.

Joseph Hooker, who became director of Kew Gardens in 1865, visited Tasmania for nearly six months in 1840–41 while surgeon and naturalist on the Ross expedition to Antarctica. He described five new species of eucalypt, including *E. gunnii*, the cider gum, so called because Palawa people and colonists obtained a fermented cider from its sap.[9] Being interested in species that were frost-tolerant and might survive English winters outdoors, Hooker went north from Hobart to the central highlands, where conditions were coldest on the island. He had heard that Aboriginal people and later stockmen drank the fermented sap of *E. gunnii* as a mild intoxicant. For example, the conciliator George Augustus Robinson, traversing the midlands in company with Tasmanian Aboriginal people, wrote on 28 November 1831:

> what interested me the most were the numerous cider trees which skirted this extensive plain and which were the first I had seen. Most of those trees had been tapped by the natives. This they had effected by perforating a hole in the tree a short distance above the ground by means of sharp stones and then making a hole at the bottom of the tree into which the liquid is conveyed and from which they extract it, sometimes if the hole is small by sucking it through a reed or twisted bark. In some of those holes I observed upwards of a quart of this juice and which my people greedily partook of. It is exceedingly sweet and well flavoured and in this

100 River red gum (*Eucalyptus camaldulensis*) alive and dead from drought. The live tree affords shade for farmers and visitors in an otherwise treeless terrain at Traveller's Rest beside the Brandewyn River, atop Pakhuis Pass in the Cederberg, South Africa, 2010.

respect resembles the flavour of cider. Some that had been dried by the sun had an apple taste. The tree in appearance resembles the blue gum [E. globulus], but the leaf when closely inspected has a different form and the bark is more of a dark blue colour. This tree grows to a large size; the wood appears brittle. The natives are very fond of the juice and I am told it frequently makes them drunk.[10]

Hooker was keen to see and collect the species in its native habitat to ascertain its suitability for English climes. He was aware of a damaging frost that occurred in the highlands in 1837 and, he wrote,

> had killed all the other and larger species of *Eucalyptus*, especially on flat grounds, similar to, but on a lower elevation than those on which we were. For many miles on our roads to the lakes, our course had been amongst the dead trunks of tall Gum trees . . . on the banks of Lake Echo, a beautiful sheet of water, a similar death-like scene met the eye. Gum trees, Leptosperma, Hakeas and Banksias, all seemed as if they had been suddenly struck with some mortal disease in the full vigour of their growth, and in the prime of life . . . the effects of the great frost of 1837 . . . proves at once how much hardier this species (*E. gunnii*) is, which, though growing at a much higher elevation, and on a marshy plain, where the effects of frost are always most severe, was almost uninjured.[11]

Subsequent research has indeed established that *E. gunnii* is among the most frost-tolerant of all eucalypts. It was introduced to the United Kingdom as far north as Scotland, at Whittingehame Castle, for example, in a glen of the Lammermoor Hills in East Lothian, overlooking the North Sea, in 1846. Seed presented to the railway entrepreneur James Maitland Balfour by James Gascoyne-Cecil, 2nd Marquess of Salisbury, were sown in 1845. The resulting tree, named *E. whittingehameii* (now a synonym of *E. gunnii* subsp. *gunnii*), was 'cut to the ground by frost in 1860–61, but sent forth shoots from its stem'.

Another Scottish estate, Kinloch Hourn to the west, overlooking the Sound of Sleat and the Isle of Skye, was owned by the much-travelled banker and botanist Robert Birkbeck, a relative of Whittinge-hame's Balfour. About twenty eucalypts were planted there, mostly Tasmanian, including *E. coccifera*, *E. gunnii* (including *E. whittingehamei*), *E. urnigera*, *E. vernicosa*, *E. coriacea* and *E. cordata*. *Eucalyptus gunnii* was planted on the hillsides in considerable numbers, affirming Hooker's observations of the species' excellent tolerance of frost.

Back in Australia, Prosper Vincent Izart Ramel – a member of the French Societé Zoologique d'Acclimatation (Zoological Society for Acclimatization) – met Ferdinand von Mueller, Victoria's govern-ment botanist, in Melbourne in 1854. Particularly taken by the appear-ance and vigour of *E. globulus*, Ramel accepted von Mueller's urging to make the blue gum and similar Australian hardwoods famous throughout Europe.

By the 1860s, at Ramel's insistence, eucalypt plantations abounded in Provence, along the Italian border and in Corsica. He had also introduced eucalypts to Algeria and Tunisia. His success in the west-ern Mediterranean relied on von Mueller's willingness to send huge quantities of seed from Australia. Von Mueller spent more than forty years advocating for eucalypts through a formidable correspondence and number of publications. He discovered, named, classified and assessed the economic potential of some 120 species, including the most famous of all horticultural exports, *yorgum* (red-flowering gum, *Corymbia ficifolia*; see illus. 3, 74, 94). One species collected in Western Australia's Little Sandy Desert in 1876 by the explorer Ernest Giles was named *E. rameliana* (see illus. 9) to honour the efforts of his French apostle. The species was lost to science and presumed extinct after its initial collection until 1991, so obscure and difficult of access is its sand-dune habitat to Western scientists and collectors.[12]

Von Mueller's energetic advocacy for eucalypts is exemplified by his activities in a single year, 1861, when he arranged to send 22 cases of plants overseas, including 31,000 live plants, 36,400 cuttings and 51,290 seed packets. He wrote exuberantly in 1879 that eucalypts were globally important

> whether viewed in their own unparalleled celerity of growth among hardwood-trees, or estimated in their manifold applicabilities to the purposes of industrial life, or contemplated as representing among them in all-overtowering height the loftiest trees in her Majesty's dominions . . . for all times to come . . . in sylvan culture.'[3]

He argued that eucalypts provide wood and health, and even 'beneficent climate changes'. These claims gained credence through the planting of either *E. camaldulensis* or *E. globulus* at the malaria-riddled monastery of Tre Fontane, south of Rome, said to be the place where St Paul was beheaded. It took a decade (1869–79), and there was at first some failure in establishing the eucalypts by the Trappist monks, but malarial infections eventually reduced as the trees grew and drained the swampy lands. This was something that Caesar and earlier Roman emperors had not managed to achieve, so – despite some scepticism – the good name of eucalypts as health providers was established. Malaria did recur at the site in the 1880s. Was it drainage or eucalypts suppressing the disease? Von Mueller let others make the claim of a direct causative role of eucalypts in curing malaria. He did hold, however, that the volatiles from live trees curtailed lung disease, as Aboriginal ceremonies using smoking leaves had shown to believers. He saw the climate improve when barren semi-arid lands were afforested with eucalypts.

Von Mueller had plans to write a flora of Australia, listing all known species with descriptions and distributional data. This plan was ultimately thwarted by Joseph Hooker, who argued that the task of necessity required access to the major international collections in European herbaria, especially that of Kew. The colonial flora was taken up by the prolific English botanist George Bentham and published in seven volumes under the title *Flora Australiensis* over the period 1863–78.

Bentham – who never set foot in Australia, basing his work entirely on herbarium specimens with the ultimate agreement and cooperation of von Mueller as a primary field-based collector and colonial botanist – recognized approximately 150 eucalypt taxa, describing 89 as new, of which 47 remain recognized today. Of necessity he had a broad species concept, accepting levels of variation within species that today most botanists would regard as too broad in many cases. Over the course of his productive career, von Mueller described 138 *Eucalyptus* taxa (species and varieties), of which 96 remain recognized today at one level or another. He also held a broad species concept, despite being able to observe eucalypts as live trees and mallees in the wild. His primary eucalypt publication appeared in 1879 as the exquisitely illustrated folio book *Eucalyptographia: A Descriptive Atlas of the Eucalypts of Australia.*

This first major phase of taxonomic research following the initial description of eucalypts by Western scientists stimulated ongoing cultivation outside Australia, led by European botanists, collectors and wealthy landowners driven by a fervent desire to improve on nature and generate new economies across the world. This worldwide trend persisted for six decades from the middle of the century. Apart from Algeria and Tunisia mentioned above, eucalypt plantations for fuel appeared in Pakistan (1843), Uruguay, California and Hawaii (1853), Argentina (1857), Peru (1860) and Ecuador (1865), and in South Africa (where conditions were suitable) late in the century.

Increasingly, during the Victorian era, plantations became large in scale and state-supported. By the end of the nineteenth century in Madagascar, for example, missionaries, settlers and foresters had begun planting eucalypts, and the French authorities there imposed a system of enforced national service on local people to ensure that vast plantations were established. The injustice of this coercion was still keenly felt by the Malagasy people into the twenty-first century.

101 A eucalypt plantation with older plants right to the summit
of a granite inselberg near Nandihizana, Madagascar, 2007.

Moreover, eucalypts have now become pernicious weeds in this island
of mystery, invading even the shallow soils of granite inselbergs and
threatening multitudes of native plants (illus. 101).

There is no doubt that eucalypts have furnished timber and shelter
for rural people in such countries as South Africa, where trees in semi-
arid environments are rare indeed. However, there are limits to the
tolerance of aridity by eucalypts (see illus. 100). Except for places with
underground water supplies, these species are incapable of surviving
in the wild in deserts.

Californian Eucalypts

Some parts of the United States were more suitable than others for
the introduction of these new species. In Texas, for example, eucalypts grew well enough at first but soon succumbed to the lethal
effects of frost, drought and alkaline soils. Eucalypts grew well in
California, however, and were promoted initially by rich landowners; the trees looked attractive and, where native species struggled,
rapidly provided shade, shelter and wood.

Interest in Californian plantations coincided with the gold rush, which began in 1849, and the University of California, Berkeley became a centre for their promotion. Gradually, government agencies took the message on board. Blue gums in particular were grown, and between 1910 and 1913 some 8 million *E. globulus* were planted in the Berkeley Hills to form a continuous strip 22 kilometres (nearly 14 mi.) long from Berkeley to Oakland (illus. 102). The value for timber of this massive enterprise proved less than expected, however. Wood from young trees split and bent rapidly as it dried. Eventually it was realized that weedy, immature gums in foreign lands were no match for old-growth Australian forest eucalypts in terms of wood quality. However, this did not dispel a boom in the early twentieth century, with more than one hundred companies buying land, managing nurseries and planting trees. The face of Californian landscapes in the central valley and southern regions was changing from grassland, chapparal and pineland to eucalypt monoculture. The U.S. Forest Service became involved in promoting eucalypts and undertaking scientific research on their establishment and uses.

The negative aspects of eucalypt plantations were downplayed. Soil moisture was depleted, as it sometimes is in Australia. The leaf litter was what is termed allelopathic, so nothing native grew under these eucalypt plantations – as is sometimes the case in Australia – and the plantations were vulnerable to fire. The wood of young trees was not durable, especially the sapwood, so rapid growth wasn't an advantage, since mature trees were best for timber. Wood for fuel was being phased out in favour of oil, electricity or gas; land was more valuable for crops than for fuelwood; and hardwood was more costly to process than softwood conifers. Almost invariably, the wrong species were planted for Californian conditions. In the 1970s foresters attempting to establish eucalypts in northern California tested 34 eucalypts that were potentially cold-tolerant and grew as trees, not mallees. Their summary stated: 'Species from Western Australia and of the subgenus *Monocalyptus* [that is, *E.* subgenus *Eucalyptus*] all failed on the site. *E. camaldulensis, E. dalrympleana, E. glaucescens* [Tingiringi gum],

E. grandis, *E. nitens*, *E. ovata* and *E. viminalis* were the species with best sur-vival and growth.'[14] Today it is recognized that species of *E.* subgenus *Eucalyptus* typically grow on nutrient-deficient upland soils, whereas those of *E.* subgenus *Symphyomyrtus* (all the rest in the quotation above) favour more fertile soils on younger landscapes in Australia.[15]

Californians fortunately lost interest in eucalypts (apart from their use as ornamentals) before the extensive industrialization of the plantation industry, with its attendant social and environmental difficulties. Some five hundred of the nine hundred eucalypt taxa have been grown in the state, largely from the efforts of a relatively small number of enthusiasts. Some Californians I have met have expressed surprise at the claim that eucalypts are native to Australia.

102 *Eucalyptus globulus* with a glaucous (bluish) wild seedling in the Berkeley Hills, California, 2009.

103 A *Eucalyptus globulus* plantation in Portugal, 2011.

Because these trees are so common locally, they regard them as native to California. This was not the case in India, Thailand, Brazil and Portugal (illus. 103).

Socio-Environmental Issues

The British East India Company actively acquired land and promoted plantations from the 1860s onwards. *E. globulus* did well in southwest and south-central India, but not in the humid lowlands. Around 105 species received trials as forestry became professionalized following the formation of an Imperial Forest Department in 1864, and half a dozen of these showed considerable promise. The Indian Forest Act 1878 broadened central control over 23 per cent of the nation, including native forests and wastelands occupied by poor subsistence farmers, with the agenda of forcing farmers to become low-paid forest workers instead. The introduction of a money economy shattered village life and many communities. Of the 170 eucalypts that were ultimately tested in India, *E. tereticornis* did best. Following independence from the British in 1947, forestry in India enjoyed enthusiastic government support and foreign aid. Some 20 per cent of the land area (64 million hectares/158 million ac) is now forest, down from 40 per cent half a century before.

In the 1980s a National Forest Policy proposed to bring an additional 5 million hectares (12 million ac) into plantations. This prompted criticism, especially of eucalypt plantations, for socio-environmental reasons: maximizing firewood was to the detriment of other wood uses by local villagers; biodiversity would be diminished, creating 'green deserts'; village solidarity would be challenged; it would replace croplands; and water supplies and erosion control by native forests were threatened. In 1983 people in Karnataka pulled up eucalypt seedlings in nurseries, replacing some with tamarind seeds. The single-minded focus of foresters and industrial-scale plantation development faced serious opposition. Robin W. Doughty wrote in 2010, 'Over the past twenty years, institutional support for eucalypts has frayed in India and in other nations whose residents had greeted them with initial enthusiasm.'[16]

A similar scenario has played out for eucalypt plantations in Thailand. Poor forest-dwellers, reliant on native vegetation for a range of products and services, are being displaced by industrial-scale eucalypt plantations, primarily for paper pulp. So, too, in Brazil and Chile. Initial promise of, and expectations for, eucalypt plantations have not been met. Too much of a divide exists between the expert foresters of state agencies and the people directly affected by the establishments of these plantations. The marked increase in scale of industrial plantations for paper pulp and wood has led to growing concern about the merits of eucalypt forestry.

To some extent, there is no looking back. In many countries, eucalypt plantations are here to stay. Well placed, containing the right species and with local cultural support, they may enjoy continued

104 River red gum (*Eucalyptus camaldulensis*) resprouting after the winter, featured in the Australia Garden prepared by the Royal Botanic Gardens, Kew, in the forecourt of the British Museum, London, 2011.

105 Young buds of *Eucalyptus caesia* subsp. *magna* grown in a pot at the Director's Garden, Royal Botanic Gardens, Kew, in 2012, and subsequently flowered under glass in December. Attempts to overwinter plants outside by wrapping them in dry moss failed.

popular interest. In horticulture, too, attempts to grow eucalypts will continue to fascinate enthusiasts keen to extend the boundaries of these species in cultivation and abroad (illus. 104, 105). We are currently in the midst of a third wave of taxonomic research, informed by DNA sequencing studies and now whole genome research. There is much more to learn about these Universal Australians, and global collaboration is the hallmark of our times in such studies. Eucalypts have become the hardwood citizens of the world.

Modern Uses of Eucalypts

Smoking ceremonies using smouldering fresh eucalypt leaves (illus. 106) evince the ancient spiritual connection between humans and eucalypts dating back 55,000–70,000 years. Before writing this chapter, I participated in a smoking ceremony at an important gathering place of Wilman Noongar families east of Perth. We were celebrating the recent publication of *Wilman Dryandra Healthy Country Plan 2023*, an evocative commitment to the future of the equally new Wilman (Dryandra) People Corporation. This commitment to country still dominated by eucalypts (Dryandra National Park) drew upon the smoke of the Western Australian flooded gum (*E. rudis*) leaves to drive away any *warra wiern* (bad spirits) and welcome the presence of *quabba wiern* (good spirits) on the banks of the ancient Hotham River.

The present book is a celebration of such ancient connections and the modern practical uses of a remarkable heritage of trees gifted by Australia to the world. We have seen the extraordinary depth and breadth of Indigenous people's connections to eucalypts across the island continent. From practical items, such as men's *gidj* (spears) and *kylie* (boomerangs) and women's *wanna* (digging sticks) to profoundly important ceremonial items, eucalypts have helped humans to enjoy rich and challenging lives for countless generations.

Medicinal uses have featured prominently in the lives of many. The antibiotic oils in eucalypt leaves and branchlets (illus. 107) have cured lung infections and helped to heal damaged skin, as Doc Reynolds relays in the Foreword to this book. Eucalypt oil is still working its medicinal magic, now produced in abundance in places far from Australia, especially China.

The house in which these words are being assembled is full of eucalypt products, again drawing on a heritage dating back to the late Pleistocene and pioneered by Aboriginal people. The Merningar/Minang *kornts* (homes) that once occupied the beachside on which I write may have been replaced by Western technology, but *jarrah* (*E. marginata*) and *karri* (*E. diversicolor*) beams still provide the structural

106 A smoking ceremony by Noongar people using eucalypt foliage (in part),
held at a gathering aiming to rid the place of *warra wiern* (bad spirits) and
encourage the presence of *quabba wiern* (good spirits).

foundations and bedeck the finishing touches, framing doors and windows and forming handrails and floors. The musical instruments we possess range from clapping sticks gifted by Noongar friends to modern guitars. The wood of eucalypts contributes to their construction and ongoing use. We have fine furniture fashioned from recycled *jarrah* that once formed the beams of the old Albany jetty. I write on a *jarrah* desk, beautifully constructed and warmly red-brown timbered.

Even the paper in the books and printers that remain so important to modern life comes from the fibres of woodchips from Tasmanian blue gum (*E. globulus*) grown in plantations a short distance away, on the south coast of Western Australia. Although controversial still, with questionable ecological impact, plantation forestry of eucalypts has gifted much to our modern lives.

Wild eucalypts arguably make an even greater contribution to human and other life. In common with all trees, eucalypts generate oxygen as they photosynthesize. They provide food for myriad insects, mammals and birds. Their bark with its soapy exudates cleans descending rainfall and liberates water-repellent soil to recharge underground aquifers (see illus. 97–8). Their roots also bind the soil, preventing erosion.

Wild eucalypts will burn, or freeze, or fall in floods and storms, but have a remarkable capacity to regenerate from such disturbances. Used wisely, fires can be beneficial to the land, an ally and friend

107 Eucalypts have medicinal oils found in the leaves and the pith of branchlets in some species. In this case, transmitted sunlight highlights leaf veins and pith glands present in *marri* (*Corymbia calophylla*, right) but not in *yorgum* (*C. ficifolia*, left).

warmly embraced by Indigenous people for countless generations. Ignored or misinterpreted by today's city-based cultures, however, fire unleashes its fury in eucalypt forests and woodlands at increasingly massive scale, exacerbated by climate change.

The world today cannot survive without eucalypts. We have attested to their spread as fast-growing sources of fuel and timber across the Earth. Their utility is unquestionable, for beekeepers or the pharmacy, the timber yard or the trade in fine furniture. Wherever wood, oil and nectar products have been needed from fast-growing herbivore-resistant trees, eucalypts have been planted.

There is much to celebrate embodied in these diverse organisms. Even more so, there is much to revere, as Australia's Indigenous people have done for so long. The future of eucalypts remains in resolving the tension between their sacred and profane uses. Aboriginal people resolved this tension long ago. Cultures based on modern Western science and economics have yet to mature enough for most people to see the wisdom in this path. Consequently, eucalypts today face challenging conservation problems, as we will now see.

nine

Eucalypt Conservation

❁

G iven the importance of eucalypts in forestry and their wide-spread use in many countries of the world, it may come as a surprise that there are many threatened species and communities of eucalypts in their native Australia. Why is this so?

Threatened Species

Of the 822 species recognized in the genera *Eucalyptus*, *Corymbia*, *Blakella* and *Angophora*, 193 (23 per cent) meet international criteria as threatened and 36 are considered to be too poorly known to assess their conservation status.[1] Some 27 per cent of the 719 species in the genus *Eucalyptus* itself are threatened. This proportion of threatened species approximates to the more than 20 per cent of threatened species estimated for all 400,000 or so plants on Earth – an alarming statistic in itself.[2]

Threatened eucalypts are not atypical, too, in that the conversion of habitat to crops and pasture is by far the major cause of decline. The greatest concentration of threatened eucalypts is therefore found in the wheat-growing area of Southwest Australia, with a secondary node in the Wimmera region of northwestern Victoria and neighbouring South Australia (illus. 108). Eucalypts thus support the recognition of the Southwest Australian Floristic Region as Australia's primary global biodiversity hotspot, the richest in endemic species under threat and first recognized as such in 2000.[3] The Temperate Forests

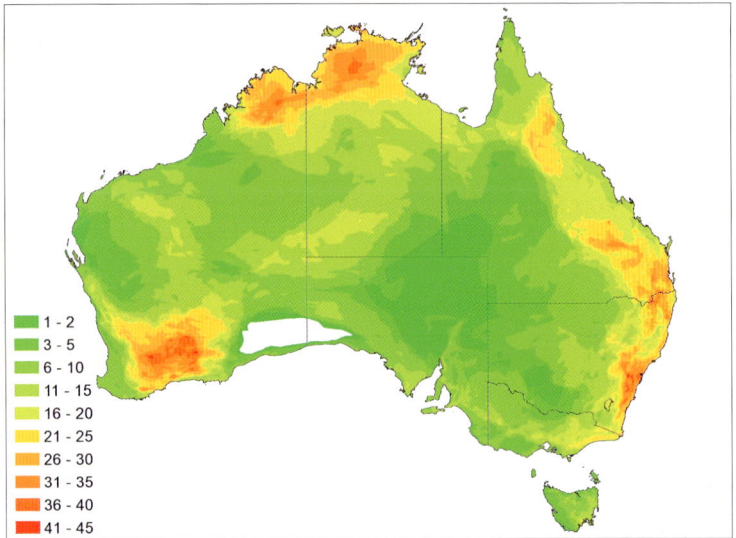

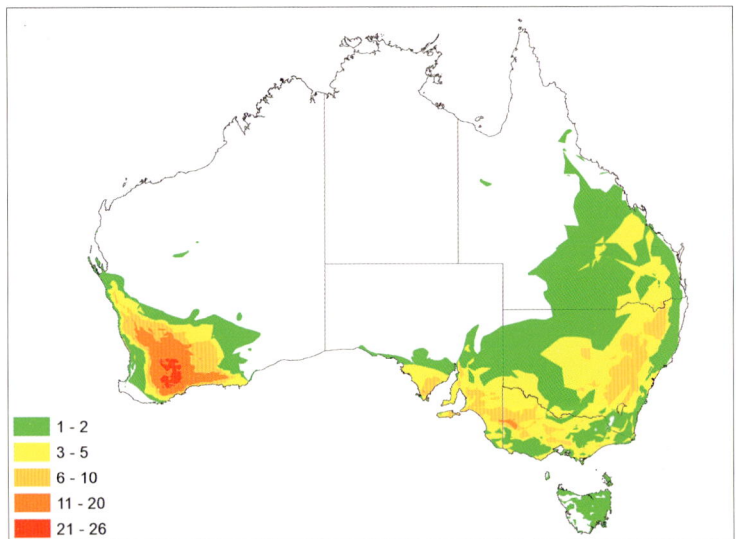

108, 109 Maps showing (*top*) the distribution of eucalypt species richness (719 in *Eucalyptus*, 57 in *Corymbia*, 36 in *Blakella* and 10 in *Angophora*) and (*bottom*) the density of 193 threatened *Eucalyptus* species classified as Critical, Endangered or Vulnerable under international criteria, out of a total of 822 eucalypts. Note the rich concentration in the wheatbelt of Southwest Australia.

of East Australia were added as a second national biodiversity hotspot in 2011.[4]

This pattern for threatened species is at variance with the places where eucalypts are concentrated in Australia. There are almost no threatened species in the tropical and subtropical regions of the northern and northeastern continent, despite these regions being moderately rich in species. This is where the 93 species of *Corymbia* and *Blakella* are concentrated, two genera that contain no threatened species. The ten *Angophora* species are also not threatened. The absence of threatened species in the north points to the tenacity of eucalypts – provided they are not bulldozed out of existence. Relatively little of the tropical regions has been cleared, although much has been extensively grazed and disturbed by fire regimes. Mining has had a relatively small effect.

By contrast, the agricultural development of Southwest and Southeast Australia has involved the complete removal of native vegetation. Eucalypts persist in agricultural landscapes in small reserves and inhospitable terrain, such as rugged rock outcrops. It is estimated that 134 of the threatened *Eucalyptus* species had more than 30 per cent of their geographical range destroyed by agricultural clearing over three generations after the European colonization of Australia in 1788. Some have lost up to 94 per cent (this figure for *E. silvestris* in western Victoria) of their distributional range. Although many of these 134 species remain numerically abundant, they are on the pathway to extinction unless they are managed differently in the future.

Mining is a threat to many of the remaining eucalypts, all of which have relatively few populations or individuals and are declining. These species include *E. cerasiformis*, *E. desmondensis*, *E. georgei*, *E. johnsoniana*, *E. jutsonii*, *E. platydisca*, *E. purpurata*, *E. recurva*, *E. rhomboidea*, *E. rugulata*, *E. steedmanii*, *E. stoatei* and *E. synandra* from Western Australia; *E. infera* and *E. nudicaulis* from Queensland; and *E. magnificata* from New South Wales. The clearing of land for urbanization is a significant threat for some species (for example, *E. petrensis* in greater Perth).

This account of threatened species is based on a recent assessment of conservation status that is considerably at variance with the present listing of eucalypts of concern by state and territory governments and the Commonwealth.[5] Numerically rare species have tradition- ally been the focus of attention (see illus. 61), and there has been little focus on rates of decline, irrespective of numerical abundance. It remains to be seen whether Australian jurisdictions take up the recent call to consider rates of decline as equally important to small population size in conservation assessments.

Examples of threatened species illustrated herein, all from South- west Australia, include the endangered *E. rhodantha* (see illus. 61), *E. longicornis, E. stoatei* (see illus. 77) and *E.* × *erectifolia* (see illus. 87), and the following vulnerable species: *E. loxophleba, E. salmonophloia* (see illus. 81, 95), *E. macrocarpa* (see illus. 35, 61), *E. wandoo* (see illus. 56–7) and *E. pyriformis* (see illus. 61). Of these species, at present only *E. rhodantha* is listed by the state government of Western Australia as threatened.

Climate change has been invoked as a major threat to eucalypts. Alarming predictions have been made regarding their future:

> We predict that within the next 60 years the vast majority of species distributions (91%) across Australia will shrink in size (on average by 51%) and shift south on the basis of projected suitable climatic space. Geographic areas currently with high phylogenetic diversity and endemism are predicted to change substantially in future climate scenarios. Approximately 90% of the current areas with concentrations of palaeo-endemism (that is, places with old evolutionary diversity) are predicted to disappear or shift their location.[6]

However, while elegant statistical approaches have been used, the model used to formulate these predictions has yet to be tested rigor- ously in eucalypts. The approach is based on bio-climate envelope models and assumes that migration is the only way for eucalypts to escape the effects of climate change. Because few eucalypts have good seed dispersal capabilities, dire consequences are predicted. This goes against empirical observations of the importance of persistence in wet local refugia as an alternative strategy.[7] In Southwest Australia, where significant extinction of south coast local endemic eucalypts is predicted, not a single species has exhibited significant climatic drought stress, let alone become extinct over the past half-century of climate change. An earlier, more conservative study of climate change and eucalypts concluded that bio-climatic models cannot be used to reliably predict 'the future distributions, the survival or extinction of specific eucalypt species'.[8] Turning the discipline of restoration ecology towards 'renovation ecology', based on foundational responses to climate change, seems premature until rigorous experimentally based understandings of eucalypt ecophysiology are well established.[9] Consequently, climate-change risks were not used in the recent assessment of threatened eucalypts.[10] However, as discussed below, very recent decline of common eucalypts on marginal thin soils associated with granite outcrops has occurred in response to prolonged spring/summer drought on the south coast of Southwest Australia. Perhaps drought stress from climate change is now approaching a critical threshold in this region.

Fire regimes are often mentioned as a significant threat for endangered species. Traditionally, eucalypts have been regarded as 'adapted' to fire because most respond to a fire event by resprouting. But some eucalypts in fact succumb to fire more readily than some rainforest species.[11] Even resprouting mallees can be killed by two fires separated by a short interval of one to three years.[12] On the other hand, tropical savanna eucalypts are tolerant of fire and unresponsive to increase in the frequency and intensity of conflagration.[13]

The members of one group of eucalypts, known as obligate seeders, are killed by canopy fire as adults and recover only through seed germination and growth. Consequently, they must flower and fruit before the next fire if the population is to be replaced. Most such species are found in semi-arid Southwest Australia, where they are known by such Noongar names as *mallet*, *maarlak* or *marlock* and *moort*. Much of this cereal-growing landscape is relatively fire-free, owing to extensive agriculture.[14] Obligate seeders are less at risk there now,

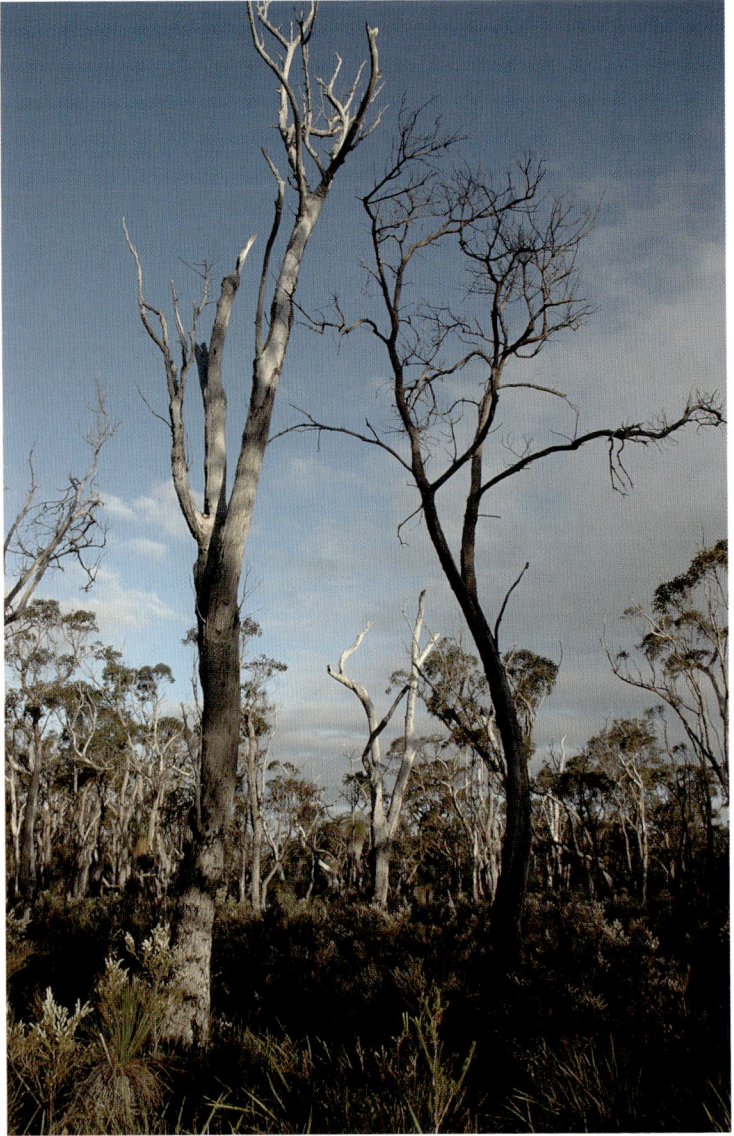

110   Healthy forests are valued and cared for by most Australians, but degraded trees threatened by introduced diseases and other causes are rife. The conservation and sustainable use of eucalypts are in our hands. Here dieback disease (caused by the fungus *Phytophthora cinnamomi*) is shown killing *jarrah* (*Eucalyptus marginata*) at Mt Lindesay National Park in Southwest Australia.

but remain vulnerable in large conservation reserves that are subjected to increasing levels of prescribed burning by land managers.[15]

Canopy dieback (illus. 110) and decline are a feature of many trees on farms, usually involving herbivorous insect outbreaks, drought and possibly pathogens. Such phenomena appear to be a legacy of extensive clearing for agriculture, and are secondary to clearing as a major threat to eucalypts.

Such agricultural development has fragmented the natural range of many common eucalypts on relatively fertile land, reducing populations to remnants in reserves or on inhospitable rock outcrops. Inbreeding effects in small vegetation remnants have been established for a few species of eucalypt. However, species that are naturally fragmented – among them those occurring on insular habitats, such as granite or sandstone inselbergs – appear to have evolved reproductive attributes that enable them to cope with small population size.[16] The effects of fragmentation require much more research and, again, were not considered in the recent review of threatened eucalypts.

Few examples of plantation eucalypts hybridizing with local endemic eucalypts have been established, and rates are relatively low (less than 2 per cent for most species). This indicates that hybridization is not at present a significant threat to most endangered species.

Threatened species of eucalypt have thus declined primarily because of agricultural development and rising saline watertables, with secondary causes including mining, urban expansion and intensifying fire regimes. Climate change may also become so severe in the future that the extinction of endemic eucalypts becomes probable.

Caring for threatened eucalypts starts with seed collections. There has been a concerted effort to do this, under the global auspices of Kew's Millennium Seed Bank Project.[17] Thereafter, conservation actions for threatened species are usually summarized and implemented in recovery plans. For example, the Rose Mallee Interim Recovery Plan 2006–2011 summarized existing knowledge and outlined future actions, many of which were implemented.[18] Farmland containing the largest remnant population, with an estimated 470+

plants, was purchased as a nature reserve by the Western Australian government in October 1995. The 4-kilometre (2½ mi.) boundary was then fenced to prevent grazing by rabbits, and a perimeter firebreak was installed. Fire was excluded from the reserve. In 1994 seedlings of rose mallee (*E. rhodantha*; see illus. 61) were planted in degraded parts of the site, seed of other genera (*Banksia*, *Calothamnus* and *Hakea*) likely to attract bird pollinators were included in supplemental plantings, and invasive weeds were removed.

Outside the fenced boundary, 1.7 kilometres (about 1 mi.) of native plant buffer was planted with local species of *Acacia*, *Allocasuarina*, *Banksia*, *Calothamnus* and *Hakea*. Research into the pollination biology, population genetics and mating system of *E. rhodantha* was undertaken by postgraduate students, and seed was collected and placed in secure long-term seed banks in Perth and at Kew's Millennium Seed Bank in the United Kingdom.

Seedlings provided by Western Australian government agencies were distributed by local shires for farmland plantings elsewhere. The shire of Three Springs adopted *E. rhodantha* as its floral emblem as a result of a public awareness programme arising from the previous recovery plan. Landowners modified their farming practices, such as reducing the use of herbicides and fertilizers, in the vicinity of *E. rhodantha*, and ongoing monitoring and maintenance programmes were undertaken by the conservation department.[19]

This may be an exceptionally well-implemented example, but it highlights similar recovery actions that have been undertaken to varying degrees across Australia. Such actions are aimed at preventing the continued decline and eventual extinction of threatened eucalypts.

Rediscovering Australia's Only 'Extinct' Eucalypt

Given the extent of agricultural land-clearing in southern Australia, and the known presence of at least 74 narrow-range endemics across the region, it remains intriguing that only a single presumed extinct eucalypt existed in 1991. The mystery species was *E. rameliana* (see illus. 9), named by Ferdinand von Mueller after his apostle Prosper Ramel, and intriguingly known only from the type collected by the explorer Ernest Giles from an obscure location in the Gibson Desert 'near/beyond Alfred and Marie Range, WA, June 1876'.[20] This is more than 1,000 kilometres (620 mi.) northeast of the cleared wheatbelt of Southwest Australia.

To be classified as 'presumed extinct' in 1991, a species had to have been neither seen nor collected over the past fifty years. Despite several futile searches in the 1980s of the Alfred and Marie Range, and one widely publicized false alarm, nothing matching Giles's single collection had materialized. The explorer's lyrical two-volume account of his desert explorations gave no clue as to the precise whereabouts of *E. rameliana*.[21] It later transpired that he was preoccupied with poisoned camels at the critical time, and about to embark on a push across unknown red sand dunes of the Little Sandy Desert, 500 kilometres (about 300 mi.) beyond (west of) the Alfred and Marie Range.

The species was recognized in the field in July 1991 by a seed collector, Nick Foote, while driving across trackless terrain in search of a well on the old Number 1 Rabbit Proof Fence.[22] Giles's mallee, once presumed extinct, had indeed been found by non-Aboriginal people again.

Of course, the species was known to the local Martu people, and called *yalpiri*. Finding its precise location led to further surveys in this least-known of Australia's deserts. It turned out to have been photographed and illustrated from a short distance away in a book of 1978 by journalists following Giles's path.[23] Other people travelling the Rabbit Proof Fence had also noted the plant without identifying the species accurately until they saw photos of *E. rameliana* in newspaper articles about Foote's adventures. A young postdoctoral student, Jane Sampson, came out on one of the subsequent Little Sandy Desert surveys and published on *yalpiri*'s mating system and population genetics using the latest forms of analysis.[24] Within a few years, Australia's only 'extinct' eucalypt had been brought into the international scientific purview of the late twentieth century. It is testament to the durability and tenacity of eucalypts that the continent now has not a single species that is presumed extinct.

Threatened Ecological Communities

Threatened ecological communities (TECs) are a special category now afforded legal protection in Australia by the Commonwealth and some state legislation. They are defined by the Commonwealth as follows:

> An ecological community becomes threatened when it is at risk of extinction. That is, the natural composition and function of the ecological community have been significantly depleted across its full range. This can occur for a number of reasons including clearing of native vegetation, inappropriate fire regimes, non-native or invasive species, climate change, water diversion, pollution and urban development. Because of these threats, many ecological communities in Australia have undergone, and continue to be affected by[,] a rapid and significant reduction in geographic distribution and/or ecological function.[25]

Eucalypt woodlands constitute some of the most extensive and yet highly cleared and degraded plant communities in Australia. Twenty-four eucalypt communities are listed as threatened under the Environment Protection and Biodiversity Conservation Act 1999.[26] These are found mostly in Southeast Australia, with just one covering the species-rich wheatbelt of the Southwest.

The Commonwealth listing of the above eucalypt TECs activates the writing of a Recovery Plan, which sets out how the TEC is defined, where it occurs, what threats it faces and what management actions are needed to reduce those threats. Essentially similar processes to those outlined above for *E. rhodantha* are undertaken. However, there are only a few of these eucalypt TECs for which a Recovery Plan has been written.

Devising ways of implementing recovery plans for TECs is also at an early stage. The landscape ecologist Nathan McQuoid and others have made a significant start in Southwest Australia.[27] The fundamental importance of differentiating landscapes occupied by TECs is emphasized by McQuoid. Uplands are host to eucalypts with very different biological attributes from those on fertile lowland sites.[28] Consequently, management prescriptions differ. It may be some time before the benefits of this approach become evident and influence mainstream land management. But what is it, specifically, about upland OCBILs that managers must take note of?

Special Vulnerability and Enhanced Resilience on Uplands Versus Lowlands

Eucalypts rely primarily on gravity for seed dispersal, assisted by wind, especially for those with winged seeds, as in some *Corymbia* (see illus. 16–19). Consequently, a common observation is that sites where topsoil is bulldozed away rarely have abundant recruitment from seeds of eucalypts. Species with lignotubers are able to sustain growth by resprouting from below ground, but obligate seeding eucalypts are especially vulnerable to dramatic soil disturbance and removal. Forestry managers of such species long ago learned the importance of not removing topsoil when logging, and of leaving mature seed trees at regular intervals in a logging coup to rain down their seed and produce the next generation of trees.

It may be that the best thing to do with eucalypts on uplands is to leave them alone, as is recommended for giant eucalypts. It is remarkable that not a single eucalypt species has become extinct over the last fifty years, despite lists of threatened species and protective legislation being established across Australia. Perhaps this is a reflection of the fact that the vast majority of rare and localized species grow on uplands, and display the accentuated resilience to more general fragmentation of landscapes alluded to above. Minimizing disturbance on uplands seems essential.

111 For the first time in a century, the common species *marri* (*Corymbia calophylla*) has succumbed on shallow granitic soils in country of highest rainfall to prolonged spring/summer drought caused by climate change. Inlet Road rock, Denmark townsite, south coast of Southwest Australia, 2024.

OCBIL eucalypts that have persisted in small, isolated populations for millions of years may well be masters of resilience and persistence. Notions of moving them around landscapes in the face of gloomy predictions from climate-change modelling may be misguided, and connecting their small, naturally fragmented populations with revegetated corridors may likewise be naive. Yet it is clear that even common species, for instance *marri* (*Corymbia calophylla*), on such tough sites as the shallow soil associated with granite outcrops are beginning to succumb to prolonged drought brought about by climate change (illus. 111). Nevertheless, recognizing the importance of leaving OCBILs be, and focusing human disturbance and the manipulation of eucalypts on species of lowland YODFELs, is a challenging new perspective for managers and conservation biologists brought up on conventional theory.

Each of the above prescriptions must be carefully and rigorously tested in studies of eucalypts. The urgency to better understand eucalypts in landscapes, with fresh eyes, has never been greater.

Commercial Forestry

Forestry has been practised since the earliest days of colonization in Australia. In the late nineteenth century, after a century of commercial exploitation, the discipline became professionalized as Forest Departments were established across southern Australia. Thereafter the trajectory of forestry followed a similar path to that outlined in the previous chapter for India, attaining its heyday in reach and power across vast landscapes in the 1970s.

Then, as in other countries, people began questioning the logging of native forests, especially when such species as *marri* (see illus. 16–20) were cut down primarily for woodchip. The ultimate separation of the views of professional foresters from those of the broader community led to less logging of native hardwoods, and substantial increases in the area of forest national parks. While this approach was strongly supported, a regrettable outcome has been the diminishing of a significant workforce in forests able to be deployed to fight fires and implement prescribed fire to protect these assets. As a consequence, increasingly frequent large-scale prescribed burns have been introduced in forest national parks, threatening biodiversity that requires long-unburnt vegetation.[29]

The history of commercial logging in Australia has been elucidated by many. The loss of government has occurred over such policy questions as the logging of old-growth forest in Western Australia. Interesting insights have emerged through oral history documenting the rich diversity of issues and attitudes towards forest management.[30] Increasingly, there have been calls for the more sympathetic management of native forests, highlighting values other than those of commercial forestry. Respecting Aboriginal cultures and learning Aboriginal ways of living sustainably with forests is an emerging call. Perhaps new ways will be found to absorb such ideas in the face of a rapidly changing world, and Australia's rich diversity of eucalypts will continue to thrive.

112 Impressionist painting from the Eucalyptus School in Southern California:
Guy Rose, *Laguna Eucalyptus*, c. 1917, oil on canvas.

Epilogue

I have tried to give a sense of eucalypts as trees with a rich diversity of life-ways and stories. In particular, perhaps for the first time in any detail, a summary is offered of the cross-cultural understanding of eucalypts from diverse Aboriginal communities and an emerging Western scientific perspective.

Many other writers have assembled accounts of the increasing insights gained by Western science into the biology and use of eucalypts. Few, however, have ensured that Aboriginal voices have been heard prominently. Even fewer explain what they mean by the terms 'species', 'subspecies' and 'hybrid', yet most celebrate the fact that eucalypts are exceptionally numerous on all such counts.

This book indicates that there is an ever more pressing need to apply Western science if we are to understand eucalypts on their own terms, as Aboriginal people have done for at least 65,000 years. Southern hemisphere landscapes and disturbance regimes are exceptionally diverse, with the greatest proportion of subdued infertile uplands on Earth. Eucalypts are born of such landscapes and the diversity of disturbance events, evolving in myriad ways we have scarcely begun to understand or synthesize as a coherent world view matching those devised by Aboriginal people.

The fact that we haven't yet learned to shed the preconceptions on eucalypt species and hybrids that arose as far back as the European Enlightenment is a comment on the conservatism of much of Western science. Eucalypts are not oaks or pine trees growing in postglacial

Eurasia or North America. They may have some common biological attributes, but many have followed surprising and unique evolutionary pathways. Recognizing this is the first step towards mainstreaming new ways of caring, conserving and living sustainably with eucalypts.

We are lucky indeed that no eucalypt has yet become extinct. Eucalypts offer a natural heritage of immense value and importance in the sciences and arts (illus. 112), deserving every care and attention we can collectively muster to live onwards with these exceptional woody plants. If this book, in some way, sets aflame a desire to learn more and better understand and care for eucalypts, to challenge and rigorously test some of the ideas raised herein, to work collaboratively with Aboriginal people in cross-cultural learning and co-management of such a rich natural heritage, it will have achieved its aim.

Timeline

59–44 million years ago	Series Eucalypteae genera first evolve – *Hindeucalyptus*, mesicalypts (*Allosyncarpia*, *Stockwellia*/*Eucalyptopsis*), newcalypt (*Arillastrum*), eucalypts (*Eucalyptus*, *Angophora*, *Corymbia*, *Blakella*)
52–47 million years ago	Eucalypt genera evolve as a group of disturbance opportunists within and outside rainforests, not solely in response to fire
Since *c.* 2 million years ago	The vast majority of eucalypt species evolved in one of the most rapid and rich diversifications seen on Earth, particularly in *Eucalyptus* subg. *Symphyomyrtus* and *E.* subg. *Eucalyptus*
75,000–55,000 years ago	Estimated colonization of Australia by Aboriginal people, and therefore incorporation of circa nine hundred eucalypts into their Dreaming, practical and medicinal uses and languages
1642	Crew of the *Zeehan* on Abel Tasman's voyage report seeing two large smooth-barked trees freshly notched with stone axes for climbing – probably today's *Eucalyptus globulus* – in Storm Bay, Tasmania
1668	Rumphius is advised of a tree he later names *Arbor versicolor* in 1743 (multi-coloured tree with bark the 'colour of a rainbow'), the *Ay Alla* or tree of God, today's *Eucalyptus deglupta* from Seram island

1697	William Dampier reports bloodwoods (*Corymbia greeniana*) for the first time in the northwest coastal desert of Western Australia. Trees dripping gum (*marri*/*Corymbia calophylla*) are also seen by Dutch explorers at the Swan River, much further south
1770	James Cook's *Endeavour* expedition lands at Kurnell, Botany Bay, where botanists Joseph Banks and Daniel Solander make the first collections of *Angophora costata* and *Corymbia gummifera*
1771	Seeds of *Corymbia gummifera* collected by Banks and Solander are germinated in England, and those raised by nurseryman James Lee first flower before 1778
1788	Captain Arthur Phillip sends seeds of red mahogany, red messmate (*E. resinifera*) from Sydney to Sir Joseph Banks in England. Seeds of other common Sydney species including *Bourrounj*, the Sydney peppermint (*E. piperita*), are soon available in England
1788	*Eucalyptus* L'Hér. is named as a genus by French botanist Charles L'Héritier de Brutelle with a single species (*E. obliqua*) from Tasmania in *Sertum Anglicum* (An English Wreath)
1790	*Eucalyptus urophylla* is grown at Bogor and Jarkarta by the Dutch, and up to sixteen species are grown independently in India's Mysore (now Karnataka), the first plantations outside of England for the genus
1792	While anchored in Recherche Bay to the southwest of Bruny Island, Tasmania, the French collect some 5,000 plant specimens, including the famous tree that naturalist Jacques-Julien Houton de Labillardière subsequently described in 1800 as Tasmanian blue gum (*Eucalyptus globulus*)
1792	The first outdoor planting of a eucalypt in mainland Europe, *E. robusta,* at the royal palace of the king and queen of Naples in Caserta, Italy

1797	The genus *Angophora* Cav. is formally named by Spanish botanist Antonio José Cavanilles
1800, 1803	*Eucalyptus globulus* is grown in Java, and *E. robusta* in Mauritius and Italy, for the first time
1801–5	Botanist-surgeon Robert Brown, aboard the *Investigator* expedition, identifies 64 Australian eucalypts, including nine new south coast eucalypts from Western Australia
1802	The type species of *E.* subg. *Eudesmia, E.* × *tetragona*, is collected at Lucky Bay (WA) by Brown, and named as *Eudesmia tetragona* in 1814 before being transferred to *Eucalyptus* by Ferdinand von Mueller in 1864
1805–9	George Caley, the assiduous Sydney-based collector, focuses on eucalypts of the region and their Aboriginal names and uses. Caley is credited with the earliest recognition of natural hybrids among eucalypts
1820	The type species of *E.* subg. *Blakella, E. clavigera*, is collected at Careening Bay (WA) by Allan Cunningham and named by Johann Schauer in 1843
1823–9	South America sees eucalypt plantations when *Eucalyptus globulus* is grown in Chile and *E. robusta* and *E. tereticornis* at the Rio de Janeiro Botanic Garden, Brazil. *Eucalyptus globulus* is grown in Cape Town, South Africa, for the first time in 1828 and at Porto, Portugal, in 1829
1832	Australia's most widespread eucalypt, *E. camaldulensis*, is named by the German gardener and botanist Frederick Dehnhardt after an order of Tuscan monks, the Camaldolese
1840	*Eucalyptus lehmannii*, the type species of the largest subgenus in *Eucalyptus* (*Symphyomyrtus*), is collected at Cape Riche (WA) by Ludwig Preiss, and named by Johann Schauer as *Symphyomyrtus lehmannii* in 1844 before being transferred to *Eucalyptus* by George Bentham in 1867

1840–41	Kew's Joseph Hooker visits Tasmania and names five new eucalypt species, including cider gum *Eucalyptus gunnii*
1843–60s	Eucalypt plantations for fuel appear in Pakistan (1843), Uruguay, California and Hawaii (1853), Argentina (1857), Peru (1860) and Ecuador (1865). These plantations also abound in Provence, along the Italian border, in Corsica, Algeria and Tunisia
1867	Colonial flora writer George Bentham of Kew publishes the first overview of Australian eucalypts in *Flora Australiensis*, vol. III (1863–78), without visiting the continent or seeing a single eucalypt in the wild
1876	Ferdinand von Mueller names *Eucalyptus rameliana,* collected by desert explorer Ernest Giles from beyond the Alfred and Marie Range in the Gibson Desert of Western Australia. This species was presumed extinct until 1991
1879–84	Ferdinand von Mueller's exquisitely illustrated folio book *Eucalyptographia: A Descriptive Atlas of the Eucalypts of Australia and the Adjoining Islands* is published in ten issues
1903–33	Joseph Maiden, director of the Royal Botanic Gardens, Sydney, publishes *A Critical Revision of the Genus Eucalyptus* (8 vols): a monumental contribution in which he examined and illustrated in detail every species then known
1910–13	374 eucalypts species are recorded in California as planted (with 202 species still present as living trees in 2008)
1929	The sole representative of *E.* subg. *Acerosae,* *E. curtisii* is collected near Plunkett, Queensland, by D. Curtis and named by W. Blakely and C. White in 1931
1934	Joseph Maiden's successor, gardener and botanist William Blakely, publishes a 'Key' to the eucalypts,

a synthesis of Maiden's and his own work. This
book cements Sydney as the epicentre of eucalypt
taxonomic research for another thirty years

1957
The importance of Tasmanian eucalypts in
exploring evolutionary theory is highlighted by
H. N. Barber and W. D. Jackson, a tradition that
has carried on to the present

1969
Denis J. Carr and S. G. Maisey Carr based at the
Australian National University make incisive
anatomical observations from the 1950s that
clarify major groups as well as smaller aggregations
of species among the eucalypts

1971
The Sydney eucalypt taxonomic mantle passes
to Lawrence A. S. Johnson, in collaboration with
Lindsay Pryor from the Australian National
University; they develop a revolutionary and
insightful but informal classification of the
eucalypts, which still prevails largely today

1973
George Chippendale publishes *Eucalypts of the
Western Australian Goldfields (and the Adjacent Wheatbelt)*,
a first in colour-illustrated regional field guides

1976
Lindsay Pryor publishes *The Biology of Eucalypts*,
a small book summarizing a career bringing
biological studies of eucalypts into the modern
era

1982
Stephen D. Hopper, Norman A. Campbell
(CSIRO) and Gavin F. Moran (CSIRO) pioneer
the investigation of rare and threatened
Eucalyptus species, and of threatened endemic
trees worldwide, in a study of morphometrics,
pollination, reproductive biology and population
genetics of the Western Australia granite rock
endemic *E. caesia*

1988
CSIRO botanists A. R. Griffin, I. P. Burgess
and L. Wolf report on patterns of natural and
manipulated hybridization in eucalypts inferred
primarily from herbarium records

1991	A decade of careful field, herbarium and literature research applying Darwinian biological species concepts leads to modern monographic recognition of 28 species in the *E.* series *Levispermae* containing *E. wandoo* and allies
1992	Dean Nicolle establishes the Currency Creek Arboretum in South Australia, today the world's largest scientific collection of living eucalypts
1995	Kenneth D. Hill and Lawrence A. S. Johnson of the Royal Botanic Gardens, Sydney, establish the genus *Corymbia*
1996	Ross G. Florence's book *Ecology and Silviculture of Eucalypt Forests* delivers a classic manual for foresters and ecologists
2000	Ian Brooker's most important taxonomic contribution formalizes and extends Pryor and Johnson's (1971) classification above the species level, and questions the merit of recognizing three genera (*Eucalyptus, Angophora, Corymbia*) rather than a broad *Eucalyptus* s.l. with twelve subgenera
2000	The multi-authored book *Temperate Eucalypt Woodlands in Australia*, ed. Richard J. Hobbs and Colin J. Yates, captures information on threatened woodlands where massive clearing for agricultural development has resulted in biodiversity loss and widespread land degradation
2001	The Australian Labor Party's Western Australian Government under Gallop is elected on a policy platform, including cessation of logging of old growth *karri/Eucalyptus diversifolia* and tingle trees/ *E. jacksonii, E. brevistylis, E. guilfoylei*
2006	Dean Nicolle publishes a classification and census of regenerative strategies in the eucalypts (*Angophora, Corymbia* and *Eucalyptus*), with special reference to the obligate seeders, offering essential insights to those interested in restoring eucalypts to landscapes

2009	Eucalypts are first posited as evolving out of OCBILs (old, climatically buffered infertile landscapes) rather than from rainforest environments
2010	*Eucalypts: A Celebration*, a beautifully illustrated and comprehensive overview of eucalypt diversity, is published by curator of the Australian National Botanic Gardens John Wrigley and Canberra-based photographer Murray Fagg
2013	*D'harawal Dreaming Stories* by traditional D'harawal custodian Frances Bodkin and supporting artist Lorraine Robertson captures the richness of continuous oral history traditions concerning eucalypts among Sydney people
2014	A comprehensive review of the biogeography of eucalypts based on national herbarium specimen data is published by Carlos E. González-Orozco et al.
2014	Alexander A. Myburg et al. first document the genome of *Eucalyptus grandis*
2015	A pioneering phylogenomic study of eucalypt diversification and hybridization by Susan Rutherford et al. establishes that recent speciation could be investigated rigorously with next-generation DNA sequencing approaches
2017	Nicole Bezemer tests for the James Effect, an OCBIL theory hypothesis, establishing that small ancient populations may persist through purging lethal genes to overcome deleterious inbreeding in wild seedlings of *Eucalyptus caesia*
2018	Lynda D. Prior, Ben J. French and David M.J.S. Bowman publish on the effect of experimental fire on seedlings of Australian and Gondwanan tree species from a Tasmanian montane vegetation mosaic, demonstrating that some eucalypts are more susceptible to fire than are some rainforest trees

2019	Exceptional insights on eucalypt taxonomy, evolution and diversification appear using DNA sequence data and dated fossils in the most comprehensively sampled study to date (Andrew H. Thornhill et al.)
2020	Arguably the most significant rethink about the conservation status of eucalypts, R.J. Fensham et al. propose that population decline as well as rarity needs consideration
2021	Tim P. Robins et al. explore, in the context of OCBIL theory, differing patterns of hybridization in two *Eucalyptus* subgenera, finding that taxon age and landscape position materially correlate with clonality and the complexity of hybrid populations
2024	The latest DNA sequences and anatomical studies by Michael Crisp et al. clarify that *Blakella* merits recognition as a fourth genus of eucalypt
2025	Dean Nicolle et al. argue for sinking *Angophora*, *Blakella* and *Corymbia* into *Eucalyptus*. Their reasons are yet to be tested in the context of the International Code on Botanical Nomenclature

References

Introduction

1 J. E. Hickey, P. Kostoglou and G. J. Sargison, 'Tasmania's Tallest Trees', *Tasforests*, XII (2000), pp. 105–21; Brett M. Mifsud, 'Victoria's Tallest Trees', *Australian Forestry*, LXVI/3 (September 2003), pp. 197–205; Richard Preston, *The Wild Trees: What If the Last Wilderness Is Above Our Heads?* (London, 2007); J. L. Williams, D. Lindenmayer and B. Mifsud, 'The Largest Trees in Australia', *Austral Ecology*, XLVIII/4 (2023), pp. 653–71.

2 John Wrigley and Murray Fagg, *Eucalypts: A Celebration* (Crows Nest, NSW, 2010); Michael D. Crisp et al., 'Perianth Evolution and Implications for Generic Delimitation in the Eucalypts (Myrtaceae), Including the Description of the New Genus, *Blakella*', *Journal of Systematics and Evolution*, LXII/5 (September 2024), pp. 942–62. To comply with the publisher's aim to use a single-word title, I adopt 'eucalypts' in this book to cover the four technical genera of *Eucalyptus*, *Corymbia*, *Blakella* and *Angophora*. This enables inclusion of traditional broad interpretations of *Eucalyptus* prior to 1995, while providing the latest insights into the four main groups today recognized by DNA studies among the true eucalypts. For alternative views to Crisp et al., 'Perianth Evolution and Implications', see M.I.H. Brooker, 'A New Classification of the Genus *Eucalyptus* L'Hér. (Myrtaceae)', *Australian Systematic Botany*, XIII/1 (2000), pp. 79–148, and Dean Nicolle et al., 'The Genus Problem – *Eucalyptus* as a Model System for Minimising Taxonomic Disruption', *Taxon* (August 2025), doi.org/10.1002/tax.13240. Controversies over precisely what is meant by the generic name *Eucalyptus* is a matter for continuing research using the best available scientific evidence and solid theory within the context of the international rules for botanical nomenclature.

3 Lindsay D. Pryor and Lawrie A. S. Johnson, '*Eucalyptus*, the Universal Australian', in *Ecological Biogeography of Australia*, ed. A. Keast (The Hague, 1981), pp. 501–36.

4 Wrigley and Fagg, *Eucalypts*; Ashley Hay, *Gum: The Story of Eucalypts and Their Champions* (Sydney, 2002).

5 Doug Benson, 'Vegetation Patterns across the Sydney Basin during the Last Glacial Maximum Based on Plant Biogeography, Ecology, Geomorphology and Climate', *Proceedings of the Linnean Society of New South Wales*, CXLVI (2024), pp. 1–47.

6 Carlos E. González-Orozco et al., 'Biogeographical Regions and Phytogeography of the Eucalypts', *Diversity and Distributions*, XX/1 (January 2014), pp. 46–58.

1 Eucalypt Dreaming on Mainland Australia

1 N. B. Tindale, *Aboriginal Tribes of Australia: Their Terrain, Environmental Controls, Distribution, Limits and Proper Names* (Berkeley, CA, 1974); D. R. Horton, 'The AIATSIS Map of Aboriginal Australia', 1996, www.aiatsis.gov.au; G. E. Ford, 'Darkiñung Recognition: An Analysis of the Historiography for the Aborigines from the Hawkesbury-Hunter Ranges to the Northwest of Sydney', MA thesis, University of Sydney, 2010; Ian Keen, *Aboriginal Economy and Society: Australia at the Threshold of Colonisation* (Oxford, 2004).

2 Peter Veth, 'Breaking through the Radiocarbon Barrier: Madjedbebe and the New Chronology for Aboriginal Occupation of Australia', *Australian Archaeology*, LXXXII/3 (2017), pp. 165–7.

3 Kathryn Coe, Nancy E. Aiken and Craig T. Palmer, 'Once Upon a Time: Ancestors and the Evolutionary Significance of Stories', *Anthropological Forum*, XVI/1 (2006), pp. 21–40.

4 W.E.H. Stanner, 'The Dreaming', in *Traditional Aboriginal Society*, ed. W. H. Edwards (South Melbourne, 1987), pp. 225–36; Cliff Goddard and Anna Wierzbicka, 'What Does *Jukurrpa* ("Dreamtime", "the Dreaming") Mean? A Semantic and Conceptual Journey of Discovery', *Australian Aboriginal Studies*, MMXV/1 (2015), pp. 43–65.

5 Yami Lester, northwestern South Australian Yakuntjara man, quoted in *Survival in Our Own Land: 'Aboriginal' Experiences in 'South Australia' since 1836 Told by Nungas and Others*, ed. C. Mattingley and K. Hampton, 2nd edn (Sydney, 1992), pp. 72–3.

6 Frances Bodkin and Lorraine Robertson, *D'harawal Dreaming Stories* (Sussex Inlet, NSW, 2013), pp. 4–42; some words and meanings in this account are also sourced from Les Bursill et al., *DHARAWAL: The Story of the Dharawal Speaking People of Southern Sydney* (Sydney, 2007).

7 Ronald M. Berndt, 'Looking Ahead Through the Past: 1982 Wentworth Lecture', in *The Wentworth Lectures: Honouring Fifty Years of Australian Indigenous Studies*, ed. R. Tonkinson (Canberra, 2015), pp. 25–58.

8 M.I.H. Brooker and D. A. Kleinig, *Field Guide to Eucalypts*, vol. 1: *South-Eastern Australia*, 2nd edn (Hawthorn, VIC, 1999).

9 Ibid.

10 Alex Roberts and Kath Schilling, *Aboriginal Women's Fishing in New South Wales: A Thematic History* (Sydney, 2010).

11 Joan Webb, *George Caley: 19th Century Naturalist* (Chipping Norton, NSW, 1995).

12 Ibid., 'Appendix D: Caley's Eucalypts', pp. 175–6.
13 I am applying here the boundaries of the Darkinyung resolved by
    G. E. Ford, 'Darkiñung Recognition'.
14 Dianne Johnson, *Sacred Waters: The Story of the Blue Mountains Gully Traditional
    Owners* (Broadway, NSW, 2007), pp. 25, 57.
15 An example of this series is Ngarul J. Nambatu et al., *Marri Ngarr and
    Magati Ke Plants and Animals* (Darwin, NT, 2009), p. 39.
16 Bonnie Deegan et al., *Jaru Plants and Animals: Aboriginal Flora and Fauna
    Knowledge from the South-East Kimberley and Western Top End, North Australia*
    (Halls Creek, WA, 2010), p. 45.
17 Carlos Parra-O et al., 'Phylogeny, Major Clades and Infrageneric
    Classification of *Corymbia* (Myrtaceae), Based on Nuclear Ribosomal DNA
    and Morphology', *Australian Systematic Botany*, XXII/5 (2009), pp. 384–99;
    Tanja M. Schuster et al., 'Chloroplast Variation Is Incongruent with
    Classification of the Australian Bloodwood Eucalypts (Genus *Corymbia*,
    Family Myrtaceae)', *PLoS ONE*, XIII/4 (2018), n.p.
18 Thomas L. Semple et al., 'Systematic Review of the Australian "Bush
    Coconut" Genus *Cystococcus* (Hemiptera: Eriococcidae) Uncovers a New
    Species from Queensland', *Invertebrate Systematics*, XXIX/3 (June 2015),
    pp. 287–312.
19 M.I.H. Brooker and D. A. Kleinig, *Field Guide to Eucalypts*, vol. III: *Northern
    Australia* (Melbourne, 1993).
20 Biddy Yingguny Lindsay et al., *Malakmalak and Matngala Plants and Animals:
    Aboriginal Flora and Fauna Knowledge from the Daly River Area, Northern Australia*
    (Darwin, NT, 2001).
21 Ibid., p. 36.
22 Jack Karadada et al., *Uunguu Plants and Animals: Aboriginal Biological Knowledge
    from the Wunambal Gaambera Country in the North-West Kimberley, Australia*
    (Kalumburu, WA, 2011), p. 33.
23 A. W. Howitt, *The Native Tribes of South-East Australia* (London, 1904), p. 433.
24 Martin Thomas, *The Many Worlds of R. H. Mathews: In Search of an Australian
    Anthropologist* (Sydney, 2011), p. 273.
25 Philip A. Clarke, 'The Aboriginal Australian Cosmic Landscape Part 1:
    The Ethnobotany of the Skyworld', *Journal of Astronomical History and
    Heritage*, XVII/3 (2014), p. 316.
26 K. L. Parker, 1896, cited ibid., p. 320.
27 Ron Murray, with permission from his father, Besley Murray, senior
    Elder, Wamba Wamba, in Arts Victoria, *Nyernila Listen Continuously:
    Aboriginal Creation Stories of Victoria* (Southbank, VIC, 2014), pp. 80–81.
28 Alan N. Williams et al., 'Holocene Demographic Changes and the
    Emergence of Complex Societies in Prehistoric Australia', *PLoS ONE*, X/6
    (2015), n.p.
29 Matthew J. Colloff, *Flooded Forest and Desert Creek: Ecology and History of the
    River Red Gum* (Collingwood, VIC, 2014), p. 198.
30 Arts Victoria, *Nyernila Listen Continuously*, pp. 52–3.
31 R. H. Mathews in Thomas, *The Many Worlds*, p. 278.

32 Ibid., p. 335.
33 J. L. Silcock et al., 'Unusual, Human-Mediated Prevalence of Epiphytes in Semi-Arid New South Wales, Australia', *Australian Journal of Botany*, LXXII/2 (2024), n.p.
34 Michelle McKemey and Harry White, *Bush Tucker, Boomerangs and Bandages: Traditional Aboriginal Plant Use in the Border Rivers and Gwydir Catchments* (Inverell, NSW, 2011).
35 Tommy Kngwarraye Thompson, Kaytetye Elder, in Colloff, *Flooded Forest*, p. 198.
36 David Brooks for Mparntwe people, *The Arrernte Landscape: A Guide to the Dreaming Tracks and Sites of Alice Springs* (Alice Springs, NT, 1991).
37 Peter Latz, *Bushfires and Bushtucker: Aboriginal Plant Use in Central Australia* (Alice Springs, NT, 1995).
38 Ibid., p. 189.
39 Ibid.
40 Ibid., p. 191.
41 Augustus Oldfield, *On the Aborigines of Australia, with an Introduction by M. Helen Henderson* (Victoria Park, WA, 2005), p. 39.
42 Ibid., p. 38.
43 Lorraine Injie, 'The Jibalarda', in *Kurlkayima Ngatha: Remember Me*, exh. cat. (Perth, WA, 2015), p. 119.
44 Libby Connors, *Warrior: A Legendary Leader's Dramatic Life and Violent Death on the Colonial Frontier* (Sydney, 2015).
45 Charles Archer, cited ibid., p. 9.
46 Scott Cane, *Pila Nguru: The Spinifex People* (Fremantle, WA, 2002); James C. Noble and Richard G. Kimber, 'On the Ethno-Ecology of Mallee Root-Water', *Aboriginal History*, XXI (1997), pp. 170–202.
47 Cane, *Pila Nguru*, p. 91.
48 Merningar Bardok Noongar Dion Cummings, personal communication, November 2024.
49 Margot Neale, ed., *Songlines: Tracking the Seven Sisters* (Canberra, 2017).
50 Ibid., pp. 108–9.

2 Noongar Sacred Cosmology and Eucalypts in Southwest Australia

1 This chapter was co-written by Merningar Bardok Elder Dr Lynette Knapp, Merningar Bardok Noongar Dion Cummings, Professor Stephen D. Hopper, Dr Alison Lullfitz, Dr Susie Cramp, Ursula Rodrigues and Anna Ischenko, a cross-cultural research team undertaking the Walking Together project (2020–24) at the University of Western Australia, Albany Campus, in collaboration with South Coast Natural Resource Management, supported by Lotterywest, Janet Holmes-à-Court and a UWA Research Priorities Fund grant. Oral history interviews were undertaken under the University of Western Australia's (UWA) Human Ethics Approvals RA/4/1/6836 and RA/2023/ ET000001. This approval

broadly follows the AITSIS Code of Ethics for Aboriginal and Torres Strait Islander Research 2022 (www.aiatsis.gov.au). The approval embraces written prior informed consent for videotaping, transcription and publication, and protects intellectual property of Indigenous participants, giving them final approval and veto for access to and publication of materials concerning their recorded knowledge, including this chapter, which may be cited as Lynette Knapp et al., 'Noongar Sacred Cosmology and Eucalypts in Southwest Australia', in Stephen D. Hopper, *Eucalyptus* (London, 2025), pp. 50–79.

2 Ngilgian, cited by Daisy Bates, *Aboriginal Perth: Bibbulmun Biographies and Legends*, ed. P. J. Bridge (Victoria Park, WA, 1992), p. 110. Translations of Noongar words come from various sources, published and oral, especially Carl G. von Brandenstein, *Nyungar Anew*, Pacific Linguistics Series C99 (Canberra, 1988); Noel Nannup, Whadjuk Elder, personal communication, 2012–18; Lynette Knapp, Merningar Bardok Elder, personal communication, 2013–24.

3 Rhoda Glover, ed., *Plantagenet: A History of the Shire of Plantagenet Western Australia* (Nedlands, WA, 1979), p. 24.

4 Noel Nannup Karda, *Moondang-ak kaaradjiny: The Carers of Everything* (Batchelor, NT, 2006); Noel Nannup, 'Caring for Everything', in *Heartsick for Country*, ed. S. Morgan, T. Mia and B. Kwaymullina (Fremantle, WA, 2008), pp. 102–14.

5 Nannup Karda, *Moondang-ak kaaradjiny*, pp. 4–6.

6 Noel Nannup, personal communication, 2014.

7 Ibid., 2013.

8 Marion Hercock, ed., *The Western Australian Explorations of John Septimus Roe, 1829–1849* (Carlisle, WA, 2014).

9 Ian Murray and Brian Goodchild, *Araluen to Zanthus: A Gazetteer of Perth Suburbs and Western Australian Towns* (Fremantle, WA, 2003), p. 127.

10 Ethel Hassell, *My Dusky Friends* (East Fremantle, WA, 1975), p. 64.

11 Hercock, *Western Australian Explorations*.

12 Sisters Muriel, Eddie and Winnie McHenry, via Mike Griffiths, personal communication, 22 February 2012.

13 George Grey, *A Vocabulary of the Dialects of Southwest Australia* (London, 1840).

14 We videotaped these stories on Country as a team, to mirror traditional Noongar teaching in the field. The text was transcribed and checked for accuracy by Lynette Knapp and Dion Cummings, and their approval given for the final text published herein. They join the four *nydiyang* (white people) conservation biologists as co-authors of the final product to ensure that their family retains its intellectual property, and to ensure appropriate cultural norms (men's business, women's business, etc.) and cultural safety are respected. In this way, due acknowledgement of the Knapp family's *wiernyert* (Dreaming) is made for present and future generations. The family retains agency and control through the generations. This section is offered as an example of contemporary cross-cultural research. It is intended to complement the preceding

chapter, which has been informed by literature in which individual
and family knowledge sources are rarely named or acknowledged.
Something is lost in this process concerning intellectual property
and cultural controls. Lynette and Dion emphasize that the following
are their family's stories. Other families will have their own stories,
which may or may not match what is published here. All such stories
have their own veracity, and none is more or less correct than the
next family's.

15 Oral history of Lynette Knapp's great-grandmother Jakbam from
Beechbeejup/Denmark was recorded by the ethnographer Daisy
Bates in the early twentieth century (www.bates.org.au, accessed
3 April 2024). When asked about the methods for obtaining water
from trees, Jakbam replied, 'Maree [*marri* (*Corymbia calophylla*)] a bole
cut out with *koj* [stone axe]'.
16 Quoted in Hercock, *Western Australian Explorations*, p. 64.
17 Goldfields Land and Sea Council, 'Locating and Recording Water
Trees', Eucalyptus Australia, www.eucalyptaustralia.org.au, accessed
1 April 2024.
18 Lynette Knapp et al., 'A Merningar Bardok Family's Noongar Oral
History of Two Peoples Bay Nature Reserve and Surrounds', *Pacific
Conservation Biology*, XXX/3 (2024), n.p.
19 Lynette Knapp, *Mirnang Waangkaniny* (Batchelor, NT, 2011).
20 Ibid., pp. 31–3.
21 Augustus Oldfield, *On the Aborigines of Australia, with an Introduction
by M. Helen Henderson* (Victoria Park, WA, 2005), p. 3.
22 Von Brandenstein, *Nyungar Anew*, pp. vi, 32; Lynette Knapp, personal
communication, 2017.

3 Tasmania, the European Naming of *Eucalyptus* and Palawa People

1 Norman Hall, *Botanists of the Eucalypts* (Melbourne, 1978); John Wrigley
and Murray Fagg, *Eucalypts: A Celebration* (Crows Nest, NSW, 2010); for a
pre-Linnean word description of an Indonesian eucalypt (*E. deglupta*) in
1743 by Rumphius, see Roderick Fensham, 'Rumphius and Eucalyptus',
Historical Records of Australian Science, XXXIII/1 (2022), pp. 23–7.
2 Charles L'Héritier de Brutelle, *Sertum Anglicum 1788* (An English Wreath):
Facsimile with Critical Studies and a Translation, ed. G.H.M. Lawrence
(Pittsburgh, PA, 1963). For an excellent account of much that follows, see
Bradley M. Potts and James B. Reid, 'Tasmania's Eucalypts: Their Place
in Science', *Papers and Proceedings of the Royal Society of Tasmania*, CXXXVII
(January 2003), pp. 21–37.
3 J. Britten and B. B. Woodward, 'Bibliographical Notes, XXXV –
L'Héritier's Botanical Works', *Journal of Botany*, XLIII (1905), p. 326.
4 F. A. Stafleu, 'L'Héritier de Brutelle: The Man and His Work',
in L'Héritier, *Sertum Anglicum*, p. xviii.
5 Ibid., p. xiii.

6   J. C. Beaglehole, ed., *The Journals of Captain James Cook on His Voyages of Discovery II*, vol. I: *The Voyage of the Resolution and Adventure, 1772–1775* (Cambridge, 1959), pp. 150–51.

7   James Cook, *A Voyage to the Pacific Ocean*, 3 vols and atlas (London, 1784), vol. III, p. 426. For a modern account of Tasmania's largest eucalypts see B. Mifsud et al. 'Tasmania's Giant Eucalypts: Discovery, Documentation, Macroecology and Conservation Status of the World's Largest Angiosperms', *Australian Journal of Botany*, LXXIII (2025), BT23088.

8   Ashley Hay, *Gum: The Story of Eucalypts and Their Champions* (Sydney, 2002).

9   Cook, *A Voyage*, vol. III, p. 426.

10   Ibid., vol. III, p. 425.

11   J.S.L. Gilmour, C. J. King and L.H.J. Williams, 'The Plants of *Sertum Anglicum*', in L'Héritier, *Sertum Anglicum*, pp. xlv–lix.

12   Jacques-Julien Houton de Labillardière, *Relation du voyage à la recherche de La Pérouse, fait par ordre de L'Assemblée Constituante, pendant les années 1791, 1792*, 2 vols (Paris, 1800), vol. I; Jacques-Julien Houton de Labillardière, *Novae Hollandiae plantarum specimen* (New York, 1804, repr. 1966).

13   Labillardière, *Relation du voyage*, vol. I, p. 174.

14   Ibid.

15   Edward Duyker, ed., *The Discovery of Tasmania: Journal Extracts from the Expeditions of Abel Janszoon Tasman and Marc-Joseph Marion Dufresne, 1642 and 1772* (Hobart, 1992), p. 13.

16   J. E. Hickey, P. Kostoglou and G. J. Sargison, 'Tasmania's Tallest Trees', *Tasforests*, XII (2000), pp. 105–21.

17   Quoted in H. L. Roth et al., *The Aborigines of Tasmania* [1899] (New York, digitally printed version 2009), p. 98.

18   Cook, *A Voyage*, vol. III, p. 425.

19   Ibid., vol. III, pp. 426–7.

20   E. Duyker and M. Duyker, *Bruny d'Entrecasteaux: Voyage to Australia and the Pacific, 1791–1793* (Melbourne, 2001), p. 37; see Potts and Reid, 'Tasmania's Eucalypts', for an illustration of the 76-metre-tall (249 ft) *E. globulus* tree, 'Big Ben', at Port Esperance, with a circumference of 25 metres (82 ft), 1.5 metres (5 ft) above ground level, and a basal cavity with interior dimensions of 6 × 7.8 metres (20 ft × 25 ft 6 in.).

21   Quoted in Cook, *A Voyage*, vol. III, p. 426.

22   Bill Gammage, *The Biggest Estate on Earth: How Aborigines Made Australia* (Crows Nest, NSW, 2011).

23   Quoted in Cook, *A Voyage*, vol. III, p. 426.

24   E. Duyker, *Citizen Labillardière: A Naturalist's Life in Revolution and Exploration (1755–1834)* (Carlton South, VIC, 2004).

25   Gammage, *The Biggest Estate*.

26   Quoted in Cook, *A Voyage*, vol. III, p. 426.

27   Hans Lambers et al., 'Plant Mineral Nutrition in Ancient Landscapes: High Plant Species Diversity on Infertile Soils Is Linked to Functional Diversity for Nutritional Strategies (Marschner Review)', *Plant and Soil*, CCCXXXIV/I (2010), pp. 11–31.

28 Quoted in Cook, *A Voyage*, vol. III, p. 426.
29 Labillardière, *Relation du voyage*, vol. I, p. 65.
30 J. Milligan, 'A Vocabulary of the Dialects of Some of the Aboriginal Tribes of Tasmania', *Royal Society of Tasmania, Papers*, III (1859), p. 280.
31 Labillardière, *Relation du voyage*, vol II: *Appendix* (Paris, 1800), pp. 43–7.
32 Milligan, 'A Vocabulary'.
33 C. Bowern, 'The Riddle of Tasmanian Languages', *Proceedings of the Royal Society Series B*, CCLXXIX/1747 (2012), pp. 4590–95.
34 William Anderson, 'A Journal of a Voyage Made in His Majesty's Sloop Resolution', in Cook, *A Voyage*, vol. III, p. 785.
35 John Albert Taylor, 'The Palawa (Tasmanian Aboriginal) Languages: A Preliminary Discussion', MA diss., University of Tasmania, Hobart, 2006; Lyndall Ryan, *Tasmanian Aborigines: A History since 1803* (Crows Nest, NSW, 2012).
36 Milligan, 'A Vocabulary'; Roth et al., *The Aborigines*; L. Thompson, *The Creation of Trowenna: A Story from the Neunone People of Bruny Island* (Melbourne, 2012); J. Cooper, *Land of the Sleeping Gods: Untold History and Mythology of the Tasmanian Aborigines, The Writings and Drawings of William Jackson Cotton* (Hobart, 2013).
37 *Poericker*: Taylor, 'The Palawa Languages', *Toilena*: Roth et al., *The Aborigines*; Cooper, *Land of the Sleeping Gods*.
38 *Lenna/line* and *toienook boorack*: Milligan, 'A Vocabulary'.
39 Taylor, 'The Palawa Languages'; Milligan, 'A Vocabulary'.
40 Thompson, *The Creation of Trowenna*.
41 Labillardière, *Relation du voyage*, vol. II, pp. 43–7; Roth et al., *The Aborigines*; Cooper, *Land of the Sleeping Gods*.
42 Thompson, *The Creation of Trowenna*, pp. 13, 15.
43 William Jackson Cotton in Cooper, *Land of the Sleeping Gods*. The authenticity of the story is contested, however; see N. D. Brodie, 'Quaker Dreaming: The "Lost" Cotton Archive and the Aborigines of Van Diemen's Land', *Journal of Religious History*, XL/3 (2016), pp. 303–25.
44 Ibid.
45 Ibid.
46 See Milligan, 'A Vocabulary'; Roth et al., *The Aborigines*; Cooper, *Land of the Sleeping Gods*; Thompson, *The Creation of Trowenna*, p. 15.
47 Quoted in Brodie, 'Quaker Dreaming'.
48 Duyker and Duyker, *Bruny d'Entrecasteaux*, p. 141.
49 M.I.H. Brooker and D. A. Kleinig, *Field Guide to Eucalypts*, vol. II: *South-Western and Southern Australia* (Melbourne, 1990); Doug J. Boland et al., *Forest Trees of Australia*, 5th edn (Collingwood, VIC, 2006).
50 J. B. Walker, 'Notes on the Aborigines of Tasmania, Extracted from the Manuscript Journals by George Washington Walker', *Papers and Proceedings of the Royal Society of Tasmania for 1897* (1897–8), pp. 145–75.
51 Noel Nannup, Eugene Eades, personal communication, 2015.

4 Modern Species, Subspecies and Hybrids

1 For this chapter, see references in Lindsay D. Pryor and Lawrie A. S. Johnson, *A Classification of the Eucalypts* (Canberra, 1971); Norman Hall, *Botanists of the Eucalypts* (Melbourne, 1978); and John Wrigley and Murray Fagg, *Eucalypts: A Celebration* (Crows Nest, NSW, 2010).

2 For detailed references and the elaboration of key ideas presented here on Joseph Hooker, see P. F. Stevens, 'J. D. Hooker, George Bentham, Asa Gray and Ferdinand Mueller on Species Limits in Theory and Practice: A Mid-Nineteenth-Century Debate and Its Repercussions', in *The Scientific Savant in Nineteenth-Century Australia: Historical Records of Australian Science*, vol. XI, ed. R. W. Home (Canberra, 1997), pp. 345–70; Jim Endersby, *Imperial Nature: Joseph Hooker and the Practices of Victorian Science* (Chicago, IL, 2008); Stephen D. Hopper, 'Royal Botanic Gardens Kew', *eLS* (April 2015), pp. 1–9. For detailed references and the elaboration of key ideas presented here on Charles Darwin, see Charles R. Darwin, *On the Origin of Species by Means of Natural Selection, or The Preservation of Favoured Races in the Struggle for Life* (London, 1859); Stephen D. Hopper, 'Evolutionary Networks: Natural Hybridization and Its Conservation Significance', in *Nature Conservation 4: The Role of Networks*, ed. D. A. Saunders, J. L. Craig and E. M. Mattiske (Chipping Norton, NSW, 1995), pp. 51–66; James Mallet, 'Subspecies, Semispecies, Superspecies', in *Encyclopedia of Biodiversity*, ed. S. A. Levin (Cambridge, 2001), pp. 523–6; James Mallet, 'Mayr's View of Darwin: Was Darwin Wrong about Speciation?', *Biological Journal of the Linnean Society*, XCV/1 (September 2008), pp. 3–16; Stephen D. Hopper and Hans Lambers, 'Darwin as a Plant Scientist: A Southern Hemisphere Perspective', *Trends in Plant Science*, XIV/8 (2009), pp. 421–35.

3 Charles R. Darwin, 'On the Specific Difference between *Primula veris*, Brit. Fl. (var. *officinalis*, of Linn.), *P. vulgaris*, Brit. Fl. (var. *acaulis*, Linn.) and *P. elatior*, Jacq.; and on the Hybrid Nature of the Common Oxlip. With Supplementary Remarks on Naturally Produced Hybrids in the Genus *Verbascum*', *Journal of the Linnean Society of London (Botany)*, X (1868), pp. 437–54.

4 Ferdinand von Mueller in 1857, cited in Stevens, 'J. D. Hooker, George Bentham', p. 350.

5 Pryor and Johnson, *A Classification*, p. 1.

6 George M. Chippendale, '*Eucalyptus, Angophora* (Myrtaceae)', *Flora of Australia*, XIX (1988), pp. 1–540.

7 Pryor and Johnson, *A Classification*, p. 1.

8 For example, Susan Rutherford et al., 'Phylogenomics of the Green Ash Eucalypts (Myrtaceae): A Tale of Reticulate Evolution and Misidentification', *Australian Systematic Botany*, XXVIII/6 (2015), pp. 326–54; Carl Gosper et al., 'Phylogenomics Shows Lignotuber State Is Taxonomically Informative in Closely Related Eucalypts', *Molecular Phylogenetics and Evolution*, CXXXV (June 2019), pp. 236–48.

9 Charles A. Gardner, 'Taxonomy and the Species Concept with Special Reference to Eucalyptus', *Australian Forestry*, IX (1945), pp. 7–11; Pryor

and Johnson, *A Classification*, pp. 21–2; M.I.H. Brooker and Stephen D. Hopper, 'A Taxonomic Revision of *Eucalyptus wandoo*, *E. redunca*, and Allied Species (*E.* Series *Levispermae* Maiden – Myrtaceae) in Western Australia', *Nuytsia*, VIII/1 (1991), pp. 1–189; M.I.H. Brooker, 'A New Classification of the Genus *Eucalyptus* L'Hér. (Myrtaceae)', *Australian Systematic Botany*, XIII/1 (2000), pp. 79–148; Dean Nicolle, *Classification of the Eucalypts* (*Angophora*, *Corymbia* and Eucalyptus) *Version 2*, 2015, www.dn.com.au; Gosper et al., 'Phylogenomics', pp. 236–48. For references and aspects of the biology of *E. caesia*, see Stephen D. Hopper, Norman A. Campbell and Gavin F. Moran, '*Eucalyptus caesia*, a Rare Mallee of Granite Rocks from South-Western Australia', in *Species at Risk: Research in Australia*, ed. R. H. Groves and W.D.L. Ride (Canberra, 1982), pp. 46–61; Margaret Byrne and Stephen D. Hopper, 'Granite Outcrops as Ancient Islands in Old Landscapes: Evidence from the Phylogeography and Population Genetics of *Eucalyptus caesia* (Myrtaceae) in Western Australia', *Biological Journal of the Linnean Society*, XCIII/1 (2008), pp. 177–88; Nicole Bezemer et al., 'Paternity Analysis Reveals Wide Pollen Dispersal and High Multiple Paternity in a Small Isolated Population of the Bird-Pollinated *Eucalyptus caesia* (Myrtaceae)', *Heredity*, CXVII/6 (2016), pp. 460–71; Nicole Bezemer et al., 'Conservation of Old Individual Trees and Small Populations Is Integral to Maintain Species' Genetic Diversity of a Historically Fragmented Woody Perennial', *Molecular Ecology*, XXVIII/14 (July 2019), pp. 3339–57.

10 This discussion draws on key references and ideas in H. N. Barber and W. D. Jackson, 'Natural Selection in Action in Eucalyptus', *Nature*, CLXXIX (1957), pp. 1267–9; Stephen D. Hopper, David J. Coates and Allan H. Burbidge, 'Natural Hybridization and Morphometric Relationships between Three Mallee Eucalypts in the Fitzgerald River National Park, WA', *Australian Journal of Botany*, XXVI/3 (1978), pp. 319–33; Hopper, 'Evolutionary Networks'; Stephen D. Hopper, 'Natural Hybridization in the Context of OCBIL Theory', *South African Journal of Botany*, CXVIII (2018), pp. 284–9; Tim P. Robins et al., 'Landscape and Taxon Age Are Associated with Differing Patterns of Hybridisation in Two Eucalyptus (Myrtaceae) Subgenera', *Annals of Botany*, CXXVII/1 (2021), pp. 49–62.

11 Pryor and Johnson, *A Classification*, p. 89.

12 Jane Sampson, Stephen D. Hopper and Sidney H. James, 'The Mating System and Population Genetic Structure in a Bird-Pollinated Mallee, *Eucalyptus rhodantha*', *Heredity*, LXIII/3 (1989), pp. 383–93; Stephen D. Hopper, 'Plant Taxonomy and Genetic Resources: Foundations for Conservation', in *Conservation Biology in Australia and Oceania*, ed. C. Moritz and J. Kikkawa (Sydney, 1994), pp. 275–6.

13 Donna Bradbury et al., 'Clonality, Interspecific Hybridisation and Inbreeding in a Rare Mallee Eucalypt, *Eucalyptus absita* (Myrtaceae), and Implications for Conservation', *Conservation Genetics*, XVII (2016), pp. 193–205.

14 James E. Holman, Jane M. Hughes and Roderick J. Fensham, 'Origins of a Morphological Cline between *Eucalyptus melanophloia* and *Eucalyptus whitei*', *Australian Journal of Botany*, LIX/3 (2011), pp. 244–52.

15 M. H. McGowen et al., 'The Origin of *Eucalyptus vernicosa*, a Unique Shrub Eucalypt', *Biological Journal of the Linnean Society*, LXXIV/3 (2001), pp. 397–405; Bradley M. Potts and James B. Reid, 'Tasmania's Eucalypts: Their Place in Science', *Papers and Proceedings of the Royal Society of Tasmania*, CXXXVII (January 2003), pp. 21–37.

16 P. A. Butcher, M. W. McDonald and J. C. Bell, 'Congruence between Environmental Parameters, Morphology and Genetic Structure in Australia's Most Widely Distributed Eucalypt, *Eucalyptus camaldulensis*', *Tree Genetics and Genomes*, V/1 (2009), pp. 189–210; M. W. McDonald, M.I.H. Brooker and P. A. Butcher, 'A Taxonomic Revision of *Eucalyptus camaldulensis* (Myrtaceae)', *Australian Systematic Botany*, XXII/4 (2009), pp. 257–85.

17 Brad M. Potts and James B. Reid, 'Interspecific Hybridization as a Dispersal Mechanism', *Evolution*, XLII/6 (1988), pp. 1245–55; H. D. Jackson et al., 'Chloroplast DNA Evidence for Reticulate Evolution in *Eucalyptus* (Myrtaceae)', *Molecular Ecology*, VIII/5 (1999), pp. 739–51; Brad M. Potts and Heidi S. Dungey, 'Interspecific Hybridization of *Eucalyptus*: Key Issues for Breeders and Geneticists', *New Forests*, XXVII/2 (2004), pp. 115–38; Matthew J. Larcombe et al., 'Patterns of Reproductive Isolation in *Eucalyptus* – A Phylogenetic Perspective', *Molecular Biology and Evolution*, XXXII/7 (2015), pp. 1833–46; Bradbury et al., 'Clonality'.

18 Dario Grattapaglia et al., 'Progress in Myrtaceae Genetics and Genomics: *Eucalyptus* as the Pivotal Genus', *Tree Genetics and Genomes*, VIII (2012), pp. 463–508; Alexander A. Myburg et al., 'The Genome of *Eucalyptus grandis*', *Nature*, DX (2014), pp. 356–62.

19 For the author's most recent taxonomic contribution on *Eucalyptus*, including an explicit definition of subspecies, see Stephen D. Hopper, '*Eucalyptus sweedmaniana* subsp. *noongaring*, a New Four-Winged Mallee (E. Series *Tetrapterae*: Myrtaceae) Endemic to *Boylya* (Granite Outcrops) of the *Kwongkan* East of Esperance, Western Australia', *Nuytsia*, XXXV (2024), pp. 225–32.

20 Lawrie A. S. Johnson, 'Rainbow's End: The Quest for an Optimal Taxonomy', *Systematic Zoology*, XIX/3 (1970), pp. 203–39.

5 Distribution and Habitats

1 Elizabeth J. Hermsen, Maria A. Gandolfo and Maria del Carmen Zamaloa, 'The Fossil Record of *Eucalyptus* in Patagonia', *American Journal of Botany*, XCIX/8 (2012), pp. 1356–74; Raman Patel et al., 'Reproductive and Vegetative Remains of an Eucalypt (Myrtaceae) from the Early Eocene of India', *Journal of Systematics and Evolution* (June 2024), doi.org/10.1111/jse.13078.

2 Robert Brown, 'General Remarks, Geographical and Systematical, on the Botany of Terra Australis', Appendix in Matthew Flinders, *A Voyage to Terra Australis*, vol. II (London, 1814), p. 533.

3 Stephen D. Hopper, 'OCBIL Theory: Towards an Integrated Understanding of the Evolution, Ecology and Conservation of Biodiversity on Old, Climatically Buffered, Infertile Landscapes', *Plant and Soil*, CCCXXII (2009), pp. 49–86; Stephen D. Hopper, Fernando A. O. Silveira and Peggy L. Fiedler, 'Biodiversity Hotspots and OCBIL Theory', *Plant and Soil*, CDIII/1–2 (June 2016), pp. 167–216; F.A.O. Silveira et al., 'Diversification in Ancient and Nutrient-Poor Neotropical Ecosystems: How Geological and Climatic Buffering Shaped Plant Diversity in Some of the World's Neglected Hotspots', in *Neotropical Diversification: Patterns and Processes*, ed. Valentí Rull and Ana Carolina Carnaval (Cham, Switzerland, 2020), pp. 329–68; Stephen D. Hopper, 'Out of the OCBILs: New Hypotheses for the Evolution, Ecology and Conservation of the Eucalypts', *Biological Journal of the Linnean Society*, CXXXIII/2 (June 2021), pp. 342–72; Doug Benson, 'Vegetation Patterns across the Sydney Basin during the Last Glacial Maximum Based on Plant Biogeography, Ecology, Geomorphology and Climate', *Proceedings of the Linnean Society of New South Wales*, CXLVI (2024), pp. 1–47.
4 Benson, 'Vegetation Patterns'.
5 Tim Hager and Doug Benson, 'The Eucalypts of the Greater Blue Mountains World Heritage Area: Distribution, Classification and Habitats of the Species of *Eucalyptus*, *Angophora* and *Corymbia* (Family Myrtaceae) Recorded in Its Eight Conservation Reserves', *Cunninghamia*, XI/4 (2010), pp. 425–44.
6 Elizabeth N. Bui et al., 'Climate and Geochemistry as Drivers of Eucalypt Diversification in Australia', *Geobiology*, XV/3 (2017), pp. 1–14.
7 Hager and Benson, 'The Eucalypts'; Benson, 'Vegetation Patterns'.

6 The Eucalypt Life Cycle

1 Based in part on and updated from Stephen D. Hopper, 'Eucalypts', in *Mountains of Mystery: A Natural History of the Stirling Range*, ed. C. Thomson, G. Hall and G. Friend (Como, WA, 1993), pp. 71–83; for good overviews of eucalypt life histories, see L. D. Pryor, *The Biology of Eucalypts* (London, 1976); papers in *Eucalypt Ecology: Individuals to Ecosystems*, ed. Jann Williams and John Woinarski (Cambridge, 1997); A. B. Wellington, 'Seedling Regeneration and the Population Dynamics of Eucalypts', in *Mediterranean Landscapes in Australia: Mallee Ecosystems and Their Management*, ed. J. C. Noble and R. A. Bradstock (Melbourne, 1989), pp. 155–67; Dean Nicolle, 'A Classification and Census of Regenerative Strategies in the Eucalypts (*Angophora*, *Corymbia* and *Eucalyptus* – Myrtaceae), with Special Reference to the Obligate Seeders', *Australian Journal of Botany*, LIV/4 (July 2006), pp. 391–407.
2 Stephen D. Hopper and Paul Gioia, 'The Southwest Australian Floristic Region: Evolution and Conservation of a Global Hotspot of Biodiversity', *Annual Review of Ecology, Evolution and Systematics*, XXXV/1 (2004), pp. 623–50; Paul Gioia and Stephen D. Hopper, 'A New

Phytogeographic Map for the Southwest Australian Floristic Region after an Exceptional Decade of Collection and Discovery', *Botanical Journal of the Linnean Society*, CLXXXIV/1 (2017), pp. 1–15.

3 D. J. Boland et al., *Eucalyptus Seed* (Brisbane, 1980).

4 Maureen Walsh, *May Gibbs: Mother of the Gumnuts: A Biography* (Sydney, 2007).

5 Hopper, 'Eucalypts'; Pryor, *Biology of Eucalypts*; Wellington, 'Seedling Regeneration'; Nicolle, 'A Classification and Census'.

6 Michael D. Crisp et al., 'Flammable Biomes Dominated by Eucalypts Originated at the Cretaceous–Palaeogene Boundary', *Nature Communications*, II (2011), art. 193.

7 R. G. Florence, *Ecology and Silviculture of Eucalypt Forests* (Collingwood, VIC, 1996); Peter Wilf and Robert Kooyman, 'Paleobotany Reframes the Fiery Debate on Australia's Rainforest Edges', *New Phytologist* (November 2024), doi.org/10.1111/nph.20301.

8 Nicolle, 'A Classification and Census'.

9 H. M. Wallace and S. J. Trueman, 'Dispersal of *Eucalyptus torelliana* Seeds by the Resin-Collecting Stingless Bee, *Trigona carbonaria*', *Oecologia*, CIV/1 (September 1995), pp. 12–16.

10 R. J. Whelan and A. R. Main, 'Insect Grazing and Post-Fire Succession in South-West Australian Woodland', *Australian Journal of Ecology*, IV/4 (1979), pp. 387–98.

11 Nicolle, 'A Classification and Census'.

12 Florence, *Ecology and Silviculture*.

13 Donna Bradbury et al., 'Clonality, Interspecific Hybridisation and Inbreeding in a Rare Mallee Eucalypt, *Eucalyptus absita* (Myrtaceae), and Implications for Conservation', *Conservation Genetics*, XVII (2016), pp. 193–205; S. D. Hopper et al., 'Plant Diversity on the Edge: Floristics, Phytogeography, Fire Responses, and Plant Conservation of Two Peoples Bay Nature Reserve in the Context of OCBIL Theory', *Pacific Conservation Biology*, XXX (2024), PC24024, doi:10.1071/PC24024.

7 How Australia Made the Eucalypts

1 Gregory P. Wilson et al., 'A Large Carnivorous Mammal from the Late Cretaceous and the North American Origin of Marsupials', *Nature Communications*, VII (2016), art. 13734.

2 R.M.D. Beck et al., 'Australia's Oldest Marsupial Fossils and Their Biogeographical Implications', *PLOS ONE*, III/3 (2008), doi.org/10.1371/journal.pone.0001858.

3 Claudia Monika Schimschal and Wilfried Jokat, 'The Falkland Plateau in the Context of Gondwana Breakup', *Gondwana Research*, LXVIII (2019), pp. 108–15.

4 Howie D. Scher et al., 'Onset of Antarctic Circumpolar Current 30 Million Years Ago as Tasmanian Gateway Aligned with Westerlies', *Nature*, DXXIII/7562 (2015), pp. 580–83.

5   Laura J. May-Collado, C. William Kilpatrick and Ingi Agnarsson, 'Mammals from "Down Under": A Multi-Gene Species-Level Phylogeny of Marsupial Mammals (Mammalia, Metatheria)', *Peer Journal*, III (2015), e805.

6   Beck et al., 'Australia's Oldest Marsupial Fossils'.

7   Stephen Gale, 'Long-Term Landscape Evolution in Australia', *Earth Surface Processes Landforms*, XVII/4 (1992), pp. 323–43.

8   Russell Ferrett, *Australia's Volcanoes* (Sydney, 2005); Ngoc Nguyen, Jessie C. Buettel and Barry W. Brook, 'A Geological Imprint on Plant Biodiversity: Eastern Australia's Cenozoic Volcanic Flora', *Journal of Biogeography* (November 2024), doi.org/10.1111/jbi.15039.

9   Hans Lambers et al., 'Plant Mineral Nutrition in Ancient Landscapes: High Plant Species Diversity on Infertile Soils Is Linked to Functional Diversity for Nutritional Strategies (Marschner Review)', *Plant and Soil*, CCCXXXIV/1 (2010), pp. 11–31.

10 Brian McGowran et al., 'Biogeographic Impact of the Leeuwin Current in Southern Australia Since the Late Middle Eocene', *Palaeogeography, Palaeoclimatology, Palaeoecology*, CXXXVI/1–4 (1997), pp. 19–40.

11 Several papers explore OCBIL Theory in detail, providing comprehensive references: Stephen D. Hopper, 'OCBIL Theory: Towards an Integrated Understanding of the Evolution, Ecology and Conservation of Biodiversity on Old, Climatically Buffered, Infertile Landscapes', *Plant and Soil*, CCCXXII (2009), pp. 49–86; Stephen D. Hopper, Fernando A. O. Silveira and Peggy L. Fiedler, 'Biodiversity Hotspots and OCBIL Theory', *Plant and Soil*, CDIII/1–2 (June 2016), pp. 167–216; Stephen D. Hopper, 'Natural Hybridization in the Context of OCBIL Theory', *South African Journal of Botany*, CXVIII (2018), pp. 284–9; F.A.O. Silveira et al., 'Diversification in Ancient and Nutrient-Poor Neotropical Ecosystems: How Geological and Climatic Buffering Shaped Plant Diversity in Some of the World's Neglected Hotspots', in *Neotropical Diversification: Patterns and Processes*, ed. Valentí Rull and Ana Carolina Carnaval (Cham, Switzerland, 2020), pp. 329–68; Stephen D. Hopper, 'Out of the OCBILs: New Hypotheses for the Evolution, Ecology and Conservation of the Eucalypts', *Biological Journal of the Linnean Society*, CXXXIII/2 (June 2021), pp. 342–72; Doug Benson, 'Vegetation Patterns across the Sydney Basin during the Last Glacial Maximum Based on Plant Biogeography, Ecology, Geomorphology and Climate', *Proceedings of the Linnean Society of New South Wales*, CXLVI (2024), pp. 1–47.

12 Paul Gioia and Stephen D. Hopper, 'A New Phytogeographic Map for the Southwest Australian Floristic Region after an Exceptional Decade of Collection and Discovery', *Botanical Journal of the Linnean Society*, CLXXXIV/1 (2017), pp. 1–15.

13 Lambers et al., 'Plant Mineral Nutrition'.

14 Ibid.

15 Lynda D. Prior, Ben J. French and David M.J.S. Bowman, 'Effect of Experimental Fire on Seedlings of Australian and Gondwanan

Trees Species from a Tasmanian Montane Vegetation Mosaic',
Australian Journal of Botany, LXVI/7 (2018), pp. 511–17; James C. Noble
and Peter J. Diggle, 'Population Biology of Coppicing Plants: Survival
of Mallee (*Eucalyptus* spp.) Populations Exposed to Contrasting Fire
and Cutting Regimes', *Australian Journal of Botany*, LXI/7 (2013),
pp. 552–7.

16 Michael D. Crisp et al., 'Flammable Biomes Dominated by
Eucalypts Originated at the Cretaceous–Palaeogene Boundary',
Nature Communications, 11 (2011), art. 193; Michael J. Bayly, 'Phylogenetic
Studies of Eucalypts: Fossils, Morphology and Genomes', *Proceedings
of the Royal Society of Victoria*, CXXVIII/1 (2016), pp. 12–24; Andrew H.
Thornhill et al., 'A Dated Molecular Perspective of Eucalypt Taxonomy,
Evolution and Diversification', *Australian Systematic Botany*, XXXII/1 (2019),
pp. 29–48; but for an alternative on fire adaptation, see Prior, French
and Bowman, 'Effect of Experimental Fire'; and Peter Wilf and Robert
Kooyman, 'Paleobotany Reframes the Fiery Debate on Australia's
Rainforest Edges', *New Phytologist* (November 2024), doi.org/10.1111/
nph.20301.

17 Benson, 'Vegetation Patterns'.

18 Hopper, 'Out of the OCBILs'.

19 Scott Ferguson et al., 'Plant Genome Evolution in the Genus
Eucalyptus Is Driven by Structural Rearrangements that Promote
Sequence Divergence', *Genome Research*, XXXIV/1 (2024), pp. 1–14.

8 Cultivating Eucalypts Abroad and Modern Uses

1 For references, see Robert Fyfe Zacharin, *Emigrant Eucalypts* (Cape
Schanck, VIC, 1978); Robin W. Doughty, *The Eucalyptus: A Natural
and Commercial History of the Gum Tree* (Baltimore, MD, 2000); Bradley
M. Potts and James B. Reid, 'Tasmania's Eucalypts: Their Place in
Science', *Papers and Proceedings of the Royal Society of Tasmania*, CXXXVII
(January 2003), pp. 21–37; Brett M. Bennett, 'The El Dorado of
Forestry: The Eucalyptus in India, South Africa and Thailand,
1850–2000', *International Review of Social History*, LV/S18 (2010),
pp. 27–50; Manuel Esperon-Rodriguez et al., 'Wide Climatic Niche
Breadth and Traits Associated with Climatic Tolerance Facilitate
Eucalypt Occurrence in Cities Worldwide', *Global Ecology and
Biogeography*, XXXIII/6 (2024), e13833, doi.org/10.1111/geb.13833.

2 Francisco Javier Silva-Pando and Rubén Pino Pérez, 'Introduction
of *Eucalyptus* into Europe', *Australian Forestry*, LXXIX/4 (2016),
pp. 283–91.

3 Ibid.

4 Ibid.

5 Emanuele Del Guacchio et al., 'Wandering among Dehnhardt's Gums:
The Cold Case of *Eucalyptus camaldulensis* (Myrtaceae) and Other
Nomenclatural Notes on *Eucalyptus*', *Taxon*, LXVIII/2 (2019), pp. 379–90.

6 Ibid.
7 Doughty, *The Eucalyptus*, p. 129.
8 Western Australian Herbarium, 'Robert Brown's Australian Botanical Specimens, 1801–1805 at the BM', https://florabase.dpaw.wa.gov.au, accessed 3 March 2020.
9 On cider gum and Robinson and Hooker, including quotations given, see Rodney Barker, 'How to Eat a Gum Tree – Part 3 The Cider Gum *Eucalyptus gunnii*', *Newsletter – Association of Societies for Growing Australian Plants*, Australian Food Plants Study Group, XIV (1992), pp. 6–12; and Potts and Reid, 'Tasmania's Eucalypts', p. 26.
10 Quoted in N. D. Brodie, 'Quaker Dreaming: The "Lost" Cotton Archive and the Aborigines of Van Diemen's Land', *Journal of Religious History*, XL/3 (2016), pp. 303–25.
11 Joseph D. Hooker, 'Note on the Cider Tree', *London Journal of Botany*, III (1844), pp. 496–501.
12 Stephen D. Hopper, 'In the Footsteps of Giles', *Landscope*, VII/3 (1992), pp. 28–34; Jane F. Sampson, Stephen D. Hopper and Sidney H. James, 'The Mating System and Genetic Diversity of the Australian Arid Zone Mallee, *Eucalyptus rameliana*', *Australian Journal of Botany*, XLIII/5 (1995), pp. 461–74.
13 Ferdinand von Mueller, *Eucalyptographia: A Descriptive Atlas of the Eucalypts of Australia and the Adjoining Islands* (Melbourne, 1879), p. 6.
14 James P. King and Stanley L. Krugman, 'Tests of 36 *Eucalyptus* Species in Northern California', *Forest Service Pacific Southwest Forest and Range Experimental Station Research Paper*, PSW-152 (Berkeley, CA, 1980), back cover.
15 Tim P. Robins et al., 'Landscape and Taxon Age Are Associated with Differing Patterns of Hybridisation in Two Eucalyptus (Myrtaceae) Subgenera', *Annals of Botany*, CXXVII/I (2021), pp. 49–62.
16 Doughty, *The Eucalyptus*, p. 144.

9 Eucalypt Conservation

1 R. J. Fensham et al., 'Rarity or Decline: Key Concepts for the Red List of Australian Eucalypts', *Biological Conservation*, CCXLIII (2020), n.p.
2 Neil A. Brummitt et al., 'Green Plants in the Red: A Baseline Global Assessment for the IUCN Sampled Red List Index for Plants', *PLOS ONE*, X/8 (2015), doi.org/10.1371/journal.pone.0135152.
3 Stephen D. Hopper and Paul Gioia, 'The Southwest Australian Floristic Region: Evolution and Conservation of a Global Hotspot of Biodiversity', *Annual Review of Ecology, Evolution and Systematics*, XXXV/I (2004), pp. 623–50.
4 K. J. Williams et al., 'Forests of East Australia: The 35th Biodiversity Hotspot', in *Biodiversity Hotspots: Distribution and Protection of Conservation Priority Areas*, ed. F. E. Zachos and J. C. Habel (Berlin, 2011), pp. 295–310.

5 Fensham et al., 'Rarity or Decline'.

6 Carlos E. González-Orozco et al., 'Phylogenetic Approaches Reveal Biodiversity Threats under Climate Change', *Nature Climate Change*, VI/12 (2016), pp. 1110–14.

7 Gunnar Keppel et al., 'Refugia: Identifying and Understanding Safe Havens for Biodiversity under Climate Change', *Global Ecology and Biogeography*, XXI/4 (2012), pp. 393–404.

8 Lesley Hughes, E. M. Cawsey and Mark Westoby, 'Climatic Range Sizes of Eucalyptus Species in Relation to Future Climate Change', *Global Ecology and Biogeography Letters*, V/23 (2006), pp. 27–8.

9 James Aronson and Andre F. Clewell, *Ecological Restoration: Principles, Values, and Structure of an Emerging Profession* (Washington, DC, 2013); Suzanne M. Prober et al., 'Facilitating Adaptation of Biodiversity to Climate Change: A Conceptual Framework Applied to the World's Largest Mediterranean-Climate Woodland', *Climate Change*, CX (2012), pp. 227–48; Suzanne M. Prober et al., 'Shifting the Conservation Paradigm: A Synthesis of Options for Renovating Nature under Climate Change', *Ecological Monographs*, LXXXIX/1 (2019), n.p.

10 Fensham et al., 'Rarity or Decline'.

11 Lynda D. Prior, Ben J. French and David M.J.S. Bowman, 'Effect of Experimental Fire on Seedlings of Australian and Gondwanan Trees Species from a Tasmanian Montane Vegetation Mosaic', *Australian Journal of Botany*, LXVI/7 (2018), pp. 511–17.

12 James C. Noble and Peter J. Diggle, 'Population Biology of Coppicing Plants: Survival of Mallee (*Eucalyptus* spp.) Populations Exposed to Contrasting Fire and Cutting Regimes', *Australian Journal of Botany*, LXI/7 (2013), pp. 552–7.

13 Fensham et al., 'Rarity or Decline'.

14 Erica Shedley et al., 'Using Bioregional Variation in Fire History and Fire Response Attributes as a Basis for Managing Threatened Flora in a Fire-Prone Mediterranean Climate Biodiversity Hotspot', *Australian Journal of Botany*, LXVI/2 (2018), pp. 134–43.

15 S. Don Bradshaw et al., 'Understanding the Long-Term Impact of Prescribed Burning in Mediterranean-Climate Biodiversity Hotspots, with a Focus on South-Western Australia', *International Journal of Wildland Fire*, XXVII/2 (2018), pp. 643–57.

16 Nicole Bezemer et al., 'Conservation of Old Individual Trees and Small Populations Is Integral to Maintain Species' Genetic Diversity of a Historically Fragmented Woody Perennial', *Molecular Ecology*, XXVIII/14 (July 2019), pp. 3339–57; Donna Bradbury et al., 'Clonality, Interspecific Hybridisation and Inbreeding in a Rare Mallee Eucalypt, *Eucalyptus absita* (Myrtaceae), and Implications for Conservation', *Conservation Genetics*, XVII (2016), pp. 193–205; M. H. McGowen et al., 'The Origin of *Eucalyptus vernicosa*, a Unique Shrub Eucalypt', *Biological Journal of the Linnean Society*, LXXIV/3 (2001), pp. 397–405.

17 Luke Sweedman and David Merritt, eds, *Australian Seeds: A Guide to Their Collection, Identification and Biology* (Melbourne, 2006); Carolyn Fry, Sue Seddon and Gail Vines, *The Last Great Plant Hunt: The Story of Kew's Millennium Seed Bank* (Richmond, UK, 2011).

18 Department of Environment and Conservation, *Rose Mallee* (Eucalyptus rhodantha) *Interim Recovery Plan 2006–2011*, Interim Recovery Plan no. 229 (Perth, WA, 2006).

19 Ibid.

20 George M. Chippendale, '*Eucalyptus, Angophora* (Myrtaceae)', *Flora of Australia*, XIX (1988), pp. 1–540.

21 Ernest Giles, *Australia Twice Traversed: The Romance of Exploration, Being a Narrative Compiled from the Journals of Five Exploring Expeditions into and through Central South Australia and Western Australia from 1872 to 1876*, vols I and II (London, 1889).

22 Stephen D. Hopper, 'In the Footsteps of Giles', *Landscape*, VII/3 (1992), pp. 28–34.

23 Graham McInerney and Alec Mathieson, *Across the Gibson* (Adelaide, 1978).

24 Jane F. Sampson, Stephen D. Hopper and Sidney H. James, 'The Mating System and Genetic Diversity of the Australian Arid Zone Mallee, *Eucalyptus rameliana*', *Australian Journal of Botany*, XLIII/5 (1995), pp. 461–74.

25 Australian Government: Department of Climate Change, Energy, the Environment and Water, 'What Is a Threatened Ecological Community (TEC)?', www.environment.gov.au, accessed 2 March 2020.

26 Australian Government: Department of Climate Change, Energy, the Environment and Water, 'Threatened Ecological Communities of Australia map', www.environment.gov.au, accessed 2 March 2020.

27 Nathan McQuoid, *Lifting the Bonnet on Wheatbelt Woodlands: A Guide to the Connection between Landscape and Vegetation in Southwest Australia* (Ultimo, NSW, 2014); Carl R. Gosper et al., 'A Conceptual Model of Vegetation Dynamics for the Unique Obligate-Seeder Eucalypt Woodlands of South-Western Australia', *Austral Ecology*, XLIII/6 (2018), pp. 681–95.

28 Stephen D. Hopper, 'Out of the OCBILs: New Hypotheses for the Evolution, Ecology and Conservation of the Eucalypts', *Biological Journal of the Linnean Society*, CXXXIII/2 (June 2021), pp. 342–72; Fernando A. O. Silveira, Peggy L. Fiedler and Stephen D. Hopper, eds, 'OCBIL Theory: A New Science for Old Ecosystems', *Biological Journal of the Linnean Society*, Special Issue, CXXXIII/2 (2021), pp. 251–644; Doug Benson, 'Vegetation Patterns across the Sydney Basin during the Last Glacial Maximum Based on Plant Biogeography, Ecology, Geomorphology and Climate', *Proceedings of the Linnean Society of New South Wales*, CXLVI (2024), pp. 1–47. Gregg Borschmann, *The People's Forest: A Living History of the Australian Bush* (Blackheath, NSW, 1999). I am indebted to Gregg Borschmann for extensive discussions on hypotheses concerning the origins of eucalypts that ultimately led to the publication of Hopper, 'Out of the OCBILs' and Silveira et al., 'OCBIL Theory'.

29 Bradshaw et al., 'Understanding the Long-Term Impact'.

30 Borschmann, *The People's Forest*; Chrissy Sharp, *Shades of Green: Finding a Middle Path through the Forest* (Fremantle, wa, 2022); David Lindenmayer, *The Forest Wars: The Ugly Truth about What's Happening in Our Tall Forests* (Crow's Nest, nsw, 2024).

.

Bibliography

Barber, H. N., and W. D. Jackson, 'Natural Selection in Action in Eucalyptus', *Nature*, CLXXIX (1957), pp. 1267–9

Barbour, Robert C., et al., 'The Potential for Gene Flow from Exotic Eucalypt Plantations into Australia's Rare Native Eucalypts', *Forest Ecology and Management*, CCLX/12 (December 2010), pp. 2079–87

Bayly, Michael J., 'Phylogenetic Studies of Eucalypts: Fossils, Morphology and Genomes', *Proceedings of the Royal Society of Victoria*, CXXVIII/1 (2016), pp. 12–24

Benson, Doug, 'Vegetation Patterns across the Sydney Basin during the Last Glacial Maximum Based on Plant Biogeography, Ecology, Geomorphology and Climate', *Proceedings of the Linnean Society of New South Wales*, CXLVI (2024), pp. 1–47

—, and Georgina Eldershaw, 'Backdrop to Encounter: The 1770 Landscape of Botany Bay, the Plants Collected by Banks and Solander and Rehabilitation of Natural Vegetation at Kurnell', *Cunninghamia*, X/1 (2007), pp. 113–37

Bentham, George, *Flora Australiensis*, vols I–VII (London, 1863–78)

Bezemer, Nicole, Siegfried L. Krauss and David G. Roberts, 'No Evidence for Early Inbreeding Depression in Planted Seedlings of *Eucalyptus caesia*, an Anciently Fragmented Tree Endemic on Granite Outcrops', *Plant Ecology*, CCXX/12 (2019), pp. 1101–8

—, et al., 'Conservation of Old Individual Trees and Small Populations Is Integral to Maintain Species' Genetic Diversity of a Historically Fragmented Woody Perennial', *Molecular Ecology*, XXVIII/14 (July 2019), pp. 3339–57

Blakely, W. F., *A Key to the Eucalypts* (Sydney, 1934)

Bodkin, Frances, and Lorraine Robertson, *D'harawal Dreaming Stories* (Sussex Inlet, NSW, 2013)

Boland, Doug J., et al., *Forest Trees of Australia*, 5th edn (Collingwood, VIC, 2006)

Borschmann, Gregg, *The People's Forest: A Living History of the Australian Bush* (Blackheath, NSW, 1999)

Brooker, M.I.H., 'A New Classification of the Genus *Eucalyptus* L'Hér. (Myrtaceae)', *Australian Systematic Botany*, XIII/1 (2000), pp. 79–148

—, and Stephen D. Hopper, 'A Taxonomic Revision of *Eucalyptus wandoo*, *E. redunca*, and Allied Species (*E.* Series *Levispermae* Maiden – Myrtaceae) in Western Australia', *Nuytsia*, VIII/1 (1991), pp. 1–189

—, and Dean Nicolle, *Atlas of Leaf Venation and Oil Gland Patterns in the Eucalypts* (Melbourne, 2013)

Carr, D. J., and S.G.M. Carr, *Eucalyptus I. New or Little-Known Species of the 'Corymbosae'* (Canberra, 1985)

—, and —, *Eucalyptus II. The Rubber Cuticle and Other Studies of the 'Corymbosae'* (Canberra, 1987)

Carr, S.G.M., and D. J. Carr, 'Oil Glands and Ducts in Eucalyptus L'Hérit. I. The Phloem and the Pith', *Australian Journal of Botany*, XVII/3 (1969), pp. 471–513

Cavanagh, Tony, 'Australian Plants Cultivated in England and Europe from 1771', *Australian Garden History*, II/3 (1990), pp. 7–10

Chippendale, G. M.,'*Eucalyptus, Angophora* (Myrtaceae)', *Flora of Australia*, XIX (1988), pp. 1–540

—, *Eucalypts of the Western Australian Goldfields (and the Adjacent Wheatbelt)* (Canberra, 1973)

Crisp, Michael D., et al., 'Perianth Evolution and Implications for Generic Delimitation in the Eucalypts (Myrtaceae), Including the Description of the New Genus, *Blakella*', *Journal of Systematics and Evolution*, LXII/5 (September 2024), pp. 942–62

Doughty, Robin W., *The Eucalyptus: A Natural and Commercial History of the Gum Tree* (Baltimore, MD, 2000)

Duyker, Edward, ed., *The Discovery of Tasmania: Journal Extracts from the Expeditions of Abel Janszoon Tasman and Marc-Joseph Marion Dufresne, 1642 and 1772* (Hobart, 1992)

Fensham, Roderick, 'Rumphius and Eucalyptus', *Historical Records of Australian Science*, XXXIII/1 (2022), pp. 23–7

—, et al., 'Rarity or Decline: Key Concepts for the Red List of Australian Eucalypts', *Biological Conservation*, CCXLIII (2020), n.p.

Ferguson, Ian, et al., *Report to the Minister for the Environment by the Ministerial Advisory Group on Karri and Tingle Management* (Perth, WA, 2001)

Florence, R. G., *Ecology and Silviculture of Eucalypt Forests* (Collingwood, VIC, 1996)

French, Malcolm, *Eucalypts of Western Australia's Wheatbelt* (Perth, WA, 2012)

George, Alex, *William Dampier in New Holland* (Hawthorn, VIC, 1999)

González-Orozco, Carlos E., et al., 'Biogeographical Regions and Phytogeography of the Eucalypts', *Diversity and Distributions*, XX/1 (January 2014), pp. 46–58

Gosper, Carl, et al., 'Phylogenomics Shows Lignotuber State Is Taxonomically Informative in Closely Related Eucalypts', *Molecular Phylogenetics and Evolution*, CXXXV (June 2019), pp. 236–48

Griffin, A. R., I. P. Burgess and L. Wolf, 'Patterns of Natural and Manipulated Hybridisation in the Genus *Eucalyptus* L'Hérit.-1 A Review', *Australian Journal of Botany*, XXXVI/1 (1988), pp. 41–66

Hall, Norman, *Botanists of the Eucalypts* (Melbourne, 1978)

Hay, Ashley, *Gum: The Story of Eucalypts and Their Champions* (Sydney, 2002)

Hill, K.D., and L.A.S. Johnson, 'Systematic Studies in the Eucalypts. 7. A Revision of the Bloodwoods, Genus *Corymbia* (Myrtaceae), *Telopea*, VI/2–3 (1995), pp. 185–504

Hobbs, Richard J., and Colin J. Yates, eds, *Temperate Eucalypt Woodlands in Australia* (Chipping Norton, NSW, 2000)

Hooker, Joseph D., 'Note on the Cider Tree', *London Journal of Botany*, III (1844), pp. 496–501

Hopper, Stephen D., 'OCBIL Theory: Towards an Integrated Understanding of the Evolution, Ecology and Conservation of Biodiversity on Old, Climatically Buffered, Infertile Landscapes', *Plant and Soil*, CCCXXII (2009), pp. 49–86

—, 'OCBIL Theory as a Potential Unifying Framework for Investigating Narrow Endemism in Mediterranean Climate Regions', *Plants*, XII/3 (February 2023), p. 645

—, 'Out of the OCBILs: New Hypotheses for the Evolution, Ecology and Conservation of the Eucalypts', *Biological Journal of the Linnean Society*, CXXXIII/2 (June 2021), pp. 342–72

—, and Paul Gioia, 'The Southwest Australian Floristic Region: Evolution and Conservation of a Global Hotspot of Biodiversity', *Annual Review of Ecology, Evolution and Systematics*, XXXV/1 (2004), pp. 623–50

—, Norman A. Campbell and Gavin F. Moran, '*Eucalyptus caesia*, a Rare Mallee of Granite Rocks from South-Western Australia', in *Species at Risk: Research in Australia*, ed. R. H. Groves and W.D.L. Ride (Canberra, 1982), pp. 46–61

Horton, D. R., 'The AIATSIS Map of Aboriginal Australia', 1996, www.aiatsis.gov.au

Knapp, Lynette, et al., 'A Merningar Bardok Family's Noongar Oral History of Two Peoples Bay Nature Reserve and Surrounds', *Pacific Conservation Biology*, XXX/3 (2024), n.p.

Ladiges, P. Y., and C. J. Humphries, 'A Cladistic Study of *Arillastrum*, *Angophora* and *Eucalyptus* (Myrtaceae)', *Botanical Journal of the Linnean Society*, LXXXVII/2 (1983), pp. 105–34

L'Héritier de Brutelle, Charles, *Sertum Anglicum 1788* (An English Wreath): *Facsimile with Critical Studies and a Translation*, ed. G.H.M. Lawrence (Pittsburgh, PA, 1963)

Lindenmayer, David, *The Forest Wars: The Ugly Truth about What's Happening in Our Tall Forests* (Crow's Nest, NSW, 2024)

McQuoid, Nathan, *Lifting the Bonnet on Wheatbelt Woodlands: A Guide to the Connection between Landscape and Vegetation in Southwest Australia* (Ultimo, NSW, 2014)

Maiden, Joseph H., *A Critical Revision of the Genus Eucalyptus*, vols I–VIII (Sydney, 1903–33)

Moran, G. F., and S. D. Hopper, 'Genetic Diversity and the Insular Population Structure of the Rare Granite Rock Species, *Eucalyptus caesia* Benth', *Australian Journal of Botany*, XXXI/2 (1983), pp. 161–72

Myburg, Alexander A., et al., 'The Genome of *Eucalyptus grandis*', *Nature*, DX
(2014), pp. 356–62

Nannup Karda, Noel, *Moondang-ak kaaradjiny: The Carers of Everything* (Batchelor,
NT, 2006)

Neale, Margot, ed., *Songlines: Tracking the Seven Sisters* (Canberra, 2017)

Nicolle, Dean, 'A Classification and Census of Regenerative Strategies
in the Eucalypts (*Angophora, Corymbia* and *Eucalyptus* – Myrtaceae),
with Special Reference to the Obligate Seeders', *Australian Journal of Botany*,
LIV/4 (July 2006), pp. 391–407

—, *Classification of the Eucalypts* (Angophora, Corymbia *and* Eucalyptus) *Version 2*,
2015, www.dn.com.au

Playford, Phillip, *Voyage of Discovery to Terra Australis by Willem de Vlamingh in
1696–97* (Nedlands, WA, 1998)

Potts, Bradley M., and James B. Reid, 'Tasmania's Eucalypts: Their Place
in Science', *Papers and Proceedings of the Royal Society of Tasmania*, CXXXVII
(January 2003), pp. 21–37

Prior, Lynda D., Ben J. French and David M.J.S. Bowman, 'Effect of
Experimental Fire on Seedlings of Australian and Gondwanan Trees
Species from a Tasmanian Montane Vegetation Mosaic', *Australian
Journal of Botany*, LXVI/7 (2018), pp. 511–17

Pryor, Lindsay D., *The Biology of Eucalypts*, London, 1976)

—, and Lawrie A. S. Johnson, *A Classification of the Eucalypts* (Canberra, 1971)

Ritter, Matt, and Jenn Yost, 'Diversity, Reproduction, and Potential
for Invasiveness of *Eucalyptus* in California', *Madroño*, LVI/3 (2009),
pp. 155–67

Robins, Tim P., et al., 'Landscape and Taxon Age Are Associated with
Differing Patterns of Hybridisation in Two Eucalyptus (Myrtaceae)
Subgenera', *Annals of Botany*, CXXVII/1 (2021), pp. 49–62

Rutherford, Susan, et al., 'Phylogenomics of the Green Ash Eucalypts
(Myrtaceae): A Tale of Reticulate Evolution and Misidentification',
Australian Systematic Botany, XXVIII/6 (2015), pp. 326–354

Sampson, Jane F., Stephen D. Hopper and Sidney H. James, 'The Mating
System and Genetic Diversity of the Australian Arid Zone Mallee,
Eucalyptus rameliana', *Australian Journal of Botany*, XLIII/5 (1995), pp. 461–74

Sharp, Chrissy, *Shades of Green: Finding a Middle Path through the Forest*
(Fremantle, WA, 2022)

Silva-Pando, Francisco Javier, and Rubén Pino Pérez, 'Introduction
of *Eucalyptus* into Europe', *Australian Forestry*, LXXIX/4 (2016),
pp. 283–91

Thornhill, Andrew H., et al., 'A Dated Molecular Perspective
of Eucalypt Taxonomy, Evolution and Diversification', *Australian
Systematic Botany*, XXXII/1 (2019), pp. 29–48

Tindale, N. B., *Aboriginal Tribes of Australia: Their Terrain, Environmental
Controls, Distribution, Limits and Proper Names* (Berkeley, CA, 1974)

Von Mueller, Ferdinand, *Eucalyptographia: A Descriptive Atlas of the Eucalypts
of Australia and the Adjoining Islands* (Melbourne, 1879)

Webb, Joan B., 'George Caley – Robert Brown's Collecting Partner',
    Cunninghamia, VII/4 (2002), pp. 617–21
Wrigley, John, and Murray Fagg, *Eucalypts: A Celebration* (Crows Nest,
    NSW, 2010)

Associations and Websites

ATLAS OF LIVING AUSTRALIA
https://bie.ala.org.au

AUSTRALASIAN VIRTUAL HERBARIUM (AVH)
https://avh.ala.org.au

AUSTRALIAN NATIVE PLANTS SOCIETY
https://anpsa.org.au

CANBR AND ANBG DATABASES
www.anbg.gov.au/cpbr/databases

CURRENCY CREEK ARBORETUM
www.dn.com.au/Currency_Creek_Arboretum.html

ENCYCLOPAEDIA OF AUSTRALIAN SCIENCE AND INNOVATION
www.eoas.info

EUCALYPT AUSTRALIA
www.eucalyptaustralia.org.au

EUCALYPTUS STUDY GROUP
https://anpsa.org.au/newsletter/eucalyptus-study-group

EUCLID EUCALYPTS OF AUSTRALIA (FOURTH EDITION)
https://apps.lucidcentral.org/euclid

FLORABASE (THE WESTERN AUSTRALIAN HERBARIUM)
https://florabase.dbca.wa.gov.au

FLORANT NORTHERN TERRITORY FLORA ONLINE
https://eflora.nt.gov.au

GLOBAL BIODIVERSITY INFORMATION FACILITY (GBIF)
www.gbif.org

INATURALIST
www.inaturalist.org

PLANTNET
https://plantnet.rbgsyd.nsw.gov.au

PLANTS OF THE WORLD ONLINE
https://powo.science.kew.org

TROPICOS
https://tropicos.org

VICFLORA (FLORA OF VICTORIA)
https://vicflora.rbg.vic.gov.au

Acknowledgements

I owe a great debt to teachers, mentors, colleagues, students, friends and family. The late Dr M.I.H. (Ian) Brooker generously guided my early ventures into eucalypt identification, leading to a productive taxonomic and field-research collaboration for two decades. Apart from taxonomy, my biological and conservation studies on *Eucalyptus* commenced, and continue, with a focus on natural hybridization, pollination, conservation genetics and ethnobiology, and on *E. caesia*. The support and interest of my late PhD supervisor, Dr Sid James, in this research were invaluable, as was the enthusiasm of fellow postgraduate students Dr Allan Burbidge and Dr David Coates. Dr Gavin Moran of the then CSIRO Forestry Division in Canberra collaborated on early work on the conservation genetics of *E. caesia* and other eucalypts. Together, we published pioneering work. For this I am ever grateful. Thereafter, many other colleagues and collaborators were essential to my broadening understanding of eucalypts, too numerous to name but some mentioned as co-authors in cited works and the Bibliography. I am grateful to my Noongar friend Dr Ron (Doc) Reynolds for generously agreeing to write the Foreword, and to Merningar Elder Dr Lynette Knapp and family for enriching Chapter Two with their incisive oral history. Help with advice and culturally acceptable captions is appreciated from John Heath (illus. 21–4) and David Foster (illus. 14). I am grateful to Jane Pye, New South Wales pastoralist and culturally modified tree enthusiast, for her recent hospitality and generous explanation of trees in trees. Discussions with Greg Borschmann led ultimately to my reinterpretation of the evolution, ecology and conservation of eucalypts as out of the OCBILs, not rainforests. The responsibility for this reinterpretation is mine alone.

I benefited by having access to the eucalypt collections of herbaria and libraries, especially at the Western Australian Herbarium, where 1,470 of my own eucalypt collections are currently housed. I also revelled in the massive collections of the Royal Botanic Gardens, Kew, and the living collections of Kings Park and Botanic Garden, maintained under the horticultural leadership of Grady Brand. At Kings Park, seed collector Luke Sweedman and senior research scientist Dr Siegy Krauss deserve thanks. Dr Nicole Bezemer completed an insightful PhD on *E. caesia* under the supervision of Krauss and myself, together with Dr Dave Roberts. Thanks, too, to contemporary colleagues and co-authors in the Western

Australian Department of Biodiversity, Conservation and Attractions, including Dr Margaret Byrne, Dr Colin Yates, Dr David Coates, Dr Stephen van Leeuwen, Dr Jane Sampson, Dr Rachael Binks and Tim Robins. Nathan McQuoid is a fine taxonomic collaborator. Along the way, eucalypts have been there, as have colleagues, inspiring, surprising, challenging and helping to advance the new understanding before you.

Funding for research came from an Australian Research Commission Discovery Outstanding Researcher Award attached to project DP140103357, and by grants from the Great Southern Development Commission and the Jack Family Trust. My most recent work on Noongar oral history with the Knapp family, especially Dr Lynette Knapp, continues to inspire and enlighten. I thank all Aboriginal people who generously shared time and stories, and who agreed to publication with due acknowledgement. Dr Alison Lullfitz and Catherine Vasiliu have provided able support through this work. Ursula Rodrigues kindly helped with reformatting references and the Bibliography.

To Michael R. Leaman, Alex Ciobanu, Emma Devlin and others of Reaktion Books, and to the artists and photographers who made their creative work available (each mentioned in the photo acknowledgements), I am deeply indebted, as I am to Chris, my companion in life. This book celebrates our 50th year of marriage.

My ancestors contributed to the destruction of eucalypt woodlands and forests for agriculture in Victoria (Wemba Wemba country) and New South Wales (Biripi lands). It is my hope that this book makes a small contribution towards reparation of such damage, and poses a way for a brighter future with eucalypts for our descendents.

Photo Acknowledgements

❋

The author and publishers wish to express their thanks to the sources listed below for illustrative material and/or permission to reproduce it:

© Batchelor Press, reproduced with permission: 44; from Claire Bowern, 'The Riddle of Tasmanian Languages', *Proceedings of the Royal Society Series B*, CCLXXIX/1747 (2012), reproduced with permission: 55; photos Andrew P. Brown: 9, 96; © Patricia Dundas, reproduced with permission: 4, 29; from R. J. Fensham et al., 'Rarity or Decline: Key Concepts for the Red List of Australian Eucalypts', *Biological Conservation*, CCXLIII (2020), reproduced with permission: 108, 109; Flickr: 82 (photo Discover Corps, CC BY-ND 2.0); illustration David Foster (www.fostertype. com) based on the AIATSIS map of Indigenous Australia, © AIATSIS 1996: 14; © Maxine Holman, reproduced with permission: 35; photos Stephen D. Hopper: cover, 1, 2, 3, 5–8, 10, 11, 13, 15, 16–18, 25, 28, 30, 31, 32, 33, 36, 37, 38, 39, 40, 41, 42, 43, 45, 46, 47, 50, 51, 56, 57, 58, 59, 60, 61 (with M. Lucks), 62, 63, 65, 66, 67, 68, 69, 70, 71, 72, 73, 74, 75, 77, 79, 80, 81, 83, 86, 87, 88, 90, 91, 92, 93, 94, 95, 97, 98, 99, 100, 101, 102, 103, 104, 105, 106, 107, 110, 111; after Stephen D. Hopper, Fernando A. O. Silveira and Peggy L. Fiedler, 'Biodiversity Hotspots and OCBIL Theory', *Plant and Soil*, CDIII/1–2 (June 2016): 89; iNaturalist Australia: 84 (photo Tony Eales, CC BY-SA 4.0); The Irvine Museum Collection at the UC Irvine Jack and Shanaz Langson Institute and Museum of California Art: 112; from Jacques Labillardière, *Voyage in Search of La Pérouse* (London, 1800), photos University of Pittsburgh Library System, PA: 52 (vol. I), 54 (vol. II); photo Clare Layman: 12; from Charles Louis L'Héritier de Brutelle, *Sertum Anglicum, seu, Plantae rariores quae in hortis juxta Londinum* (Paris, 1788): 48; photos Keith Lightbody: 34, 85; Mitchell Library, State Library of New South Wales, Sydney: 49; Shutterstock.com: 64 (Ilya Images), 78 (EagleEye Photos); State Library of New South Wales, Sydney, Thomas Dick Birrpai Photograph Collection, courtesy Thomas Dick Birrpai Family Stakeholder Group: 21 (BCP 04737), 22 (BCP 04759), 23 (BCP 04784), 24 (BCP 05039); State Library of Queensland, South Brisbane: 53; photos Luke Sweedman: 19, 76; photos Glenn Wightman: 26, 27; Wikimedia Commons: 20 (photo Hesperian, CC BY-SA 3.0).

Index

❀

Illustration numbers are indicated by *italics*